Business Process Driven SOA using BPMN and BPEL

From Business Process Modeling to Orchestration and Service Oriented Architecture

Matjaz B. Juric

Kapil Pant

[PACKT]
PUBLISHING

BIRMINGHAM - MUMBAI

Business Process Driven SOA using BPMN and BPEL

First published: August 2008

Production Reference: 1220808

Published by Packt Publishing Ltd.
32 Lincoln Road
Olton
Birmingham, B27 6PA, UK.

ISBN 978-1-84719-146-5

www.packtpub.com

Cover Image by Vinayak Chittar (vinayak.chittar@gmail.com)

Credits

Authors

Matjaz B. Juric

Kapil Pant

Reviewer

Frank Jennings

Senior Acquisition Editor

Louay Fatoohi

Development Editor

Nikhil Bangera

Technical Editor

Aanchal A. Kumar

Copy Editor

Sumathi Sridhar

Editorial Team Leader

Akshara Aware

Project Manager

Abhijeet Deobhakta

Project Coordinator

Patricia Weir

Indexer

Monica Ajmera

Proofreader

Dirk Manuel

Production Coordinator

Rajni Thorat

Cover Work

Rajni Thorat

Foreword

More and more organizations are turning to Business Process Management in their quest for practical ways to create new business value and to streamline their operations, and to ultimately become flexible, responsive and efficient organizations.

For the last 30 years, the business world has become more process aware, and BPM has come a long way since initial iterations that relied heavily on static flowcharts to map out corporate processes in mostly unchanging organizations.

Today, BPM has become a discipline in its own right. It applies sophisticated software and best practices to model, simulate, automate, manage, and monitor processes, in order to coordinate operations with dynamic business priorities. This has given rise to unprecedented process flexibility and scalability, wherein workflows (both human and automated) are determined in real-time by events and/or outcomes within the process, and effective knowledge transfer is made possible as processes become well-documented business artifacts on which employees can be trained.

The introduction of an independent process tier represents BPM's first major contribution to business computing. It puts the management of business logic in the hands of business managers, without threatening the integrity of the application logic.

To enjoy the full benefits of BPM, processes must integrate with existing applications and systems. They require access to the functions that are locked in application silos. Today's IT organization is complex, consisting of many different applications and systems built using heterogeneous technologies, on various types of middleware, using multiple databases and running on many platforms. Hard-coding point-to-point integration with these applications is not a good solution as it creates tight coupling with the application and makes the process brittle and inflexibleThis can make the processes expensive to change and may therefore defeat the entire purpose of BPM.

This is where Service Oriented Architecture (SOA) comes in. It provides the technical ability to create that process independence. The goal of SOA is to expose an organization's IT assets as re-usable services that can communicate and integrate more readily. SOA's aim is to provide a common communication framework to organize and describe the capabilities, usage policies and service provider locations without exposing the implementation details. It allows organizations to plug in new services or upgrade existing services in a granular fashion in order to address new business requirements, while providing the possibility of making the services consumable across different channels, and at the same time enabling existing legacy applications as services. The goal is to eliminate the integration headache common to many organizations today, while leveraging existing IT investments.

BPM and SOA are a natural match — together they facilitate the next phase of business process automation, deriving higher value from services. Business automation will no longer be about hard coding a function that is to be repeated infinitely.

Today, business automation through BPM and SOA is all about creating services that are re-usable in many different ways, in multiple processes that can be continually improved. Through this synergy, organizations will achieve better business and IT results than were ever possible through either discipline alone.

This book provides adequate coverage of BPM in the context of SOA, as well as a pragmatic approach to carrying out the analysis, execution and monitoring of business processes from end-to-end, using Business Process Modeling Notation (BPMN), and the automatic mapping of BPMN to the Business Process Execution Language (BPEL) for executing business processes in SOA.

Geoffroy de Lamalle
Business Development Manager, SOA — Europe, Middle East & Africa,
IDS Scheer AG

About the Authors

Matjaz B. Juric holds a Ph.D. in computer and information science. He is Associate Professor at the University of Maribor and the director of Science Park project. In addition to this book, he has authored or coauthored *SOA Approach to Integration, Business Process Execution Language for Web Services* (English and French editions), *BPEL Cookbook: Best Practices for SOA-based integration and composite applications development, Professional J2EE EAI, Professional EJB, J2EE Design Patterns Applied, and .NET Serialization Handbook*. He has published chapters in *More Java Gems* (Cambridge University Press) and in *Technology Supporting Business Solutions* (Nova Science Publishers). He has also published articles in journals and magazines, such as SOA *World Journal, Web Services Journal, Java Developer's Journal, Java Report, Java World, eai Journal, theserverside.com, OTN*, ACM journals, and has presented at conferences such as OOPSLA, Java Development, XML Europe, OOW, SCI, and others. He is a reviewer, program committee member, and conference organizer.

Matjaz has been involved in several large-scale projects. He has been a consultant for several large companies on SOA projects. In cooperation with the IBM Java Technology Centre, he worked on performance analysis and optimization of RMI-IIOP, an integral part of the Java platform. Matjaz is also a member of the BPEL Advisory Board.

Matjaz is the chair of SOA Competency Centre, and the author of courses and consultant for the BPEL and SOA consulting company BPELmentor.com. For more information, please visit http://www.bpelmentor.com/

My efforts in this book are dedicated to my family. Special thanks to my dear beautiful Ana. Thanks to my friends at Packt Publishing and University of Maribor and to Ales Frece.

Kapil Pant is an accomplished BPM consultant and Public speaker with extensive experience in Products and Professional Services consulting. He currently manages Wipro Technologies' BPM/SOA practice in Europe, and leads consulting engagements including Business Process Improvement workshops, BPMS and SOA Tools Study and Recommendations, and BPM Architecture, Implementation and Governance.

Over the years, Kapil has been extensively involved in conducting successful workshops on Process Improvement, Requirements Analysis, BPM/SOA and Enterprise Architecture for clients in Telecom, Banking, Securities and Insurance industry verticals. He has also worked closely with leading System Integrators such as Wipro, Tata Consulting, HCL and Satyam to conduct technology enablement programs for client projects across industry verticals.

As a recognized Public Speaker, Kapil is known for his well-researched programs delivered in his high-energy, enthusiastic, and down-to-earth style. He has presented keynote speeches, workshops, seminars, and over 40 road-shows across the Asia Pacific, Europe and the USA. He was also nominated by the Government of India to lead seminars as a part of a 25-member working committee for E-Governance Enterprise Architecture and Standards Taxonomy.

He has a Masters Degree in Computer Applications, a Bachelors Degree in Business Studies, and a TOGAF Certification.

Kapil presently lives in Hampshire, UK with his wife and enjoys blogging in his free time.

I would like to express my thanks to my colleagues in Wipro Technologies, specifically my senior colleagues Gopalakrishna Byllahalli and Gunendra Patil for their firm support, guidance and encouragement.

Ashish Sharma for his technical understanding and help with some of the key sections in the book.

Louay Fatoohi and Patricia Weir from Packt Publishing for their continued support, patience and understanding during the course of this project.

Finally, I am grateful to my parents and grandmother for their blessings and my wife Ekta for her constant encouragement and critical advice without which this book would not have been possible.

About the Reviewer

Frank Jennings works in the Information Products Group of Sun Microsystems Inc. He has more than 9 years of experience in Java, SOA and System Design. He is an Electronics Engineer from Madras University and has worked for several open-source projects.

Frank has written regular columns for leading Java journals including Java Developer's Journal and Linux Developer's Week. Frank is also the co-author of the book *SOA Approach to Integration* focusing on SOA design pattern for enterprises. Frank also is involved in technical publications for Sun Microsystems in the fields of Solaris and Developer AMP Stack. His blog can be read at `http://blogs.sun.com/phantom` and he can be reached at `theghost@sun.com`. He also holds a Post Graduate Diploma in Computer Science and an Advance Diploma in Computer Integrated Management from University of Indianapolis

Table of Contents

Preface

Modeling business processes for SOA and developing end-to-end IT support for these processes have become top IT priorities for many organisation. The SOA approach is based services and on processes. Processes are focused on composition of services and in that sense services become process activities.

Experience has shown that the implementation and the optimization of processes are the most important factors in the success of SOA projects. SOA is so valuable to businesses because it enables process optimization. In order to optimize processes, we need to know which processes are relevant and we have to understand them – something that cannot be done without business process modeling. There is a major problem with this approach – a semantic gap between the process model and the applications.

This book will show you how to bridge this gap. It describes a pragmatic approach to business process modeling using the Business Process Modeling Notation (BPMN) and the automatic mapping of BPMN to the Business Process Execution Language (BPEL), which is the de-facto standard for executing business processes in SOA. The book will also cover related technologies such as Business Rules Management and Business Activity Monitoring, which play a pivotal role in achieving closed-loop Business Process Management.

What This Book Covers

Chapter 1 looks at the relation between SOA and business processes. SOA provides the technology platform for the implementation of business processes, and the development of applications that provide end-to-end support for business processes. This chapter also covers the long-term association of SOA with business processes and BPM.

Chapter 2 gives an overview of the role of business process modeling for SOA. It outlines the importance of BPM and its life-cycle, which consists of business process design, process implementation, process execution and control, and process optimization. It discusses each of these stages in brief. It also briefly discusses ARIS the methodology, BPMN notations, and process simulation.

Chapter 3 covers the concepts of business process modeling, and the use of BPMN as a standard in providing a consistent, process vocabulary to any business. It discusses the essential components of BPMN using some examples, which will enable you to start creating BPDs. It also introduces the Oracle Business Process Analysis Suite.

Chapter 4 addresses some general guidelines for process modeling before taking a deep dive into some complex constructs of BPMN, especially the length and breadth of Events, and the role they play in creating and visualizing BPDs. It also covers support for workflow patterns in BPMN and their use during process execution using BPEL.

Chapter 5 covers two important aspects in the BPM process: process analysis using simulation and process transformation for implementation. It emphasizes the importance of tools to extend support for some of the gaps in the current standards and transformation to reduce the issues of synchronization and process round-trips.

Chapter 6 covers business process modeling using BPMN and process analysis using simulation techniques. It covers process transition from BPMN to BPEL, followed by process orchestration and execution using process engines such as Oracle's BPEL Process Manager. It also evaluates some of the best practices for implementing various technology components to make the end-to-end process of BPM and SOA seamless.

Conventions

In this book, you will find a number of styles of text that distinguish between different kinds of information. Here are some examples of these styles, and an explanation of their meaning.

A block of code will be set as follows:

```
if(  income < 10000 )
{
    declineLoan = true;
}
return declineLoan;
```

New terms and **important words** are introduced in a bold-type font. Words that you see on the screen, in menus or dialog boxes for example, appear in our text like this: "The **parallel instance generation** check box is also set to signify creation of multiple parallel tasks ".

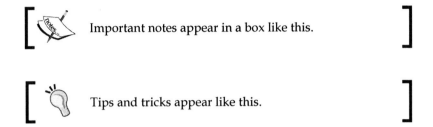

Important notes appear in a box like this.

Tips and tricks appear like this.

Reader Feedback

Feedback from our readers is always welcome. Let us know what you think about this book, and what you liked or may have disliked. Reader feedback is important for us to develop titles that you really get the most out of.

To send us general feedback, simply drop an email to feedback@packtpub.com, making sure to mention the book title in the subject of your message.

If there is a book that you need and would like to see us publish, please send us a note in the **SUGGEST A TITLE** form on www.packtpub.com or email suggest@packtpub.com.

If there is a topic that you have expertise in and you are interested in either writing or contributing to a book, see our author guide on www.packtpub.com/authors.

Customer Support

Now that you are the proud owner of a Packt book, we have a number of things to help you to get the most from your purchase.

Errata

Although we have taken every care to ensure the accuracy of our contents, mistakes do happen. If you find a mistake in one of our books—maybe a mistake in text or code—we would be grateful if you would report this to us. By doing this you can save other readers from frustration, and help to improve subsequent versions of this book. If you find any errata, report them by visiting http://www.packtpub.com/support, selecting your book, clicking on the **let us know** link, and entering the details of your errata. Once your errata are verified, your submission will be accepted and the errata added to the list of existing errata. The existing errata can be viewed by selecting your title from http://www.packtpub.com/support.

Piracy

Piracy of copyright material on the Internet is an ongoing problem across all media. At Packt, we take the protection of our copyright and licenses very seriously. If you come across any illegal copies of our works in any form on the Internet, please immidiately provide us the location address or website name, so we can pursue a remedy.

Please contact us at copyright@packtpub.com with a link to the suspected pirated material.

We appreciate your help in protecting our authors, and our ability to bring you valuable content.

Questions

If you are having a problem with some aspect of the book, you can contact us at questions@packtpub.com and we will do our best to address it.

1
SOA and Business Processes

The main objective of information technology is to provide support for business operations. IT has successfully automated various functions such as payroll, general ledger, and invoices through the introduction of application systems. Although this has been very valuable for companies, there has also been an understanding that automation of such activities is not all that IT can provide. Therefore, information systems have tried to cover more and more functions. As a result, **ERP (Enterprise Resource Planning)**, **CRM (Customer Relationship Management)**, **SCM (Supply Chain Management)**, and similar systems have emerged.

Through the introduction of these systems, companies have started to realize that the ultimate objective would be to automate business processes – in other words, to develop applications that would provide support at each and every step of a business process, from its beginning until its completion.

Although fulfilling this objective might sound simple, it is not! There are at least two major challenges:

1. Each company has its unique business processes (and application systems should be designed around the business processes, not vice versa).

2. Business processes are not constant; they change with time. Every change in the business process has to be reflected in the enterprise systems. This requires the enterprise systems to be highly flexible, so that they can be modified quickly and efficiently.

Fulfilling both requirements requires a highly flexible IT architecture, which would allow changes to be made to the software quickly and efficiently. Business processes are also required to relate more closely to the application systems, which has not been the case so far. Usually, business processes have been modeled "on paper", resulting in nice pictures. However, there has been a semantic gap between those pictures of business processes and the actual application systems, and changes in the processes have not produced clear dependencies to the changes required in application systems.

Service Oriented Architecture (SOA) has emerged as a solution to these problems. In this book, we will show you how we can use SOA along with **Business Process Management (BPM)** to solve these and other related challenges. We will look at its complete life cycle, starting with the business process modeling and ending with the application that implements such processes. We will see that SOA introduces 'new approach' technologies and languages such as **BPMN (Business Process Modeling Notation)**, **BPEL (Business Process Execution Language)**, **ESB (Enterprise Service Bus)**, services, rule engines, registries/repositories, and others, to fulfill the objectives.

In this chapter, we will look at business processes and their relevance to IT, application systems, and SOA in particular. We will:

- Explain why we have to care about business processes
- Discuss how business processes emerge
- Think about the relationship between business processes and IT
- Discuss the importance of IT flexibility
- Explain why we need SOA
- Introduce the SOA approach to business processes and explain the major benefits of the SOA approach
- Explain the role of a SOA competency centre
- Discuss SOA's inception
- See an overview of the SOA forces and their significance for IT departments
- Explain the changes in the development approach, required by SOA
- See an overview of the technical aspects of SOA
- Briefly introduce BPMN, BPEL, services, interfaces, messages, synchronicity, loose coupling, and quality of service
- Discuss the role of the ESB, Registry and Repository, Rules Engines, Business Activity Monitoring, and User Interactions
- Explain how SOA, BPMN, and BPEL fit together

Why Care about Business Processes?

Business processes are essential for every company — large or small. Companies rely on business processes. Let us look at what business processes are.

[A business process is a set of coordinated activities that are performed either by humans or by tools with an objective to realize a certain business result.]

A business process consists of a set of coordinated activities that accomplish a particular business goal. The order of these activities and the efficiency of those who perform the activities determine the overall performance of a business process. It is very much in the interest of every company to have business processes that are efficient and include only necessary activities, because this will allow them to work faster.

As business processes define the order of work, they are related directly to the efficiency and effectiveness of a company. The better the business processes are defined, the more efficiently a company can operate. In today's competitive market, the efficiency of a company is a key criterion for success, because in addition to innovation, operating efficiency is key to improving the company's competitive advantage in the market.

Knowing and understanding the details of business processes is important, because this gives us the opportunity to identify the bottlenecks and optimize business processes. Optimizing business processes make them more efficient, our customers happier, will reduce the workload on the employees, and will reduce the utilization of resources.

Managing business processes is, therefore, very important. Each company should know how its business processes are defined, who is involved in the various related activities, and how long it takes to execute a certain process.

We have already mentioned that the objective of IT is to support and automate business activities using application systems. On the one hand, this reduces the load on the employees, and on the other, it guarantees that the activities and tasks are performed efficiently as compared to manual tasks and activities.

The focus, therefore, has to be on the process itself. The level to which a business process is optimized is directly related to efficiency of such a process. Today, having highly-optimized business processes is one of the most important priorities of companies.

Optimized business processes are increasingly important for companies as they provide the company with a competitive advantage. With SOA, companies can optimize business processes easily, with less effort, and in a shorter time than with previous approaches.

However, it's not only the competitive advantage that matters; companies also need to react to changes in the global market, to new opportunities, and to threats from other companies. They react with modifications to their business processes.

The more efficient business processes a company has, the more efficient its operations will be. This will allow the company to have a competitive advantage over other companies and possibly become a leader in a certain area. Many of you might say that this is trivial to understand. Indeed, it is. But if we put emphasis on these topics, you will see that optimizing business processes is not easy, and not all companies define a systematic approach to business process optimization. Optimizing processes is also related to information systems. Each change in the process requires changes in application systems.

 Often, business processes are classified into internal or private business processes, and public or global business processes. Internal business processes are related to a single company. Global business processes connect two or more companies. Both types of processes are important and can be modeled and automated by SOA.

Examples of Business Processes

Before we dig into these topics, let us first look at some examples of business processes. Some examples of common business processes are supply, marketing and sales, procurement, and so on. Such processes take place in almost every company. They are called support processes.

However, the most important thing for each company is its "core" business processes — those processes that are directly related to the core business activities of the company. For example, a marketing company that manages advertisement boards relies on efficient processes that start with an order for advertising, and end when the advertisement is published on boards throughout the country or abroad. The faster the company can realize the orders, and the faster it can react to new requirements from customers, the better it is.

Business processes are always specific to a company. This is particularly true for core business processes. Companies, therefore, cannot buy IT support for these processes in the market, but have to custom develop it to address their specific needs.

A company that produces car seats requires an efficient production process. Such a process can be automated, starting with the cutting of leather, continuing with the gluing of seat pillows, assembly of the seat carrying construction, and so on. In addition to production tasks, we can also automate other related tasks. Production can also be linked to the supply, which will open up new opportunities for supply chain management and help reduce stock levels. It is obvious that we are limited only by our own creativity.

A clothing company's core processes are design, production, and sale of clothes. The faster the turnaround between design and production, the more flexibility the company has to react to customers' wishes, and the better it can adapt to new opportunities. The better the connection between production and sales, the better the company can adjust its production to actual demand in the market.

A stockbroker company provides services related to buying and selling stocks. It also provides capital management services. Using the Internet, the company can develop applications that will allow customers to observe price changes in real-time and place orders online. This will change the processes dramatically and provide new opportunities for services that such companies offer their clients. At the same time, it will allow tighter integration with clients and closer observation of their needs. IT can help business processes change in order to get the maximum value from new technologies.

 SOA introduces new horizons in business processes optimization, where the only limit is our creativity. Business processes can provide an important competitive advantage.

In some industries, best practices related to business processes have been gathered and published. Such business process frameworks can be used for various reasons:

- To standardize business processes in an industry
- To ease integration between different companies from the same industry/sector
- To use them as benchmarks to compare our own processes
- To follow and improve our processes

Some experts are of the opinion that the best practices represent the average state in the industry. If our company is benefiting from such processes, it means that our processes are no better than average. Usually, companies that are above average keep their business processes confidential, because they know that their business processes reflect their true competitive advantage.

In the telecommunication sector, a well-known business process framework is **Enhanced Telecom Operations Map (eTOM)**. eTOM defines best practices process frameworks for different aspects related to telecommunication business, such as:

- Customer relationship management
- Marketing fulfillment
- Order handling
- Problem handling
- Customer SLA/QoS management
- Invoice management
- Service management
- Service configuration and activation
- Problem management
- Resource management and operations
- Resource provisioning
- Partner relationship management
- Marketing and offer management
- Sales development
- Service development and retirement
- Supply chain development and management
- Human resources management
- Financial and asset management

We could find many more examples. However, the fact is that business processes are always specific to a single company, and are quite complex. A birds-eye view of the processes (as provided above) only tells half the truth. We can get a complete understanding of a business process only when we look at the details. It's in these details that the complexity hides.

How Business Processes Emerge

When a company is established, its business processes are often not defined in a systematic way. Rather, they arise in a spontaneous way. It is the employees who often define the various activities and tasks. As the company grows, more and more people get involved in the processes, and processes become more and more complex. Processes in a large company differ from the processes in a small company.

In the real world, however, no single person can give a complete overview of an organization's business processes. The knowledge about how a process works is usually in the heads of employees and very often each person only knows about his or her own part of the process. The management does not motivate employees to think about the process, or even to think of optimizing it. Therefore, processes remain unchanged and are far from optimal.

If we agree with this, we can very simply conclude that if there is no single person in the company who could give an overview of the whole business process, then how can we know whether the company's operations are optimal. The management definitely wants to have the answers for the following questions:

- Are the tasks and activities of a process organized in an optimal way?
- Which tasks and activities require the most time to complete?
- How are the activities and tasks distributed among employees?
- How efficient are the employees?

We need to understand the business process in order to answer these questions. First, we should understand how business processes work. To do this, the usual approach has been business process modeling, which uses graphical (visual) languages to represent process flows, roles, and related documents. Business process modeling is not something very new. It has been around for quite a while and is a matured and well-understood discipline.

We can model business processes in a variety of visual languages; the most widely used are **EPC (Event Process Chain)**, **eEPC (Extended Event Process Chain)**, UML Activity Diagrams, and recently BPMN.

We use business process models to understand the processes. This gives us the opportunity to modify and improve them, and to optimize them. Business process optimization and re-engineering are very important and it is up to our imagination to improve processes and integrate them to gain synergic benefits, and use other approaches to optimize them. We will not go into the details of business process optimization right now, because we will come back to this topic later in this chapter, and will discuss it again in the next chapter.

However, we will emphasize that business process re-engineering and optimization are related to several important topics that should not be overlooked. We will mention just three here:

1. Changing business processes requires changing the way people work. And people do not like change. Therefore, in order to be successful, we need to be careful how we apply the changes to the real world, and how we motivate the employees to change their way of working. Otherwise, a theoretical process, even if highly optimized, will not work in the real world.

2. Changing business processes does not mean changing only the behavior of the employees, but requires changing the IT support and related application systems. This topic is of particular interest for us, and we will look at it in detail in the next section.

3. Finally, changing the business processes only once is not the key to long-lasting success. If a company wants to have long-lasting success, it should develop an environment where business processes can be continuously optimized. This is a particularly difficult task, because continuous change in business processes also requires continuous change in the way employees work, and in the way IT supports the business.

How Business Processes and IT Relate

We have defined business processes as a set of coordinated activities. We have also seen that most often employees perform these activities. Usually employees use applications to support their work. Sometimes, these applications fully support some activities, and the employee's intervention is not required.

With each new application that is introduced into a company, more activities become supported by IT. In other words, business processes are highly dependent on these applications, and vice versa. In addition, applications gradually start to impersonate business processes.

 Usually, business processes are tightly coupled with applications. Companies rely on IT applications in order to function. IT not only provides support for business operations, but has actually become an essential part of every business.

Today, businesses depend on IT. Can you imagine a business without IT? Can you imagine how any major company would operate, if IT does not function for one day?

Up to here, everything looks good. Nevertheless, we have not thought about the fact that business processes change over time. If the business processes are constant, we can afford to tightly couple them with application software. The fact, however, is that business processes are not constant and need to change. They need to be flexible. Therefore, IT also has to be flexible. In the next section, we will look at IT flexibility.

IT Flexibility

If each change in a business process requires a corresponding change in the IT system and in one or more applications, then the crucial question is: How quickly can we modify the applications?

The fact is that the time needed to modify the applications is crucial. In the eyes of the managers, this is 'lost' time, because the company needs to wait until the IT system is modified, before it can start using the new processes. Moreover, new processes might be better equipped to offer new or modified products or services. Therefore, the management will always put IT under pressure to do the modifications as quickly as possible — to minimize the **IT gap**.

To get a better understanding, let us look at a few examples. If an insurance company wants to offer a new insurance product, it has to upgrade the IT system before it can launch this new product in the market. The insurance company has to modify all the applications related to offering/ordering insurance products. This includes the applications on the office counters, the applications on the notebooks of insurance agents, the web site where insurance products can be bought online, in the call center for phone orders, and so on. Next, the applications for invoicing have to be modified. Various reports have to be modified too, in order to obtain information on how well the new product sells, who buys it, and how satisfied the customers are.

If a telecommunication operator introduces a new service or modifies an existing service, does this require changes to the IT applications? Yes, it does. It requires changes similar to those discussed earlier. In a telecommunication company however, such changes might also require modification in the software that runs the network. Today, there are many businesses where the IT support has infiltrated so deep into the company operations, that not only do support services rely on the application systems, but the whole core business operation has become dependent on the software.

Therefore, it is quite understandable that the management requires its IT systems to be flexible.

On the other hand, we know that IT systems in companies are usually very complex. We also know that complex systems require time to change. We can easily see that we are talking about two contradictory forces. One is the requirement from the management that changes should happen as quickly as possible. The other is the requirement from engineers, who require time to change complex systems.

In the real world, the request from management is usually of higher priority. This is why engineers are forced to change applications in a short time. Therefore, they do not have enough time to plan and design the changes. Even worse, they often need to apply modifications to software under pressure of time. In such conditions, they might be able to implement the changes, but changes may be done in a manner that negatively influences the overall software architecture and the entire information systems.

When such changes happen repeatedly, the overall software architecture becomes less robust. The changes get more difficult to implement, and hence require more time. This becomes a vicious circle. At a certain point, the architecture might even get so fragile that changes can compromise the integrity of the whole system. The dependencies and relations between the various software parts become almost unmanageable, and it takes so long to apply changes that it cannot fulfill the business requirements any more.

This is related to other impact factors, including:

- The heterogeneous architecture of a typical information system
- The usage of traditional software life cycles, which have not anticipated change

Heterogeneous Architecture

A typical information system today consists of a mix of heterogeneous application systems that have been developed over time. The application systems in a company are usually a mixture of:

- Self-developed solutions
- Custom-built, but outsourced solutions
- Commercial systems such as ERP, CRM, SCM, and similar solutions

These systems use different architectural styles (client/server, multi-tier), different technologies, and languages (C++, Java, C#, Visual Basic, COBOL, and so on). It is quite unlikely that this mix of different systems was designed in a unified manner —it just grew, and will continue to grow. The fact is that companies rely on these systems and cannot afford to turn them off overnight.

Over time, some integration was achieved between the application systems, but it was not properly designed. This resulted in point-to-point integrations and the use of several different integration middleware products, including RPC, message brokers, distributed object models, proprietary integration servers, and in the recent years, web services.

Point-to-point integrations are very problematic, because as the number of involved systems starts to grow, the number of connections starts to grow exponentially. As point-to-point integrations are tightly-coupled integrations, they are very difficult to maintain. Changes in one system provoke a 'domino effect', whereby changes have to be applied in all related systems. Often, the complexity of maintaining the integrations becomes very high, and so does the cost.

To get a feeling for the number of necessary connections, let us presume that several applications have to be connected to each other. We will count only unidirectional connections, that is, if application A has to be connected to B, and B to A, then these are counted as two connections. With fifty applications, we would need an unbelievable 2,450 connections if we integrate applications on a point-to-point basis. To be honest, in the real world, we will probably not need to connect each application with the others. However, this does not change the fact that we will have to manage and maintain a large number of individual connections.

These issues are manifested whhile dealing with:

- Combinations of monolithic, client/server, and multi-tier applications
- A mix of procedural and object oriented solutions
- A mix of programming languages
- Different types of database management systems (relational, hierarchical, and object)
- Different middleware solutions for communication (message oriented middleware, object request brokers, remote procedure calls, web services, and so on)
- Multiple information transmission models, including publish/subscribe, request/reply, and conversational models
- Different transaction and security management middleware
- Different ways of sharing data
- Possible usage of EDI, XML, and other proprietary formats for data exchange

All of these issues make applying changes to information systems even more difficult and time consuming, thus increasing the IT gap even further.

Traditional Software Lifecycles

Existing applications have most likely been developed using traditional software life cycles. These consist of various stages, including:

- Requirements specification
- Analysis and design
- Implementation
- Testing
- Deployment

Depending on the development process, these stages are either sequential, partially parallel (Waterfall model), or iterative-incremental (Rational Unified Process). No matter which development process is used, they all are based on the following two facts:

- The requirements are specified in advance. These requirements should be specified as precisely as possible, because the architectural design depends on the requirements. Real-world experience, however, shows that in most of the cases, it is difficult to define the requirements in advance. It is also very common that the requirements change, even throughout the development.

- Traditional software development processes were not designed for continuous change. Rather, they relied on certain precise requirements. Modifications to the requirements need to be run through the whole development cycle again (because requirement gathering is usually the first stage), which is very time consuming. This is not aligned with business expectations, which require quick changes.

With this, we do not want to say that requirement specifications are not necessary. In contrary, it is very important to specify the requirements. The key is to develop a software architecture that will anticipate change and be flexible to change. Only such an architecture can fulfill the requirements of the next generation of information systems—information systems that will provide end-to-end support for business processes. Existing software architectures have not fulfilled these expectations.

Why Do We Need SOA?

Service Oriented Architecture (SOA) is the architecture of the next generation of information systems. It provides answers to the problems identified in the existing software architecture. SOA enables the development of applications that are more flexible, and more adaptable than applications built using traditional architectures. SOA applications are, therefore, much easier to modify and adapt.

SOA also enables better alignment between the business processes and the applications. As we will see later in this chapter, SOA minimizes the semantic gap between the business process models, and the actual application software. SOA achieves this with the introduction of new technologies and languages, most importantly, **BPEL**.

All of this is in line with our primary objectives:

- To minimize the IT gap, and the time required to modify the information system in response to the changes in business processes
- To make the information system more flexible and adaptable to change through a loosely-coupled approach
- To provide end-to-end support for business processes
- Finally, to make the company more agile, more flexible, and to allow it to adapt more easily various forces, such as competitive pressures, new opportunities, changes in the global market, and so on

Why Should We Believe This?

The fact is that in the past there have been several attempts to make software architectures more flexible. There have also been several attempts to align business process modeling with software development (and vice versa). However, the fact is that the problems continue to exist even now.

To be able to answer this question, we will first look at the business processes, and how they are managed today. We have already identified that:

- Business processes in a company usually emerge in a nonsystematic way
- Business processes are dynamic and change over time
- Often there is no single person who has all of the details of all of the business processes in a company

The classical approach to BPM foresees the cataloguing of all business processes and drawing the exact specifications of each business process. The output of such projects are "nice pictures" of processes. We have used the phrase "nice pictures" because capturing a business process can only result in a snapshot of a process at the time when the snapshot was taken. However, business processes are dynamic and change over time. Therefore, such pictures of processes cannot correspond to the real processes for more than a limited period.

Larger companies usually face two additional problems:

- Modeling business processes (specified as one-time projects), can take quite a while. It can happen that even before we complete the project, some process specifications might be out-of-date (this is particularly true for processes that have been modeled at the beginning of the project).

- Business processes are also usually quite complex. Whhile specifying them, the most difficult part is to provide in-depth specifications. The complexity usually hides in the details. Therefore, we might get high-level process specifications. However, such specifications may be very simplistic, and may not include important details. This could influence our understanding of the processes. Very often, process specifications do not include exceptional scenarios, and do not foresee how to react to such scenarios.

The following figure provides an example of a process specification:

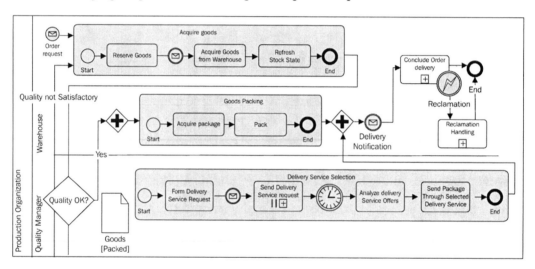

Even if we succeed in modeling business processes in detail, and in a relatively short span of time, there is another huge problem we have to face with the traditional approach – the business process activities and tasks are performed by the employees and the software. There is a huge *semantic gap* between what goes on in the information systems and the process model diagrams. This semantic gap exists because it is very difficult to relate the changes in the processes with the changes required in the information systems, and vice versa. Therefore, it is also very difficult and time-consuming to maintain the business process models in-sync with the actual software. This is very time-consuming because it has to be done manually, and is therefore not done in real-world environments, where time is valuable.

Part of the problem is hidden by the fact that enterprise systems are still developed at a relatively low level. Even if we use modern software platforms, such as Java EE or .NET, we are still required to develop in languages such as Java and C#. These are object-oriented languages, which use concepts such as classes, objects, inheritance, delegation, and so on. These concepts are not synchronized with business processes. Java, C#, and similar languages are still relatively low-level, compared to business processes. Therefore, we sometimes refer to them as 'programming-in-the-small'.

SOA has introduced several new approaches to software development that we will look at, in the next section.

SOA Approach to Business Processes

The SOA approach differs considerably from traditional approaches, although this may not be obvious at first sight.

SOA introduces technologies and languages that reduce the semantic gap between the business processes (pictures) and the actual applications (code). Particularly important here are **BPMN**, which is used for modeling business processes, and **BPEL**, which is used for the execution of business processes. With these two technologies, plus some additional ones (which we will mention later in this chapter), SOA provides:

- A language — BPEL — for direct execution of business processes
- Round-trip mapping between the process models in BPMN, and their executable representation in BPEL

With this, SOA considerably reduces the semantic gap between the business processes and application systems. BPMN enables us to draw the representation of a business process, which is then mapped into the executable BPEL code, and executed directly on the SOA platform.

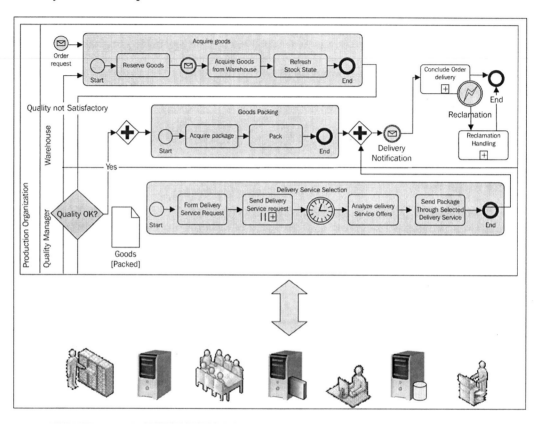

The other major difference in SOA, as compared to the traditional BPM, is the approach to business process automation. SOA takes a path different from the traditional approach which was based on the "big bang" approach, where processes were first modeled, then optimized, and finally the application software was rewritten to support the new processes. SOA has learned from the major mistakes of the traditional BPM approach:

- Modeling of business processes has taken too long and has not been done in enough detail. Therefore, the business models have not been accurate enough, were usually without exceptional scenarios, and have been a little out of date.

- The optimization has been done "in the heads" of the analysts. Although optimizations looked good on the model, there has been no proof that they would work in the real world.

- As there has been no evidence that the optimizations are acceptable, the modifications in the software, which had to be done in order to support the optimizations, have not been justified enough.

- Finally, the introduction of new optimized processes, together with the modified application software, has often represented a huge change in the operations procedures. This has resulted in changes in the behavior of employees. Such changes, particularly if they have been huge, have often met with resistance from at least a few employees, which ensured that the fragile model did not work anymore.

Major Improvements in the SOA Approach

These are the three major lessons SOA has learned:

- Business processes are so complex that we could approach them all over.

- Business processes are too valuable to a company to be merely optimized "on paper" (even if there has been support from tools that enable simulation).

- Changes in business processes are not simple and particular attention has to be paid to the fact that changes in business processes require changes in people's behavior.

 People do not like to change their behavior. Changes to business processes require that people change their behavior. Therefore, the human aspect of process optimization must never be underestimated.

The SOA approach to business process automation therefore relies on the process-by-process approach:

- First, we identify the business process that we would like to automate. Here, we focus on the business value of the process, the visibility, and other factors. We also asses the real value of process automation and possible optimizations.

- Then, we model the process. Here we use a visual notation. In this book, we will explain why it makes sense to use BPMN while modeling business processes for SOA. The process modeling for SOA has to be done in detail. It is important that we model the process in detail so that we identify individual activities that are atomic from the perspective of execution. It is also important that we model the exceptional scenarios.

Exceptional scenarios define how the process behaves when something goes wrong. In the real world, business processes can go wrong. Therefore, it is important to model processes so that they can react to exceptional situations and recover appropriately. Modeling exceptional scenarios may be even more complex than modeling the regular process flow.

- Next, we automate the process as it is, without any major modifications. In SOA, this requires mapping the BPMN process model into the executable representation in BPEL, and connecting the BPEL process with partner links, that is, with services. In other words, it is required that we relate process activities to the various services. This step is best carried out if we have a portfolio of existing services that are re-usable and in conformance to other SOA characteristics (which we will describe later in this section). If we do not have existing services, we will also need to implement the services, where we have three options:
  - To implement new services
  - To expose the business logic from existing applications
  - To use user tasks to delegate the activities to employees, and possibly automate these tasks in the future
- Once we automate the process, we will take up process optimization.

The SOA approach to process automation is a step-by-step approach. This is possible, because SOA considerably reduces the development time and complexity, and allows changes to the existing processes to be done quickly and efficiently.

- The step-by-step approach to optimization is much more efficient and friendly to the people involved in the processes. We have already mentioned that people do not like to change their behavior. Therefore, it is much wiser to implement changes in phases. This is sometimes called the evolutionary approach to business process optimization.
- The SOA approach has **another important advantage**. As we have automated the process (as described in bullet three), we can obtain some measurements about the different process activities, and how long in average they need to execute. Such quantitative metrics, which are calculated automatically by modern SOA platforms, can provide valuable information that can be used to decide where to start process optimization: we can focus on activities where we can gain the largest improvements. Gathering quantitative data about process activities is called **Business Activity Monitoring (BAM)**.

BAM, which is a part of modern SOA platforms, provides valuable quantitative data about process execution, which can then be used to decide on the point from which process optimization should start.

We can see that the SOA approach to business process automation is iterative and incremental, as shown on the figure below:

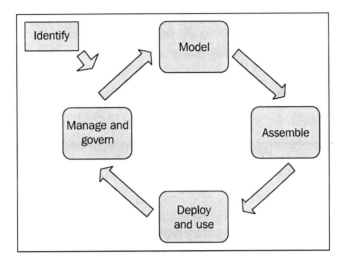

When done properly, the usual duration of one circle (iteration) is three to four months. In other words, the SOA approach can produce new automated processes or optimized versions of already automated processes in approximately three- to four-month intervals. This is very important, because the SOA approach delivers results in relatively short intervals. This way, the whole company will recognize that IT delivers useful results. This can improve the position of IT, particularly if IT has not been efficient enough in the past.

There are other important benefits to the SOA approach:

- It allows step-by-step identification of important business processes, and the in-advance assessment of the benefits of process automation and optimization.

- It allows the in-advance assessment of costs and benefits, and **ROI (Return on Investment)** calculation. It also allows continuous monitoring of total costs throughout the process.

- Owing to the reduced semantic gap between the business and IT, the communication of requests to IT becomes more precise and efficient, thus minimizing misunderstandings.

- The systematic approach to process optimization requires less adoption for the employees, who therefore, becomes more amenable to changes.

- The real-time monitoring of process performance (through BAM) provides valuable insights into the efficiency of the current processes, and helps in identifying points of optimization.

- With SOA, IT becomes more flexible and can respond faster to changes in business. This makes the whole company more agile, which improves its competitive position, reduces its response time to market changes and reduces competitive threats. It also allows the company to react faster to new opportunities.

Focus on Content, Not Technology

We have seen that SOA focuses on business processes. The business processes are the content of the business. This means that SOA shifts the focus of IT from technology to business content. This is good, because the technology should be seen merely as an enabler. The less we are aware of the technology itself, the better it serves its purpose.

In the traditional IT approaches that are in common use today, the focus has been more on technologies than on content, as shown in the following figure:

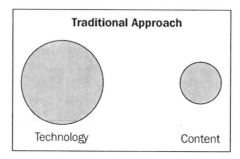

The Improvements in the performance of computers have allowed us to think about software development at higher levels of abstraction. This has started with the shift from assembler to higher -level programming languages and has since then continued with the introduction of new layers, which have simplified the development and made it less complex.

SOA continues this journey with an important addition. It raises the level of abstraction in the direction of the business content, and away from the technologies. Although some technology-oriented IT people may not like this scenario, businesses may find it useful as they can now focus more on their business' content. The following figure shows how SOA has changed the focus of IT:

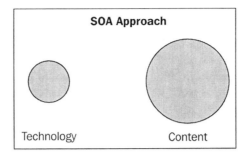

SOA, therefore, puts focus on the content of business.

 Who in the company is responsible for the business content? Is it the IT department? Usually not! SOA shifts the focus of IT from technology to business. SOA is not the domain of the IT department alone.

This brings us to the conclusion that SOA is not the domain of the IT department alone. As the focus is on business processes, it is important for SOA to outgrow the boundaries of IT departments and involve other departments as well. For success, we should involve the whole company, starting with the management.

Management Support

SOA is about business content, business processes, aligning IT with the business, and optimizing the business processes.

For an SOA project to succeed, it is very important to gain management's support. Without support, it is unlikely that we will be able to implement all of the required changes. Particularly problematic are the changes relating to the behavior of employees. Often, such changes are possible only if approved by the top management.

The other important reason why management support is necessary is that IT alone does not have the required knowledge about how business processes work in a company. It has to obtain this knowledge from the employees, who have to provide information on how the processes work.

Finally, SOA is also about business process optimization. The IT department usually does not have the authority to decide about changes in business processes. Therefore, process owners have to be involved in the SOA project. For this, orders have to come from the management.

SOA Competency Centre

We have seen that because of its focus on business content, SOA requires the involvement of not only IT, but also the other departments in a company. We have already mentioned that management and process owners have to be involved. Employees with knowledge about the business processes, the so-called key users, should also be involved.

Nevertheless, as the SOA projects usually arise from the IT departments, we could face some organizational barriers that prevent the people mentioned below from working together efficiently. Therefore, SOA will most likely require organizational changes.

The solution to these challenges can be a new organizational unit, called the SOA Competency Center. The SOA Competency Center should involve the following people:

- SOA project leader
- Business process analyst
- Process owner
- Key user
- Technical architect
- Process developer
- Service developer
- Integration and test expert
- Representative for SOA governance

SOA Inception

So far, we have seen that SOA is a comprehensive project that includes:

- Business aspects
- Technical aspects
- Organization aspects

The most important business aspects, based on an SOA survey that the author has conducted among 283 IT departments of large and medium-sized companies, are:

- Faster adaptability to changes and better adaptation of business process
- Improved efficiency of business processes
- Better alignment with IT and business requirements

This results of the survey are shown in the following figure:

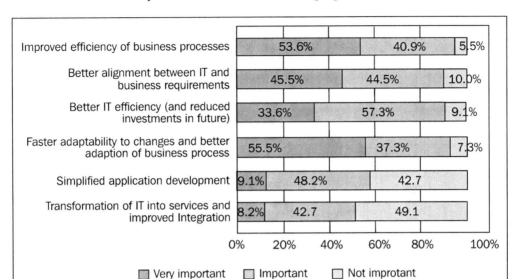

SOA is a long-term project, and it is very important that it is seen as such. In other words, SOA is a long-term development of the overall IT architecture. To be successful, we have to plan the project carefully:

1. We have to set the objectives. We have to identify the goals of SOA. It is important that we articulate the objectives very precisely. Just saying that we would like to improve the efficiency of business processes is not adequate. We have to identify which processes we would like to improve, why, when, and by how much. Only when we have a deep understanding of this, will we be able to move forward.

2. We have to identify the risks. There are many risks involved with the SOA project, starting with the organizational aspects, selection of processes, technology-related risks, and so on.

3. We have to take the necessary organizational steps and also educate the SOA team members at the same time. Here it is very important to understand that SOA introduces many changes to all aspects of application development. Team members have to understand these changes. They also have to understand the new technologies and languages.

4. We have to select an appropriate SOA platform. Major vendors today offer SOA platforms that differ in several important aspects. Careful selection is therefore necessary. We have to take into account specific aspects of the environment, existing systems, and existing knowledge in order to make a good decision.

An SOA project is usually started with a pilot project, which should be done with the help of external SOA experts. Within the SOA pilot, several aspects can be addressed. The most important aspect is probably that our team has to get used to the round-trip development of business process modeling, and their transition into executable BPEL processes. In other words, the SOA team has to feel comfortable with the composite approach to development.

SOA Forces

We have seen that SOA aligns the business and IT aspects. Listed here are the five most important business aspects:

- Business models
- Business processes
- Organizational structures
- Workforce
- Business functions such as marketing, finance, and so on

The following are the most important IT aspects:

- IT architecture
- Application systems
- Security
- Transactions
- Databases
- Hardware infrastructure

There are four major categories of forces that influence business process automation using IT:

- Business aspects such as agility, competition, new opportunities, customer demands, and customer contact
- Organizational aspects such as the need for optimization, improvements in efficiency, and cost reduction
- Increased complexity, integration demands, and standards
- Introduction of new technologies, such as Web 2.0, new devices, and architecture

This is illustrated in the following figure:

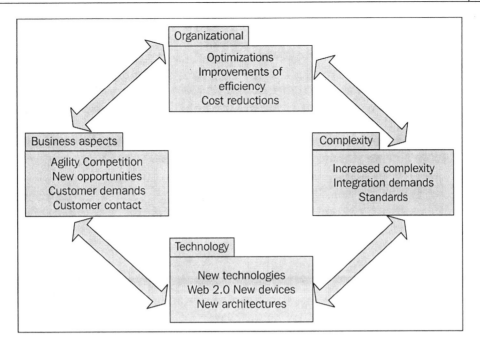

Value of SOA for IT Departments

Besides having business value, SOA also introduces important benefits to the
IT departments:

- IT departments are under constant pressure due to frequent changes. SOA
  makes such continuous changes easy, and reduces the negative effects
  of changes.

- Duplication of data across different databases and systems is quite common
  in existing systems. SOA fosters consolidation of data and introduces master
  data management solutions based on SOA concepts, services, and loose
  coupling.

- In existing applications, we usually face duplicated functionalities. SOA
  fosters consolidation of such duplicated functionalities. Using services, we
  can expose composed functionalities.

- When talking about business processes, companies often have variants of
  business processes that differ only in details. SOA enables support for such
  variants and their modifications with a common base process.

- With the diversity of devices, it becomes more and more important to enable
  access to applications and data through different channels (PCs, palmtops,
  cell phones, voice, and so on). SOA enables access to processes through
  different channels.

- IT departments often do not develop everything in-house. With the existing approaches, it is quite difficult to separate the roles of the external partners (outsourcing partners) and in-house development. Too often, the outsourcing partner has gained control over the application it has developed, and the IT department (and the company as a whole) has become dependent on the partner. SOA enables easier separation of responsibilities, whereby services can be outsourced while their integration into business processes stays in-house. In this way, IT departments retain control over the most valuable know-how a company has: the business processes know-how.

- Finally, SOA enables the development of service networks, which in turn enable the development of virtual value chains, not only within the company, but also between companies. This can open completely new possibilities in how IT can be used to optimize the business.

Changes in the Development Approach

SOA has also learned from the experiences of the existing software development methods. These methods were based on the specification of requirements, and had foreseen the analysis, design, implementation, testing, deployment, and maybe some other phases. However, the core assumption was that requirements had to be specified as precisely as possible. Changing the requirements has always been seen as something that is undesirable.

The fact today, however, is that changes are expected.

SOA has considered change from the start. Therefore, it has introduced some important modifications to the development approach. Instead of the classic approach shown here:

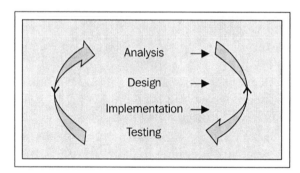

SOA introduces a modified approach, which consists of the following phases:

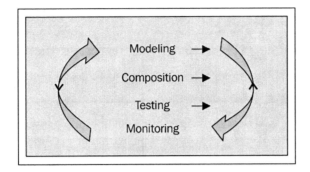

We can see that the phases are quite different. Instead of the analysis, the SOA approach foresees modeling, which refers to business process modeling. This way, the development is aligned better with the actual needs of the business. This is the first advantage of the SOA approach.

The second phase in the SOA approach is composition. Composition refers to the way business processes are developed. Instead of traditional implementation in a programming language, such as Java or C#, in the SOA approach, we have to develop business processes so that we can re-use services and compose (orchestrate) them into processes. This approach works best when we already have a portfolio of services such as:

- Services from existing applications, where we expose business logic as services
- Services that are bought, or for which development is outsourced, to external companies
- Services developed in-house

In all three scenarios, we have to follow certain guidelines. The most important one is that we develop services that are **re-usable**. This is not an easy task and we will talk more on this later in this section, when we describe the technical characteristics of SOA.

Re-usable services are very important for SOA, because they represent "big" building blocks, which contain business logic. Developing applications (processes) with such existing building blocks is much faster compared to the traditional approach in Java or C# (even if we have some libraries available). Therefore, the SOA approach to development is sometimes called *programming-in-the-large*. Composition of services (using BPEL) has been designed for such a purpose.

The third phase of SOA development approach is testing. Testing SOA applications refers to testing of the process and related services. However, we re-use services that have already been tested. Therefore, the effort required for testing is also reduced, as services do not have to be unit-tested again. Although, processes may still have to be tested (integration testing), the overall effort for testing is reduced.

Finally, we come to the monitoring phase. This phase refers to run-time monitoring of the process performance and includes:

- Monitoring of business activities, say BAM, which provides valuable information about the performance and efficiency of business processes, and can serve to identify future optimization points.

- Monitoring of QoA aspects of processes and services, such as response time, security, availability, and so on. This is often related to the definition of a **SLA (Service Level Agreement)** for processes and services.

Leading SOA platforms from vendors such as Oracle, IBM, Microsoft, and others support both these aspects of process monitoring.

Reduced Complexity

The changes in the development approach described above considerably reduce the overall complexity of the development. According to some estimates, SOA reduces the complexity by approximately 50%. This is very important because the increased complexity of application systems has been a significant source of the problems related to the long response time, needed for application modifications.

Technical Introduction to SOA

The development of composite applications is one of the major contributions of SOA, which brings us to the technical aspects of SOA. In this section, we will look at the technical background of SOA.

To be able to develop composite applications, that is, to compose business processes out of services, we need technologies that will allow us to develop services. The obvious answer to this are 'web services', as they are best aligned with the concepts of SOA. With this, we want to emphasize that SOA is not bound to specific technologies. What matters are the concepts. The most important thing from the perspective of a developer is the service description, the **WSDL (Web Services Description Language)**.

We also need a language and a technology to perform the composition of services into processes, and an environment in which to execute the processes. You may argue that we could use well-known programming languages such as Java or C# for this. It turns out that the process composition differs somewhat from traditional programming. With composition, we merge services into larger services and processes. In other words, we represent the high-level state transition logic of a process. Using programming languages such as Java, C#, and so on for these purposes is likely to result in inflexible solutions, particularly because there is no clear separation between the process flow and the business logic, and these should not be tightly coupled. However, we continue to use traditional programming languages to develop services.

In addition to these facts, the composition of business processes has other specific requirements such as support for many process instances, long-running processes, compensation, fault handling, correlation, parallel flows, complex dependencies, asynchronous invocations, and so on. All of these make it reasonable to use a specific language and a specific environment for business processes.

In SOA, the language used is **BPEL** and the environments for executing processes are called process servers (sometimes called BPEL engines). Process servers provide additional valuable features, such as an overview of the running processes, completed processes, faulted processes, and so on. They provide a complete history of process execution and insight into process activities.

BPEL is an executable language. We are emphasizing this because, in order to execute BPEL processes, we have to specify details such as interfaces, messages, variables, types, and so on. These details are usually not needed at the time when we model the business processes. Therefore, for modeling, we will use a modeling notation, the **BPMN**. BPMN has been designed explicitly for process executions. Therefore, it provides round-trip mapping from BPMN to BPEL.

This brings us to the simplified SOA architecture, as shown in the following figure:

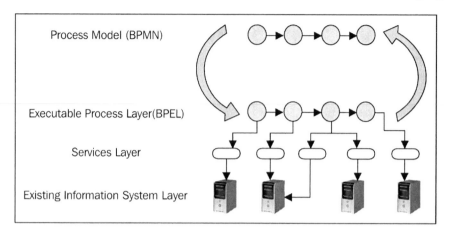

Let us now look briefly at the different building blocks. First we will look at the BPMN, then at the BPEL, and finally at the services.

BPMN

BPMN is a graphical notation used for business process modeling. We use BPMN to draw business process diagrams. These diagrams present the activities and tasks of a process and their relations. The diagrams use flowchart concepts to represent the logic of business processes.

BPMN is a visual language, and uses a set of graphical elements. Activities are represented as rectangles, and decisions as diamonds. BPMN successfully joins the simplicity of the diagrams with expressive power, which allows BPMN to be used for complex processes and specification of details.

We will take a closer look at the syntax of BPMN in the next chapter.

 BPMN has been designed specifically for SOA.

BPEL

BPEL has been adopted as the de facto standard for developing executable business processes. The main goal of BPEL is to standardize process automation between services.

With BPEL, we can describe business processes in two distinct ways: we can either specify the exact details of business processes, or specify the public message exchange between parties. The former processes are called **executable business processes** and can be executed by a process server. The latter processes are called **abstract processes**. They do not include the internal details of process flows, and are not executable. In the real world, BPEL has been used predominantly for executable processes.

Executable business processes are processes that comprise a set of existing services and specify the exact algorithm of activities, along with the input and output messages. With BPEL, we can define business processes that make use of services, and business processes that externalize their functionality as services. When we define an executable business process in BPEL, we actually define a new service that is a composition of existing services.

Within enterprises, BPEL is used to standardize enterprise application integration, and extend the integration to previously isolated systems among business partners. Between enterprises, BPEL enables easier and more effective integration with business partners. Further, BPEL encourages enterprises to define their business processes, which in turn leads to business process optimization, re-engineering, and selection of the most appropriate processes, thus further optimizing the organization. Definitions of business processes described in BPEL do not influence existing systems, thus stimulating upgrades. BPEL is the key technology in environments where functionalities already are, or will be, exposed via services.

BPEL represents a convergence of two early workflow languages, **WSFL (Web Services Flow Language)** by IBM, and XLANG by Microsoft. IBM, BEA, and Microsoft jointly developed the first version of BPEL in August 2002. Since then, several other partners have joined. Version 1.1 was adopted in March 2003. In April 2003, BPEL was submitted to **OASIS (Organization for the Advancement of Structured Information Standards)** for standardization purposes, where the **WSBPEL TC (Web Services Business Process Execution Language Technical Committee)** has been formed. In 2007, WS-BPEL version 2.0 was adopted.

BPEL uses an XML-based vocabulary to specify and describe business processes, and is based on WSDL, XML Schema, and XPath specifications. Familiarity with these specifications will be helpful while learning BPEL.

Features

With BPEL, we can define both simple and complex business processes. BPEL offers constructs such as loops, branches, variables, assignments, and so on, which allow us to define business processes in an algorithmic way. The most important BPEL constructs are related to the invocation of services. BPEL makes it easy to invoke operations of services either synchronously or asynchronously. We can invoke operations either in sequence, or in parallel. We can also wait for callbacks. BPEL provides a rich vocabulary for fault handling, which is very important, as robust business processes need to react to failures in a smart way. BPEL also provides support for long-running process and compensation, and allows us to undo partial work done by a process that has not terminated successfully. The following are the most important features that BPEL provides:

- Describing the logic of business processes through composition of services
- Composing larger business processes by combining smaller processes and services
- Handling synchronous and asynchronous (often long-running) operation invocations on services, and managing callbacks that occur later
- Invoking service operations in sequence, or in parallel
- Selectively compensating completed activities in case of failures
- Maintaining multiple long-running transactional activities, which are also interruptible
- Resuming interrupted or failed activities to minimize re-work
- Routing incoming messages to the appropriate processes and activities
- Correlating requests within and across business processes
- Scheduling activities based on the execution time and defining their order of execution
- Executing activities in parallel and defining how parallel flows merge based on synchronization conditions
- Handling message-related and time-related events

Services

SOA and BPEL approaches rely on services. We compose services into processes. To be able to take advantage of this approach, we need services. Services are discrete self-contained building blocks of SOA that contain business logic. Services expose business logic through well-defined interfaces.

Services provide business functionalities such as applications for business travel, applications for loans, and so on. This differs considerably from technology-oriented functionalities such as retrieving or updating a table in a database. Services in SOA must provide business value, hide implementation details, and must be autonomous. Therefore, in SOA we usually organize services in several layers. In the top-most layer, we have business services.

[Business services should represent activities of a business process. At the same time, they should be generic, so that they can be used in different business processes.]

Such business services cannot be developed in an ad-hoc manner. They require a lot of planning and designing. The success of SOA relies on services and the ability to define these services at the right level of abstraction, to make them re-usable, and to use them in different processes. From this perspective, we could say that SOA is the development of the overall IT architecture.

Business servers are usually composed of lower-level services. At the bottom, we have technical services. For example, these can be stored procedures, exposed from the database, or functions or methods of an existing application, and so on.

Defining the right services and positioning in the right layers requires some planning and designing. It also requires us to be familiar with good practices and patterns. This should lead us to the architecture as shown in the following figure:

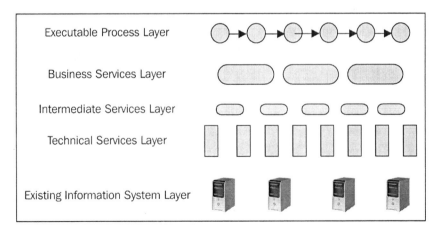

From the technical perspective, processes and services do not differ. They both expose interfaces, which are described in WSDL. Therefore, we can develop composed services using different approaches (BPEL, programming languages, and so on). We can also re-use services and/or processes. As they look similar from outside, they give us the opportunity to develop multiple layers of services and processes, from the simplest services to the complex end-to-end processes.

Service Interfaces

It is also important to know how service interfaces are defined. The interface of a service defines a set of public operation signatures. The interface is a contract between the service provider and the service consumer. Interface is separated from the implementation, is self-describing, and is platform-independent. In order to define business services, we need to focus on the correct granulation of operations. SOA services are best modeled with coarse granulation.

Messages

Service operations are defined as a set of messages. Messages specify the data to be exchanged and describe it in a platform-and language-independent way, using schemas. Services exchange only data, which differs considerably from object oriented and component approaches, where behavior (implementation code) can also be exchanged. Operations should also be idempotent (operations are idempotent if repeated invocations have the same effect as one invocation).

Synchronicity

Service consumers can use synchronous or asynchronous communication modes to invoke operations of services. In synchronous mode, a service operation responds to the service consumer after the processing is complete. The service consumer has to wait for its completion. Usually, we use synchronous mode when operations complete processing after a short period of time. In asynchronous mode, a service operation does not respond to the consumer, although it may return an acknowledgement so that the consumer knows the operation has been invoked successfully. If a response is needed, a callback from the service to consumer is used. In such a scenario, message correlation is needed.

Loose Coupling

Loose coupling of services is achieved through self-describing interfaces, coarse granulation, the exchange of data structures, and support for synchronous and asynchronous communication modes. Loosely-coupled services are services that expose only the necessary dependencies and reduce all kinds of artificial dependencies. This is particularly important where services are subject to frequent changes. When a service is modified, minimal dependencies ensure that changes made to other services are minimal. Such an approach improves robustness, makes systems more resilient to changes, and promotes re-use of services.

Quality of Service

For developing truly re-usable services, it is also important that we care about attributes, such as availability, performance, security, and so on. These are called quality of service attributes. Quality of service attributes are important in large information systems. In web services, quality of service attributes are covered by WS-* specifications such as WS-Security, WS-Addressing, WS-Coordination, and so on.

Other Important Parts of SOA

The scenario described above with BPMN, BPEL, and services covers only the most essential parts of SOA. For a full-blown SOA, other important parts are required. These include:

- Enterprise Service Bus
- Registry and repository
- Rules Engine
- BAM
- User interactions (human workflow)

SOA is also related to the following:

- Unification of presentation layer, which is related to portals
- Security and identity management

These layers are shown in the following figure:

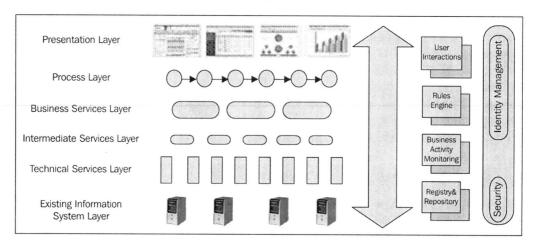

In the coming sections, we will describe the building blocks of a full-blown SOA architecture, starting with the Enterprise Service Bus.

Enterprise Service Bus

The Enterprise Service Bus (ESB) addresses the communication between the services and the processes. We have already mentioned that for services, we can use various technologies. In most cases however, we will use web services. Web services communicate using the SOAP protocol, which can be mapped to one of the transport protocols, most likely to HTTP. HTTP is an unreliable protocol, and is therefore not well-suited to mission-critical applications.

ESB addresses this problem and provides a reliable mechanism for communication between services. In addition, it offers protocol mapping capabilities. This means that ESB can translate different protocols, such as SOAP to **JMS (Java Message Service)** or vice versa. This is important because in enterprise information systems, we usually have some components already developed in different technologies. We might even have a kind of middleware, such as a message broker. ESB helps to connect and integrate these systems.

ESB can also enable reliable message delivery and provide other value-added features, which are very useful in mission critical systems. Usually, ESB also addresses aspects of security and transaction management. It allows us to configure secure access to the services and processes, and to monitor the access. It also allows the definition of services that should participate in transactions. Some ESBs even allow us to choose between ACID (WS-AtomicTransactions) and compensating transactions (WS-BusinessActivity).

Services in SOA are described in WSDL, and use input and output messages, which are formatted using XML Schema. In the ideal world, all services would use the same schema definitions. In the real world however, this is not the case. Therefore, we often have to transform the XML payload from the output schema of one service to the input schema of another service. For such transformations, we often use XSLT, XPath, or XQuery. ESB provides the ability to do such transformation transparently, on the bus, without having to modify existing services or processes. This capability to transform XML payloads is particularly valuable when new versions of services or processes are deployed. New versions might change the interface or the message schemas somehow. With ESB, we can mask these differences without having to modify all related clients.

Related to transformations is message enhancement. Sometimes, it is not enough just to transform the XML payload. We may need to add or even alter certain information in order to make the message compliant with the service definition. Such alterations may can be simple, such as altering the representation of date, or perform more complex operations such as calculating data, translating types, and so on.

ESB can also serve as a message router. Sometimes, we might want to route messages to certain services. Such routing is usually done based on some deterministic business rules, or can be based on message content, user information (which user created the message, or which user is the receiver of a message), or the time when the message was created. Routing messages on the bus gives us the advantage of doing this in the Good ESBs are integrated with Rules Engines, and allow us to use the rules from the engine for routing.

Routing is related to service mapping. ESBs can also be used to dynamically map a service implementation to the corresponding WSDL interface. On ESBs, this can be done in run time, which gives us greater flexibility over which implementation we will use. If this feature is used with care, it can improve overall flexibility.

In future, we believe that SOA will introduce another important concept: **business events**. This will extend the way services and processes interoperate. Instead of invoking services by calling their operations, we will simply trigger a business event. Such events will be consumed by those services and processes that have subscribed to the event. ESB will play a central role in this scenario, because it will monitor, route, and manage events in the same way as service invocations.

Registry and Repository

A very important aspect of SOA is re-use. Re-use at the service level means that when we compose executable processes (in BPEL), we re-use existing services as far as possible. Successful re-use is not easy to achieve and requires at least the following:

- The developers are motivated to develop re-usable services. Developing a re-usable service initially takes longer than developing a single-purpose service. Re-use pays off in the second step, when the service is actually re-used. The more it is re-used, the more justifiable this initial longer development becomes.

- Developers also have to be motivated to search for services and to identify the most appropriate services to use. They may also need to modify the behavior of the service slightly. In such a case, they need to know who else uses the services, and the boundaries within which they can make changes.

- To achieve maximum re-use and keep the architecture sound, it is useful to have some sort of governance in place. Governance procedures require information on who uses a service, how many times a service has been re-used, what level of re-use is achieved in processes, and so on.

Another very important aspect is the deployment process. A professional deployment has three environments:

- development
- test
- production environment

When an application is ready for production use, it is deployed into the production environment. Controlled deployment of processes requires that a process starts using the production version of services instead of the development or test version. If references to services (partner links) are hard-coded into the BPEL processes, such migration can be very painful, as it might, in the worst case scenario, require manual changes to URL addresses. When deploying a service, we might want to know which processes use this service, because we might want to retest those processes.

Addressing all of the aspects mentioned above is very difficult if we have no list of the available services, or when processes and services are tightly coupled (for example, when a process uses the direct URL of a service in the partner link).

Registries and repositories address these aspects. They are used to register services in a central location. Once registered, we can search and locate appropriate services at design time and at run-time. The more metadata we include for a service, the better the search capabilities that the registry and the repository can provide.

The rule of thumb is that once we have more than 50 services, we will desperately start needing the registry and the repository. However, sometimes it might be wise to introduce it from the beginning, because once developers get used to a certain development process, it will be very difficult to change their behavior.

> The current notion about the role of registries and repositories in SOA has changed considerably. A few years ago, we believed that a relatively simple registry — UDDI would cover all our needs. Today, we have identified that a registry alone is not powerful enough for SOA, because in many cases it makes sense to store service metadata as well (WSDL interfaces, XSD schemas, and many more). Therefore, today we talk about registries and repositories.

A powerful registry and repository should have the following features:

- Classification capabilities to categorize and classify services and processes based on one or more classification schemas. This simplifies queries and enables easier location of the most appropriate services for re-use.

- Governance functions to enable the definition of proprietary service/process lifecycles together with the conditions to go from one stage of the life cycle to another. Stage transition can trigger automatic actions such as execution of validators.

- Access control to define who can perform which operations against the registry and repository, and for which registered services/processes. Such access control could be based on **XACML (eXtensible Access Control Markup Language)**.

- User, programming, and administration interfaces.

Rules Engines

Business rules are an important part of each enterprise. Experience has shown that business rules change; sometimes very often, sometimes not that often. Today, business rules are coded into different applications and are tightly-coupled with the implementation of an application system. Changing business rules is therefore very difficult, and requires modifications to applications. Each modification requires testing and deployment, which makes things even more complicated. The major challenge today, however, is to identify the applications into which the same business rule is coded, and to modify all applications where this rule has been used. If we forget some applications, this could lead to unpredictable results, which we do not want to happen.

Business rules are very common in business processes. The idea of SOA has been to extract these rules from the executable code (from BPEL, Java, C#, and so on) and to store them in a central place, where:

- Business rules can be re-used from different processes, services, and applications
- User friendly interfaces exist, which enable us to change and modify business rules

Often, business processes manage business rules. Therefore, putting business rules into a central place, the Rules Engine, is appropriate because the same rule is used very often in more than one process. This might not be obvious at the start, when we will have just a few processes automated, but it will become important when the number of processes start to grow. However, similar as it is to the registry and repository, it makes sense to introduce business rules early. This is because if rules engines are introduced after we have implemented several processes, we will have to:

- Change the way development team works
- Extract the rules from the existing processes and services, which will require significant changes to these processes and services

With the introduction of Rules Engines, SOA now addresses the particular challenge of changes in business rules.

Business Activity Monitoring

Business Activity Monitoring (BAM) helps in answering the question "Where to optimize business processes? Once a process is automated end-to-end, we can use the SOA platform to provide quantitative data about the performance of the process.

A BAM solution gathers information about the time required to complete different activities of a process. It can then provide reports with average values for each activity. Having these numbers can be very helpful, because we can use them to identify which activities take the longest time to execute. With this, we can identify those parts of a process, where we will realize the largest benefits from optimization.

BAM solutions can provide other useful information. They can show us how many process instances are active at a specific time, and how long, on an average, it takes to complete a process. They can also show us which users (employees) have started how many process instances, and so on.

Please note that BAM is not just related to automatic activities (those implemented by services). It can be related to human activities as well. In such a case, we can use BAM to observe the productivity of the employees.

This brings us to the next important part of SOA — the human activities or user tasks: user interactions.

User Interactions

User interactions in business processes are very common. It is true that SOA's objective is to automate as many activities as possible. However, this cannot be done overnight. Therefore, we will need to model certain activities of a process as user interactions — human tasks.

User interactions in business processes can be simple, such as approving certain tasks or decisions, or complex, such as delegation, renewal, escalation, nomination, or chained execution. Task approval is the simplest and probably the most common user interaction. For example, in a business process, say for opening a new account, a user interaction might be required to decide whether the user is allowed to open the account. If the situation is more complex, a business process might require several users to make approvals, either in sequence, or in parallel. In sequential scenarios, the next user often wants to see the decision made by the previous user. Sometimes, particularly in parallel user interactions, users are not allowed to see the decisions taken by other users. This improves the decision's potential. Sometimes, a user does not even know which other users are involved, or even whether any other users are involved at all.

A common scenario for involving more than one user is workflow with escalation. Escalation is typically used in situations where an activity doesn't fulfill a time constraint. In such a case, a notification is sent to one or more users. Escalations can be chained, going first to the first-line employees and advancing to senior staff if the activity is not fulfilled.

Sometimes it is difficult or impossible to define in advance which user should perform an interaction. In this case, a supervisor might manually assign the task to an employees. A group of users or a decision-support system can also assign a task.

In other scenarios, a business process may require a single user to perform several steps that can be defined in advance, or during the execution of the process instance. Even the simplest processes might require that one workflow is continued with another workflow.

User interactions are not limited only to approvals. They may also include data entries or process management issues such as process initiation, suspension, and exception management. This is particularly true for long-running business processes where, for example, user exception handling can prevent costly process termination and related compensation for those activities that have already been successfully completed.

As a best practice for human workflows, it is usually not wise to associate human interactions directly with specific users. It is better to connect tasks to roles and then associate those roles with the individual users. This gives business processes greater flexibility, allowing any user with a certain role to interact with the process, and allowing changes to users and roles to be made dynamically.

User Interaction in BPEL

To interleave user interactions with BPEL processes, we can use a workflow service, that interacts with BPEL processes using standard WSDL interfaces, as any other service. This way, the BPEL process can assign user tasks and wait for responses by invoking the workflow service using the same syntax as any other service. The BPEL process can also perform more complex operations such as updating, completing, renewing, routing, and escalating tasks.

After the BPEL process has assigned tasks to users, users can act on the tasks by using the appropriate applications. The applications communicate with the workflow service by using WSDL interfaces or another API (such as Java) to acquire the list of tasks for selected users, render the appropriate user interfaces, and return the results to the workflow service, which then forwards them to the BPEL process. User applications can also perform other tasks such as reassigning, escalating, routing, suspending, resuming, and withdrawing tasks. Finally, the workflow service may supports other communication channels such as email and SMS, as shown in the following figure:

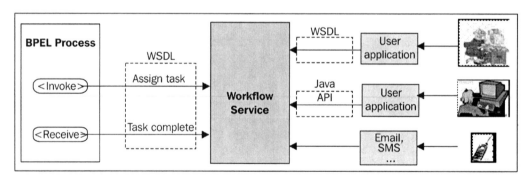

BPEL4People

In the coming years, it is likely that we will see further development of user interactions in business processes with the objective of standardizing the explicit inclusion of human tasks in BPEL processes. This standardization effort is called the BPEL4People specification, which was originally developed jointly by IBM and SAP.

The most important extensions introduced in BPEL4People are people activities and people links. A people activity is a new BPEL activity used to define user interactions, in other words, tasks that a user has to perform. For each people activity, the BPEL server must create work items and distribute them to users eligible to execute them. People activities can have input and output variables and can specify deadlines.

To specify the implementation of people activities, BPEL4People introduced tasks. Tasks specify actions that users must perform. Tasks can have descriptions, priorities, deadlines, and other properties. To assign tasks to users, we need a client application that provides a user interface and interacts with the tasks. The interface can query available tasks, claim and revoke them, and complete or fail them.

To associate people activities and their related tasks with users or groups of users, BPEL4People introduced people links. People links are somewhat similar to partner links -they associate users with one or more people activities. People links are usually associated with generic human roles such as process initiators, process stakeholders, owners, and administrators.

The actual users that are associated with people activities can be determined at design, deployment, or run time. BPEL4People anticipates the use of directories such as LDAP, (lightweight Directory Access Protocol) to select users. However, it does not define the query language used to select users. Rather, it foresees the use of LDAP filters, SQL, XQuery, or other methods.

How SOA, BPMN, and BPEL Fit Together

SOA provides the technical architecture to develop end-to-end support for business processes. SOA achieves this objective by exposing an organization's IT assets as re-usable business services that can be composed into processes on the one hand, and can integrate and communicate more easily on the other hand.

From the bottom-up perspective, SOA is integration architecture. It provides technologies and approaches for the systematic integration of existing applications and the development of new solutions. With SOA, software architects develop a high-level integration architecture that uses common concepts to share data, information, and business logic between applications in a controlled, transactional manner using a service bus or other supporting technologies, such as rules engines, registries and repositories. SOA is based on typed communication with messages that confirm to common schemas. In new-generation SOA, business events have been introduced, that provide an alternative approach to the realization of one of the most important goals of SOA—**loose coupling**. Loose coupling is an approach where different software services and components share the lowest common denominator of dependencies. This makes application architecture more robust and resistant to changes. This will allow applications, components, and services to evolve and change with, or without minimal effects on other applications, components, and services.

SOA is also the architecture for designing, automating, and optimizing business processes. The objective of SOA is to provide end-to-end automation of business processes. Business processes in SOA are based on the composition of services and processes using programming-in-the-large technologies, most importantly BPEL. BPEL business processes enable fast development, and are flexible and easy to change and modify in the future, as shown in the following figure:

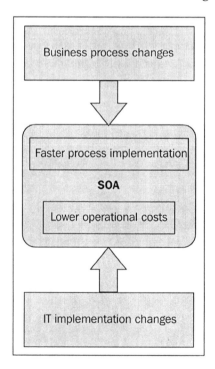

Another important feature of SOA is that it minimizes the semantic gap between process models and executable code. It achieves this objective by providing a common language to business analysts, IT architects, and developers. BPMN has become the new notation for business process modeling. An automatic round-trip mapping between BPMN and BPEL has also been developed. In this context, we should not forget the importance of **re-use**, which is the key to fast development of new solutions, and minimized testing efforts (due to re-use of existing artifacts), as shown in the following figure:

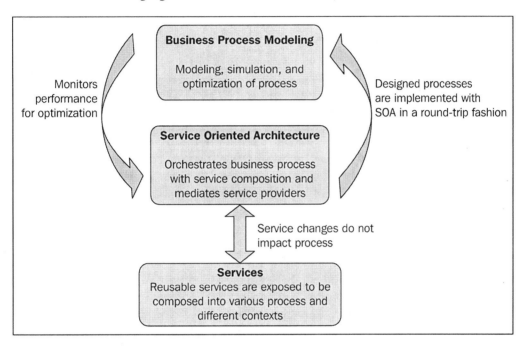

Companies that use SOA to develop end-to-end automation of business processes will benefit in terms of agility, flexibility, resilience, quality of service, better collaboration between business and IT, and better chances to develop new innovative business models.

 Innovation is the key objective of SOA and end-to-end business process automation. SOA will open up new opportunities for the development of new and innovative business models. Therefore, SOA will become a new key competency factor and an important tool for raising the competitive advantage of companies.

Let us look at some of the benefits of this approach.

Agility

SOA can improve the agility of the whole company by enabling the development and adaption of business processes quickly and efficiently using the composition of services, that is, through programming-in-the-large. As SOA services are designed for re-use and integration, the design, development, and test efforts are considerably reduced. SOA promotes re-use, which leads to increased standardization and compliance at the enterprise level. SOA also minimizes the business-to-IT gap, with the introduction of round-trip mapping between business process models (BPMN) and executable processes (BPEL).

Resilience

SOA is concerned with the development of loosely-coupled information architecture, which shields business processes and services from changes, and functions independently of versions, locations, or technical details of applications systems. SOA also enables easier and less painful migration from legacy systems, consolidation of duplicated resources, master data management, multi-channel access to applications, and the flexibility to develop variants of processes from the same base. Loose coupling enables IT assets to develop and evolve without the limitations imposed by interdependencies and point-to-point integrations.

Alignment Between Business and IT

SOA introduces a new dimension to application development with a major consequence – that of better aligning business with IT. SOA raises the level of abstraction from technologies to business services. SOA introduces business vocabulary to the IT, which simplifies the connection between IT and business people, and enables them to better understand each other. Above all, SOA talks about applications in terms of business processes. Therefore, it does not require complex mapping of requirements to actual software representation. Further, SOA provides the ability to achieve two-way mapping between the business process model and the executable processes (and services). This guarantees better alignment between business and IT in the long run—even after several maintenance and upgrade cycles.

As SOA is related to BPM, it will encourage companies to think about business processes and achieve better collaboration between business analysts and IT. Business will discover that the SOA architecture is agile enough to adapt to requirements quickly, and IT will better understand the needs of the business. This will lead to business process optimizations, improvements, and to overall process excellence, which will have important impacts on the overall efficiency of the company.

New Business Models

SOA has become the new key competency factor across companies. It has achieved this by combining the business requirements with IT capabilities. SOA uses technologies, which enable modeling, execution, configuration, and adaptability of business processes using service composition. These technologies enable better alignment of business and IT, which improves the efficiency of IT, and enables improvement of IT services on one hand, and cost savings on the other. These cost savings can be used for development of new innovative services and products, which will improve the efficiency of the whole company.

SOA also allows easier outsourcing of services, and opens up opportunities for new business models in which the business processes of a company can be exposed to customers and suppliers to achieve much tighter integration with business partners.

How the Puzzles Fit Together

This brings us to the overall picture of SOA architecture, which connects the following technologies:

- BPMN for business process modeling
- BPEL for business process execution
- Services, which represent business logic at various levels of abstraction, and are the basic building blocks of SOA
- The ESB for managing the communication between processes and services over the bus
- The registry and repository for registering services, and processes for re-use and governance
- The rules engine, which is a central place for definition of business rules
- Human interaction using user tasks, which is used for human workflow in business processes
- BAM, which is used to monitor activities and processes and to learn about process performance

In addition, SOA is typically related to the following:

- A presentation layer, which could be a portal providing a unified user experience for all integrated applications
- Security and identity management, together with single-sign-on, which becomes even more important with the introduction of SOA

The complete SOA architecture is shown in following the figure:

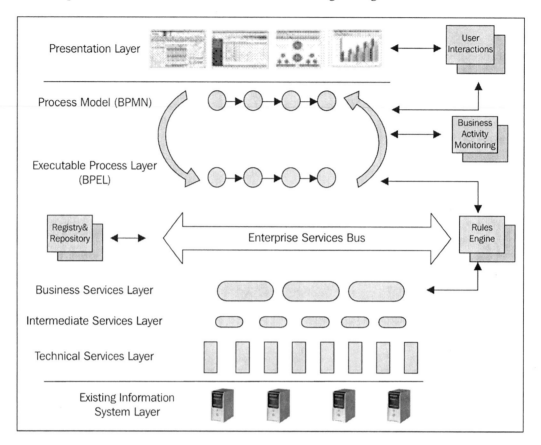

SOA Vendors

The technologies described above are part of SOA platforms, that are offered by major software vendors. Here are some major SOA vendors, which offer complete solutions:

- Oracle SOA Suite, BPA Suite, BAM, and related products including BEA (recently acquired by Oracle), AquaLogic and WebLogic
- IBM WebSphere Process Server, Business Modeler, Integration Developer, Process Monitor, ESB, Registry&Repository, and related products
- Microsoft **WCF (Windows Communication Foundation), WF (Workflow Foundation)**, BizTalk, and the forthcoming Microsoft Oslo
- Software AG webMethods
- SAP NetWeaver SOA Middleware

We can find several other companies in the market that offer separate products such as BPEL engines, ESBs, rules engines, and so on. We have not listed them here, as this information can be obtained on the Internet.

An alternative to commercial vendors is an open source implementations. SOA can be developed around open source software. One of the most popular is JBoss Enterprise SOA Platform. We can also use a mix of products such as the Glassfish application server, Open ESB, BPEL engine (such as ActiveBPEL, Apache Agila or Bexee), Drools rules engines, and many more.

Summary

In this chapter, we looked at the relation between SOA and business processes. We saw that SOA and BPM are closely related. SOA provides the technology platform for the implementation of business processes, and the development of applications that provide end-to-end support for business processes. SOA is an architecture that has introduced several important new concepts into application development. One of the most important concepts is the composition of services into business processes. With this, SOA has provided an architecture that is flexible enough to accommodate business needs related to agility, adaptability, along with other aspects related to the optimization of operations and improvement of business process efficiency.

We have seen that we have to look at SOA from three different perspectives: business, technical, and organizational. Only if we address SOA from all the three can we minimize the risks and maximize the benefits of SOA inception. The benefits are: improved flexibility, better alignment of IT and business, faster and simplified application development with reduced complexity, and most importantly, end-to-end automation of business processes, and a reduced semantic gap between business and IT. Risks are related to various organizational, technology, and business issues, which we also discussed in this chapter.

We learned that SOA is a long-term project connected with business processes and BPM. This is important because it means that we have to understand business processes in order to be able to use SOA for their implementation. Therefore, in the next chapter, we will look at how we should manage and model business processes for SOA.

2
Modeling Business Processes for SOA

Modeling business processes is a part of the overall business process management. **Business process management (BPM)** is a very important discipline, which is closely related to the operating efficiency and competitive position of a company, and its ability to grow. Business processes are also very well connected with IT. Today, IT is the driver of business processes. Imagine how any company would operate if the IT system is turned off for a week or even a day. You will quickly see that IT has become the engine that drives business processes.

SOA provides huge opportunities to better align business processes with IT and applications. To be able to achieve this, we have to understand the role of business process modeling and BPM in SOA.

In this chapter, we will:

- Discuss the role of SOA and BPM, and understand the business process life cycle
- Focus on business process modeling for SOA and discuss the methodologies and notations used
- Understand the process design and the results of process design such as process map, roles, relations, and so on
- Discuss process simulation
- Understand modeling principles
- Identify common problems in process modeling
- Discuss the process implementation phase and understand the role of SOA
- See an overview of process execution and control
- Discuss **Business Activity Monitoring (BAM)**
- Briefly discuss process optimization, key performance indicators, and typical problems in process optimization

Business Process Management

Achieving the highest level of efficiency in terms of time and cost in performing any business activity has been the guiding principle of successful businesses for a long time. In 1911, Frederick Winslow Taylor, the father of scientific management, published the following four principles of scientific management:

- Replace rule-of-thumb work methods with methods based on a scientific study of the tasks

- Scientifically select, train, and develop each employee rather than leave them to train themselves

- Provide detailed instructions and supervise how each worker performs in his or her discrete task

- Divide work equally between managers and workers, so that the managers apply scientific management principles to plan the work, and the workers actually perform the tasks

These ideas of sequencing tasks and allocating them to workers to produce results with business values are known today as business processes.

Taylor defined ideas precisely on how to implement business processes efficiently. His belief was that this is possible only through enforced standardization of methods, adoption of best practices and working conditions, and cooperation.

Today, these thoughts are grouped under BPM, which is a method for aligning a business organization with the needs of its clients. BPM fosters business effectiveness and efficiency while striving for innovation, flexibility, and integration with technology. The major objective of BPM is to continuously improve the processes, both within the company and with other companies (such as in supply chain management).

IT and BPM

As companies started to use IT to automate tasks and make work more efficient, IT started to influence business processes. To understand this, let us briefly elaborate on how IT was used in companies to automate tasks. The simplest usage of IT was the automation of simple tasks such as sending invoices or other documents by email rather than over fax or mail, calculating interest, getting stock information on different products, and so on. However, such simple automation influenced only distinct business activities and not the business processes as a whole.

Soon it was recognized that the role of IT could be larger than just automation of business tasks. IT could provide support for all business processes. Once IT became more integrated into business processes, three important things happened:

1. IT could not be considered just as system and data anymore. It had become a central element of business processes.

2. With IT's support for business processes, it became apparent that IT influenced processes. This made more sense, if business processes changed — they could be re-engineered at the same time they were supported by IT technologies. In this way the value of IT could be better leveraged.

3. IT also opened new opportunities in public business processes (those processes that spanned several companies such as supply chain), and in global processes.

The facts mentioned here have, together with changes in global economy (which in turn required changes in companies), resulted in an increased awareness of the value of business processes.

Interestingly, in many companies, awareness of the value of business processes has been most evident in the IT departments. Sometimes, IT departments have a better understanding of the value of business processes and design than the management. This is in contrast to "common sense" and the findings of professionals such as Taylor. Instead of discussing whether this is appropriate or not, let us think about the new opportunities for IT departments to evolve from technology centers to the most important core of each company: innovation centers.

To be able to understand business processes and improve them, it is first necessary to understand how the existing processes work. Hence, it is necessary to develop the **as-is** model of business processes. Developing the as-is model is also called business process modeling. Only when we understand how business processes work, can we carry out the following steps:

- Develop applications that provide end-to-end support for business processes
- Optimize business processes to make them better

Of course, it is not necessary to perform these two tasks sequentially. We can optimize some processes and then develop applications. Alternatively, we can even develop applications and optimize processes in parallel. It is particularly important to understand that business processes are not static. Business processes evolve over time because companies have to adapt and change the way they perform business operations in order to stay competitive.

Finally, IT opens new perspectives for business opportunities. This way, it can be seen as a catalyst of new, innovative business processes, which can open new customer channels, define innovative ways to collaborate with business partners, and use IT for establishing better connections with customers, and sensing their wishes.

To sum it up, the role of IT in business processes is three-fold. It can be used for:

- Automation of tasks and activities
- End-to-end automation of business processes
- Definition of innovative business processes that leverage the IT technologies in new ways

SOA and BPM

The SOA approach provides huge benefits in BPM. In older IT architectures, the business processes and applications were not linked together. Business processes were "nice drawings", and applications very complex and resistant to change. If the process needed to change, which was quite often, it took a very long time to adapt all applications. The SOA approach provides huge savings as applications are much better aligned with business processes. This reduces the time required for adoption and makes the IT system more flexible.

With this flexibility, another common problem is solved. Optimizing business processes means changing them. Changes in business processes are directly related to changes to the tasks of those employees that are involved with the processes. The fact, however, remains that people do not like changes.

In the traditional approach to business processes optimization, projects have often failed because people tried to carry out very large modifications of several processes all at once. This resulted in resistance to changes. A joke says that if a business process change doesn't make at least three people angry, it is not a change. The reason for making large changes to processes is obvious—it is easier to develop IT system for the final state of business processes than to modify the system each time a process changes.

SOA flexibility, on the other hand, enables modifications to business processes to be done in small steps. This enables a much easier and more natural evolution of processes from the **as-is** state to the **to-be** state. With step-by-step transitions, IT can follow without a lot of effort and time delays.

Such a systematic approach also introduces another benefit. Optimizing processes step-by-step allows us to gather feedback on implemented changes and adapt processes to real needs. Therefore, it is more likely that the to-be processes will be really useful and efficient, than if we take a huge step from the as-is to the to-be process model.

Business Process Lifecycle

So far, we have seen that business processes are dynamic. To express the various stages of the, the business process life cycle has to be defined. A business process lifecycle has to cover the following four phases:

1. Process modeling is related to the definition of the process model, using the selected methodology and the notation.

2. Process implementation is related to the activities required to implement end-to-end IT support for the process. SOA provides technologies and tools to make the implementations phase quick and efficient.

3. Process execution and control is related to the actual running of the process, and the supervisors controlling the process execution and taking necessary corrective actions.

4. Process monitoring and optimization is related to gathering data about the process execution. SOA approach provides the ability to gather real-time quantitative data using process monitoring or BAM tools. Optimization is responsible for interpreting these monitoring numbers and identifying optimization points.

The following figure shows how a process enters this circle and goes through various stages:

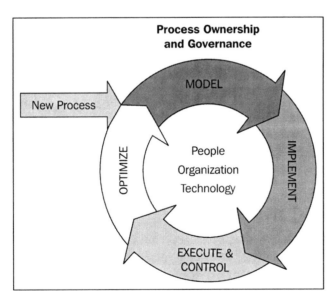

Process modeling is the phase where process analysts, together with process owners, analyze the business process and define the process model. They define the activity flow, the information flow, roles, and business documents. They also define business policies and constraints, business rules, and performance measures. Performance measures are often called **Key Performance Indicators (KPI)**. Examples of KPIs include activity turn-around time, activity cost, and so on.

Process implementation is the phase where IT developers (SOA developers), together with process analysts, implement the business process with an objective of providing end-to-end support for the process using IT (applications). The process implementation phase using the SOA approach includes process implementation with BPEL and process decomposition in to the services, identification of service, implementation or re-use of services, and integration.

Process execution and control is the actual execution phase, where the process participants execute the various activities of the process. For end-to-end support in business processes, it is very important that IT drives the process and directs process participants to execute activities—and not vice versa, where the actual process drivers are employees. An important part of this phase is process control, where process supervisors or process managers monitor whether the process is executing optimally. If delays occur, exceptions arise, resources are unavailable, or some other anomalies occur, process supervisors or managers can take corrective actions.

Process monitoring and optimization is the final and a very important phase. In this phase, process owners monitor the KPIs of the process. Process analysts, process owners, process supervisors, and key users examine the process and analyze the process execution metrics. They also need to take into account the changing business conditions. They examine business issues and identify ways to improve the business processes to eliminate these issues.

Once optimizations have been identified and selected, the process returns to the modeling phase to apply them. Then the process is re-implemented, and the whole lifecycle is repeated. We talk about an iterative-incremental lifecycle, because the process is improved in each stage.

BPM and SOA—A Perfect Fit for the Lifecycle

We have seen that business processes are dynamic and that they need to be changed quite often. As today's business processes are supported by IT, this also requires that the appropriate IT support is developed and/or changed.

With its direct support for business processes, SOA is a perfect fit for BPM. It enables quick and efficient development of applications that provide end-to-end support for business processes. SOA also provides the means to execute, control, and monitor business processes. BPM with SOA can therefore be used to support the full process lifecycle.

BPM and SOA enable business agility, as shown in the following figure:

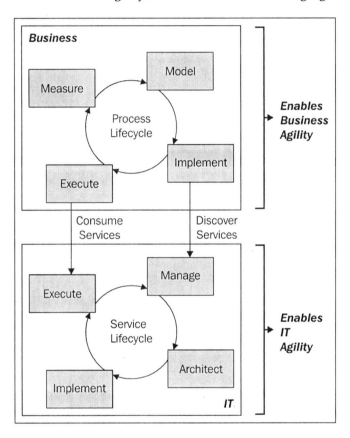

As we can see from the above figure, SOA has a crucial role in the:

- Process implementation phase
- Process execution and control phase

We will talk more about these phases later in this chapter, and also in the rest of the book.

Business Process Modeling

In the business process modeling phase, the main objective is to develop the process model, which will define the existing process flow in detail. The transparency of the process flow is crucial, as this gives the process owners, process analysts, and all others involved an insight into what is going on. An understanding of the as-is process flow also ensures that we can judge the efficiency and the quality of the process.

The main objective of process modeling is the definition of the **as-is** process flow. Process modeling needs to answer the following questions:

- What is the outcome of the business process?
- What activities are performed within the business process?
- What is the order of activities?
- Who performs the activities?
- Which business documents are exchanged within the process?
- How foolproof is the process, and how can it be extended in the future?

After answering these and some other questions, we get a good insight into how the process works. We can also identify structural, organizational, and technological weak points and even bottlenecks, and identify potential improvements to the process.

We will model business process to satisfy the following objectives:

- To specify the exact result of the business process, and to understand the business value of this result.
- To understand the activities of the business process. Knowing the exact tasks and activities that have to be performed is crucial to understanding the details of the process.
- To understand the order of activities. Activities can be performed in sequence or in parallel, which can help improve the overall time required to fulfill a business process. Activities can be short-running or long-running.
- To understand the responsibilities, to identify (and later supervise) who is responsible for which activities and tasks.
- To understand the utilization of resources consumed in the business process. Knowing who uses which resources can help improve the utilization of resources as resource requirements can be planned for and optimized.
- To understand the relationship between people involved in the processes, and their communication. Knowing exactly who communicates with whom is important and can help to organize and optimize communications.

- To understand the document flow. Business processes produce and consume documents (regardless of whether these are paper or electronic documents). Understanding where the documents are going, and where they are coming from is important. A good overview of the documents also gives us the opportunity to identify whether all of the documents are really necessary.

- To identify potential bottlenecks and points of improvements, which can be used later in the process optimization phase.

- To introduce quality standards such as ISO 9001 more successfully, and to better pass certification.

- To improve the understandability of quality regulations that can be supplemented with process diagrams.

- To use business process models as work guidelines for new employees who can introduce themselves to the business processes faster and more efficiently.

- To understand business processes, which will enable us to understand and describe the company as a whole.

A good understanding of business processes is very important for developing IT support. Applications that provide end-to-end support for business processes, can be developed efficiently only if we understand the business processes in details.

Modeling Method and Notation

Efficient process modeling requires a modeling method that provides a structured and controlled approach to process modeling. Several modeling methods have been developed over the years. Examples include IDS Sheer's the ARIS methodology, CSC's Catalyst, Business Genetics, SCOR and the extensions PCOR and VCOR, POEM, and so on. The ARIS methodology has been the most popular methodology, and has been adopted by many software vendors. In the next section, we will describe the basics of the ARIS methodology, which has lately been adapted to be conformant with SOA.

ARIS

ARIS is both a BPM methodology, and an architectural framework for designing enterprise architectures. Enterprise architecture combines business models (process models, organizational models, and so on) with IT models (IT architecture, data model, and so on).

ARIS stands for **Architecture of Integrated Information Systems** and comprises of two things, the methodology and framework, and the software that supports both. Here, we will give a brief introduction to ARIS methodology and framework, which dates back to 1992.

The objective of ARIS is to narrow the gap between business requirements and IT. The ARIS framework is not only about process models (describing business processes), although process models are one of the most important things of ARIS. As enterprise architecture is complex, ARIS defines several views that focus on specific aspects such as business, technology, information, and so on, to reduce the complexity. The ARIS framework describes the following:

- Business processes
- Products and services related to the processes
- The structure of the organization
- Business objectives and strategies
- Information flows
- IT architecture and applications
- The data model
- Resources (people and hardware resources)
- Costs
- Skills and knowledge

These views are gathered under the concept of ARIS House, which provides a structured view on all information on business processes. ARIS House offers five views:

1. The process view (also called the control view) is the central view that shows the behavior of the processes, how the processes relate to the products and services, organization, functions, and data. The process view includes the process models in the selected notation, and other diagrams such as information flow, material flow, value chains, communication diagrams, and so on.

2. The product and service view shows the products and services, their structures, relations, and product/service trees.

3. The organizational view shows the organizational structure of the company, including departments, roles, and employees. It shows these in hierarchical organizational charts. The organization view also shows technical resources and communication networks.

4. The function view defines process tasks and describes business objectives, function hierarchies, and application software.

5. The data view shows business data and information. This view includes data models, information maps, database models, and knowledge structures.

The ARIS House is illustrated in the following figure:

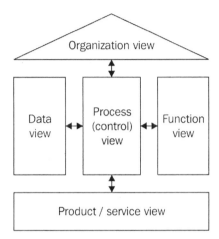

In ARIS House, the process view is the central view of the dynamic behavior of the business processes and brings together the other four static views, the organizational view, data view, function view and product/service view.

 In this book, we will focus **primarily** on the process view.

Each ARIS view is divided further into phases. The translation of business requirements into IT applications **requires** that we follow certain phases. Globally, three general phases are likely to be used:

- Requirements phase
- Design specification phase
- Implementation phase

ARIS is particularly strong in the requirements phase, while other phases may differ depending on the implementation method and the architecture we use. We will talk about these later in this chapter.

Let us now look at the other important aspect, the business process modeling notations.

Modeling Notation

Process modeling also requires a notation In the past, several notations were used to model processes. Flow diagrams and block diagrams were representatives of the first-generation notations. Then, more sophisticated notations were defined, such as **EPC (Event Process Chain)** and **eEPC (Extended Event Process Chain)**. UML activity diagrams, XPDL, and IDEF 3 were also used, in addition to some other less-known notations. A few years ago a new notation, called **Business Process Modeling Notation (BPMN)** was developed. BPMN was developed particularly for modeling business processes in accordance with SOA. In this book, we will use BPMN for modeling processes.

BPMN

BPMN is the most comprehensive notation for process modeling so far. It has been developed under the hood of **OMG (Object Management Group)**. We will provide a detailed introduction to BPMN in the next chapter. Here, we will only give a brief introduction to the most important BPMN elements so that you can read the diagrams presented later in this chapter.

The most important goals while designing BPMN have been:

- **To develop a notation, which will be understandable at all levels:** In business process modeling different people are involved, from business users, business analysts, and process owners, to the technical architects and developers. The management reviews business processes at periodic intervals. Therefore, the goal of BPMN has been to provide a graphical notation the is simple to understand, yet powerful enough to model business processes at the required level of detail.

- **To enable automatic transformation into executable code, that is, BPEL, and vice-versa:** The gap between the business process models and the information technology (application software) has been quite large in existing technologies. There is no clear definition on how one relates to the other. Therefore, BPMN has been designed specifically to provide such transformations.

To model the diagrams, BPMN defines four categories of elements:

- **Flow objects**, which are activities, events, and gateways. Activities can be tasks or sub processes. Events can be triggers or results. Three types of events are supported: start, intermediate, and end. Gateways control the divergence of sequential flows into concurrent flows, and their convergence back to sequential flow

- **Connecting** objects are used to connect flow objects together. Connectors are sequence flows, message flows, and associations.

- **Swim lanes** are used to organize activities into visual categories in order to illustrate different responsibilities or functional capabilities. Pools and lanes can be used for swim lanes.

- **Artifacts** are used to add specific context to the business processes that are being modeled. Data objects are used to show how data is produced or required by the process. Groups are used to group together similar activities or other elements. Annotations are used to add text information to the diagram. We can also define custom artifacts.

The following diagrams show the various notations used in BPMN:

Activities are the basic elements of BPMN and are represented by rectangles with rounded corners. Plus A plus sign denotes that the activity can be further decomposed:

Decisions are shown as diamonds. A plus sign inside the diamond denotes a logical AND, while an x denotes a logical OR:

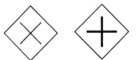

Events are shown as double circles:

Roles are shown as pools and swim-lanes within pools:

Pool name	Swimlane
	Swimlane

A Document is shown as follows:

The order of activities is indicated by an arrow:

The flow of a document or information is shown with a dashed line:

○------▷

BPMN can be used to model parts of processes or whole processes. Processes can be modeled at different levels of fidelity. BPMN is equally suitable for internal (private) business processes, and for public (collaborative) business-to-business processes. Internal business processes focus on the point of view of a single company, and define activities that are internal to the company. Such processes might also define interactions with external partners.

Public collaborative processes show the interaction between all involved businesses and organizations. Such processes models should be modeled from the general point of view, and should show interactions between the participants.

Process Design

The main activity in process design is the recording of the actual processes. The objective is to develop the as-is process model. To develop the as-is model, it is necessary to gather all knowledge about the process. This knowledge often exists only in the heads of the employees, who are involved in the process. Therefore, it is necessary to perform detailed interviews with all involved people. Often, process supervisors might think that they know exactly how the process is performed. However, after talking with those employees who really carry out the work, they see that the actual situation differs considerably. It is very important to gather all this informaion about the process, otherwise it will not be possible to develop a sound process model, that reflects the as-is state of the process.

The first question related to the as-is model is the business result that the process generates. Understanding the business result is crucial, as sometimes it may not be clearly articulated.

After the business result is identified, we should understand the process flow. The process flow consists of activities (or tasks) that are performed in a certain order. The process flow is modeled at various levels of abstraction. At the highest level of abstraction, the process flow shows only the most important activities (usually up to ten).

Each of the top-level activities are then decomposed into detailed flows. The process complexity, and the required level of detail, are the criteria that instruct us how deep we should decompose. To understand the process behavior completely, it makes sense to decompose until atomic activities (that is, activities that cannot be further decomposed) are reached.

 When developing the as-is process model, one of the most important things to consider is the level of detail. In order to provide end-to-end support for business processes using SOA, detailed process modeling should be done. The difficulties often hide in the details!

In the process design, we should understand the detailed structure of the business process. Therefore, we should identify at least the following:

- Process activities at various levels of detail
- Roles responsible for carrying out each process activity
- Events that trigger the process execution and events that interrupt the process flow

- Documents exchanged within the process. This includes input documents and output documents
- Business rules that are part of the process.

 We should design the usual (also called optimal) process flow and identify possible exception scenarios. Exceptions interrupt the usual process flow. Therefore, we need to specify how the exceptions will be handled.

The usual approach to the process design includes the following steps:

1. Identifying the roles
2. Identifying the activities
3. Connecting activities to roles
4. Defining the order of activities
5. Adding events
6. Adding documents

We should also understand the efficiency of the business process. This includes resource utilization, the time taken by involved employees, possible bottlenecks and inefficiencies. This is the reason why we should also identify metrics that are used to measure the efficiency of the process. While some of these metrics may be KPIs, other metrics relevant to the process should also be identified.

We should identify if the process is compliant with standards or reference processes. In some industry domains, reference processes have been defined. An example is the telecommunications industry where the **TMF (Telecom Management Forum)** has defined NGOSS. Part of NGOSS is **eTom (Enhanced Telecom Operations Map)**, which specifies compliant business processes for telecom companies. Other industries have also started to develop similar reference processes.

We should also identify the business goals to which the process contributes to. Business goals are the same as the process results. A business process should not only have at least one result, but should also contribute to at least one (preferably more than one) business goal. Here, we can look into the company strategy to identify the business goals.

We should also identify the events that can interrupt the process flow. Each process can be interrupted, and we should understand how this happens. If a process is interrupted, we might need to compensate those activities of the process that have already been successfully completed. Therefore, we should also specify the **compensation logic** related to different interruption events.

Finally, we should also understand the current software support for the business process. This is important because existing software may hide the details of process behavior. This information can also be re-used for end-to-end process support.

Once we have identified all of these artifacts, we will have gathered a good understanding of the process. Therefore, let us now look at the results of the process modeling.

Results of Process Modeling

The results of the process modeling phase are:

- Process map, which shows the relationship between various business processes and the interactions between these processes.

- Roles and relations structure diagram, which shows the roles involved in business processes, and the relationships between the roles.

- An as-is process model model for each individual process. This describes in detail the existing business process, including the process flow, activities, roles, and documents (discussed later in this section). It can also contain the identified optimization points.

Process Map

The process map includes all business processes in the company. If the existing processes are redesigned, the process map is updated with the newly-identified processes. The process map gives an overview of all of the processes, and is very important for understanding the structure of processes in the company.

The process map also shows the relationship between business processes and their points of connection. Usually, business processes are not isolated, but interact with other processes. The connection points show where this interaction occurs.

The process map also shows the document flow. It shows which documents are consumed by each process, and which documents are generated by each process. This includes process-specific documents and general purpose documents such as standards, regulations, internal acts, and so on.

The following figure shows an example of a process map for project management:

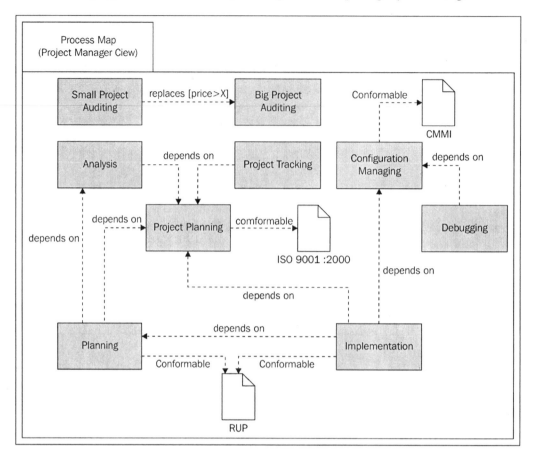

Roles and Relations Structure

The roles and relations structure diagram shows the roles and groups, and their relations. This is not a hierarchical diagram, such as an organizational diagram. Rather, it shows the relations in the style of network diagram. It shows relationships such as participations in a group, supervisions, communications, substitutions, and so on.

The following figure shows an example of a roles and relations structure:

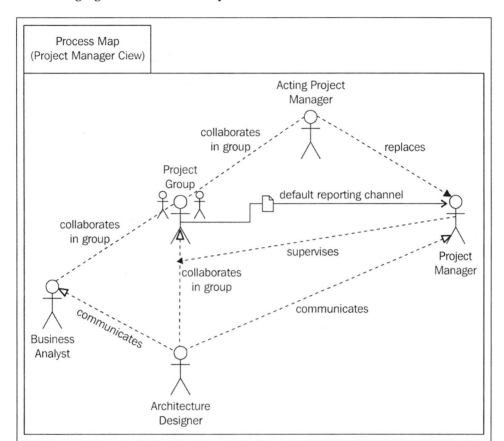

As-is Process Model

The as-is process model for each business process consists of the following:

- Process environment diagram, which shows the relationship of this process to other processes.

- Top level process model, which shows the high-level activities and the flow of these activities, along with the responsibilities of the roles involved in the process.

- Detailed process maps for each high-level activity, with detailed representations of process activities. The detail process map may have several decomposition levels, depending on the complexity of each high-level activity.

- Exception handling diagram. When modeling a business process, it is very important that we don't end up modeling only the optimal process flow. We must not forget to identify the possible exceptions that might occur, and specify how these exceptions are handled. An exception handling diagram shows exactly this.

In the following sections, we will describe the process environment diagram, top-level process modeling, detailed process maps, exception handling diagram, and responsibilities diagram. Let's start with the top-level process model.

Process Environment Diagram

The process environment diagram shows the highest-level process view, where the whole process is shown as a single activity. In this way, we look at the process as a black box. In the process environment diagram, we show:

- Process trigger, which tells us how the process is triggered to start the execution

- Necessary input information required in the process

- Process result or results

- Roles involved in the process or responsible for the process

- Responsibilities of the roles within the process (such as 'responsible-for', 'executes', 'participates', 'supervises', and so on)

- Metrics used for measuring process efficiency

- Events that can interrupt the regular process flow, and the compensation logic required to handle these interruption events

- Compliance with standards, or reference processes

- The business goals a process contributes to

The following figure shows the general layout of the process environment:

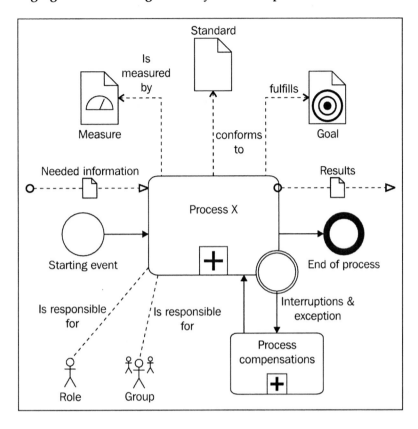

In a specific process, we define the process-specific information as shown in the following figure:

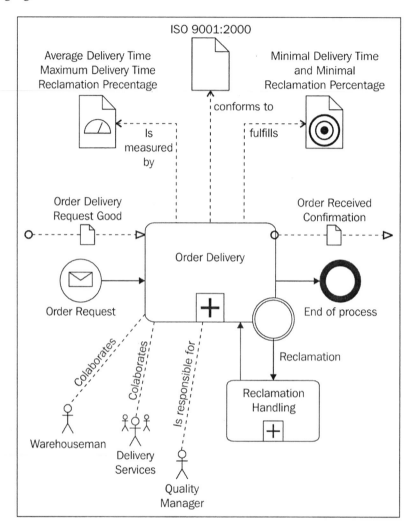

The process environment diagram does not show the process flow details. This is shown in the process model, which is described in the next section.

Top-level Process Model

The top-level process model shows the highest-level view of the process activities. Usually, the top-level process model shows a limited number (for example, up to ten) of well-structured activities that represent the high-level process flow.

The top-level process model also shows the roles that participate in the process, the main decisions taken during execution of the process and the most important exceptions.

The following figure shows a general top-level process model:

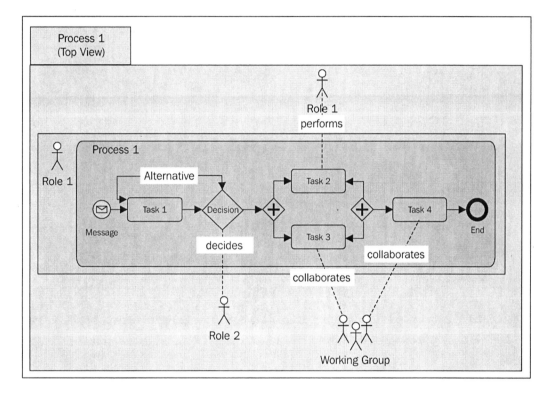

An example top-level process model for procurement business process is shown in the figure that follows:

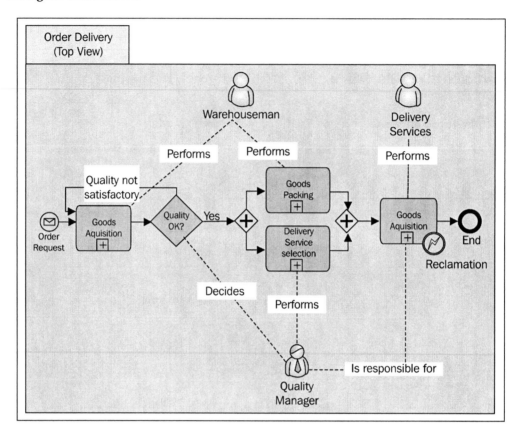

The top-level process model does not show the details of the process activities. These are shown on the detailed process maps.

Detailed Process Maps

Detailed process maps show the detailed process decomposition. (The top-level process activities included in the top-level process model are decomposed into detailed sub-processes.) The decomposition is done from the perspective of individual roles involved in the process.

For each top-level activity, a detailed process map is developed. (If a process is more complex, then these process maps are further decomposed into more detailed process maps, until the atomic activities are reached). Atomic activities are activities that do not need to be decomposed further. Atomic activities are well understood, and can be seen as distinct software operations, that will be implemented in order to provide end-to-end support for the process. Atomic activities can also be human tasks.

While modeling processes for SOA, it is very important to achieve the correct level of details. This means that the process should be decomposed to a low level of detail. This is important because the difficulties are often in the details. It is also important because, as developing SOA services we need to understand the details in order to implement them successfully.

The detailed process map also shows the conditions and the business rules. It is important to identify the business rules. In SOA, business rules are extracted and implemented within **Business Rules Management Systems (BRMS)**. Identification of business rules should be done in their generic forms so that the business rules can be re-used in other processes. Therefore, we should strive to write down the generalized rules.

We should also identify the events that occur in the process. Events can interrupt the process flow. Events can also be generated by the process. It is important that we identify all relevant events.

When designing the detailed process flow, we put activities into swim-lanes to show the roles that are responsible for carrying-out specific activities. We also show which documents are inputs to certain activities, and which documents are generated by the activities.

The following figure shows an example of a detailed process map:

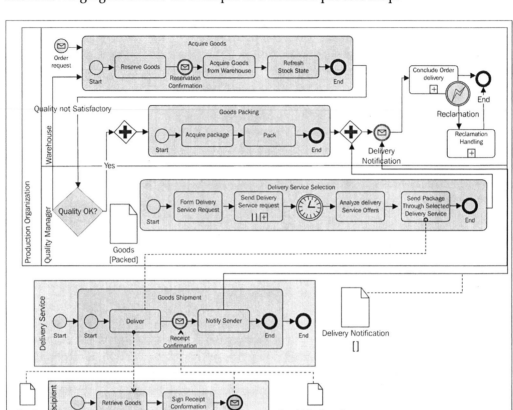

Exception Handling Diagram

When designing the process, it is also particularly important that we should identify not just the regular process flow, but also the exception flow that each process has.

If an exception occurs, it should be handled. The exception handling diagram should show how to handle these exceptions. We should specify how exceptions are handled and by whom, and where the process goes on after the exception has been handled.

Often, exceptions require that we compensate activities of the process flow that have already been completed successfully. We might also want to compensate activities if an event interrupts the process flow.

The exception handling diagram is shown separately (separate from the regular process flow). The following example shows an exception in a process flow:

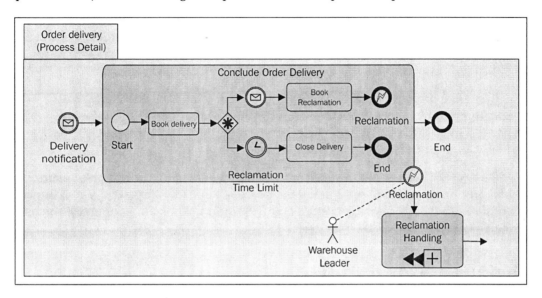

The following exception handling diagram shows how to handle exceptions and compensate:

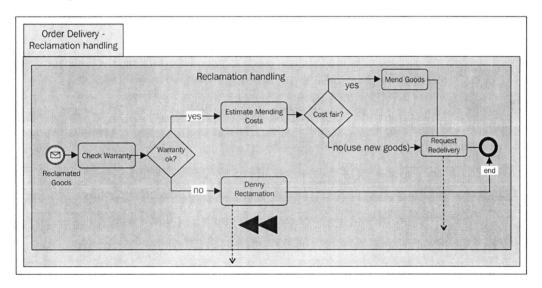

Publishing and Communicating Process Models

An important part of business process modeling is communicating the models to all interested parties. This includes company management, unit management, supervisors, employees, quality assurance, and all other interested employees, all of whom can use the process model to better understand what is going on within the organization. They can also use the process model as work instructions.

Publishing the process model and communicating it to all interested employees is also important, because this way, we can gather feedback on the process and improve it even further. Publishing a process on the company's intranet is usually a good way to give visibility to process models.

Feedback on the process models can improve the quality, and can be a good source of ideas for improving and optimizing the process. This is the first step in building a continuous awareness about processes and their optimization among process owners and all others involved in the process.

Process Simulation

Process simulation is a useful feature that can help us verify an existing process model, identify bottlenecks, and prepare ideas for process optimization. Simulation is a proven approach to identifying possible bottlenecks, assessing the costs of running a process, and identifying potential problems with resources and their allocation.

 The results of the simulation are used to define the optimizations in the process and to model the so-called **to-be** process, which will help the company to work more efficiently and produce better value.

For efficient simulation, we must have enough knowledge about the process itself, such as:

- How many instances of the process are started in a certain period?
- How are these distributed over the day, week, or month?
- How long does it take, on average, to execute a particular activity
- How much cost (other than time) is incurred by the activity?
- What quantity of which resources are utilized?
- Is there any start-up cost or waiting cost for an activity?
- How are the outcomes of decisions distributed (for example, if process behavior differs from the type of contract)?

Gathering this information can be time-consuming and can also lead to results that are not completely relevant. Sometimes, it is very difficult to assess the average execution time of a certain activity. This is particularly problematic if an activity takes a variable amount of time in the real world. If you ask an employee, he or she might not give you relevant information, because people simply don't measure the time it takes to complete an activity and do not calculate averages. In addition, there are many practical problems, for example, interruptions in the form of emails, phone calls, or a colleague knocking on the office door during the activity execution.

 Most of the simulation-related problems are omitted in SOA because we can measure real quantitative data about process execution, calculate averages, and use such data in a simulation. We shall talk more abut this later in this chapter.

Tools for Simulating Processes

To make simulation efficient, we also need good tools, that can support simulation. Most SOA platforms such as Oracle, IBM, and BEA have built-in support for process simulation, which offers good capabilities and are likely to improve further in the future versions. In the market, we can also find several other tools, some of which are specialized in process simulation.

To identify the characteristics of a good tool, the following guidelines should be taken into account:

- **Ease of developing the process model**: Ease of use allows people other than process analysts to be involved in the development of the process model and to make changes themselves.

- **Verification and correctness of the process model**: Good tools should allow automatic verification of models to assess their validity.

- **Different perspectives and support for process patterns**: A good tool should support process, resource, and data perspectives. The process perspective shows the process flow, the resource perspective shows the resource utilization, and the data perspective describes the documents used in the process.

- **Flexibility:** Tools should provide means to specify the costs of activities, start-up costs, waiting costs, resource utilization, and all other relevant aspects. It should also provide support for distribution of incoming requests, support for queues, overload, and so on.

- **Animation:** Graphical animation of simulations can be very useful and can give insights into how the process executes. Visualization can reveal bottlenecks and all other problems that might occur in the process.

- **Scenarios:** Support for different scenarios within a simulation is useful. We can change the load patterns and the behavior patterns of activities while leaving the general flow of the process as it is. This can help simulate different
real-world cases.

- **Results:** A good tool should give various types of results, such as statistics. Results should be presented in an easy-to-understand format. Good tools also provide *what-if* analysis support and conclusion-making support.

Modeling Principles

When modeling business processes, our objective should be to develop sound process models. Soundness of the process models can be achieved if we follow some basic principles:

- **Syntax**: Our model must have correct syntax as defined by the modeling notation. If we use BPMN, we should follow the BPMN syntax rules. Most tools can check the syntax.

- **Semantics**: Our model should also be semantically correct. This means that we have included all relevant activities, decisions, events, documents, and other elements. This also means that the process flow is correct, and we have defined how to react to events, how to handle exceptions, and how to compensate, if necessary. We should also use the correct names for all elements. Achieving semantic correctness is more difficult than achieving syntactical correctness. Usually, it helps if we follow a selected method such as ARIS.

- **Relevance**: We should model only those processes that are relevant to the problem domain. In modeling processes, we could easily get carried away because one process will typically relate to other processes. Sometimes, it is difficult to draw a line between what we should include and what we should not. The most basic principle is to include only those artifacts that are relevant from the perspective of the process and the problem domain we are focusing on. Too much modeling is a waste of time.

- **Cost versus benefit**: We model processes to achieve specific benefits. We should therefore weigh the amount of effort aginst the anticipated benefits. Usually, the 80/20 rule applies here as well. 80% of the benefit comes from 20% of the effort, and vice versa. Therefore, it is important to know the level of detail and when it is better to stop modeling. The required level of detail can differ. If we are performing process modeling for quality assurance, a lower level of detail is required than if we are performing process modeling for an SOA implementation.

- **Usability**: The model should be usable and understandable. Otherwise, the model is worth nothing. Business processes are complex. To achieve usability, we should decompose the model into various levels of detail. How we do the decomposition is important, as the parts should be understandable. We usually prefer simple models over more complex ones.

- **Standards**: While modeling business processes, we should use and apply certain standards. First, we should use good practices and patterns. Second, we should use naming conventions. In some industries, standard or reference process models exist (such as eTom for Telecom operators). We should look for compliance, if it can add business value.

- **Integration**: We should integrate different models that look at the same or similar process domains from different perspectives. The integrated model will reveal all aspects of the process. We should also design a process map, where all processes and relationships between them are listed.

Using these and some other more specific principles will help make our process models better, and more usable over a longer period of time. We should, however, be aware that modeling processes is not easy, although it might look easy at first sight. Therefore, in the next section, we shall list common problems that we are likely to face.

Common Problems in Process Modeling

When modeling business processes, we will face several challenges. We have identified some of these in the following paragraphs.

Modeling business processes should be aligned with the overall business strategy. If the objective of process modeling is not related to some specific business goals, then it is a waste of time for all people involved. Therefore, it is crucial, that we define, from the beginning, what the goals of process modeling are. The goal can be, for example, to provide end-to-end IT support for a specific process. The goal can also be to improve the efficiency of the process. It is however important that we do not stick to such high-level goals. We should precisely articulate the specific goals of the company. We should know the exact process for which we want to develop end-to-end support for, where we want to improve the efficiency, and by how much. Without clearly defined goals with measurable outcomes, we should not start process modeling.

When we start process modeling, we should clearly define the responsibilities. In process modeling, people from different organizations participate. They must see value in participating, otherwise, they will not be willing to dedicate their time. Communicating the benefits of process modeling is therefore important. Even more important is to have support from the top-management. Only the top-management can order all employees to participate in the project.

We should define teams that will participate in the process modeling. Here is one possible structure of the team, which has proven to be efficient:

- Process owner
- Two persons to assist the process owner, coming from the same department
- Process quality representative
- Business process analyst (or analysts)
- IT representative
- Optionally, an external consultant

We also have to define measurable goals to assess whether process management has been done the right way, and what the benefits have been.

To be successful, we also need enough knowledge in process modeling. Business analyst should have multidisciplinary knowledge. They should be experts in the process modeling method and notation used. They also have to be familiar with the business domain. Otherwise, they will not be able to convert received information into process models.

Good knowledge about the existing process is also crucial. We should therefore be sure that we have included all of the people who can contribute:

- People who have a detailed knowledge of the as-is model (existing process)
- People with a vision for future development and optimization of the process

- People who are aware of real limitations and resource restrictions
- People who generate ideas

We should also not underestimate the effort required for process modeling. The number of processes in your company can be relatively high.

 After processes are modeled, we should not just put the models into a drawer and forget about them. We should enforce the whole BPM cycle; otherwise, we will not realize the benefits related to continuous process optimization.

We should be aware that even with the best notation, such as BPMN, we cannot model all of the details, particularly the non-functional requirements such as security, costs, and so on.

When modeling processes, it is also crucial that in the first phase we stick to modeling the existing **as-is** state. It can easily happen that we start to model wishes. This way, we do not get a representative as-is model. Rather, we get a list of wishes that have not been verified in the real-world.

With this, we have concluded our discussions on process modeling. In the next section, we will talk about process implementation.

Process Implementation

After we have successfully modeled the business process, it is time for process implementation. Nowadays, it is important that IT provides end-to-end support for business processes. In the past, software offered distinct functionalities that employees had to select. Although these functionalities were helpful, the process was driven by the employees. They had to know which steps to take and when to do what. This had several drawbacks. As the process knowledge was in the heads of employees, finding replacements for these employees that had the required knowledge was difficult. Then, there was no real control on what is going on. The visibility into process execution was limited. It also happened that when information on a process activity was handed over by one employee to another, it was lost and eventually forgotten untill the customer noticed a gap in service. If the process flow is not well documented, it might be difficult even to introduce new employees .

Visibility into process execution can have a positive impact on a company's revenue, besides other obvious benefits. For example, when FedEx introduced packet tracking over the Internet, this increased the number of customers who selected FedEx as their courier. When BMW enabled online visibility for customers into car assembly processes, and enabled them to change car configuration until the very last moment, customers opted for optional equipment resulting in an average 10% increase in revenue for the company.

If a business process is implemented end-to-end, using IT, the visibility into process execution flow can be greatly improved. The end-to-end business process implementation focuses on mapping of process activities and other process requirements into applications. Today, applications and business processes are tightly related. This means that if we change a business process, we also need to change the applications. It is the time, this take the **IT-gap time**, which is crucial here. The IT gap is the time required for IT to modify the applications so that they reflect the required changes in business processes. Obviously, the management wants to minimize the IT gap, but the IT department needs adequate time.

We all know that software is complex and requires time to be modified. Information systems in companies are usually very complex, and consists of several applications that use different technologies. These applications may be integrated to a certain degree.

Generally speaking, up to now, three possibilities existed for information system development:

1. Classic (non-SOA) software development with well-known approaches, including multitier architectures and component-based software development
2. Implementation of standardized ERP solutions
3. SOA

Classic Software Development

Developing applications to support required functionality using traditional software engineering is a well-understood approach that follows the software lifecycle roughly through the following steps:

- Requirements gathering
- Analysis
- Prototyping (optional)
- Design

- Implementation
- Testing
- Deployment

Irrespective of the process model used (be it traditional, such as **RUP (Rational Unified Process)**, or agile, such as **XP (Extreme Programming)**), traditional software development has several drawbacks, that make them unsuitable for developing software with end-to-end support for business processes. Some of these drawbacks are:

- Traditional software development is focused on software requirements, which are not directly aligned with business processes. Software requirements, written as **SRS (Software Requirements Specification)** documents, are focused on functional and non-functional requirements of applications. Such requirements first have to be derived from business processes.

- The gap between business process models and software functions is evident. This is particularly problematic in the maintenance phase, when software needs to be modified to accommodate changing business needs.

- Software, developed with traditional approach, is not as flexible, as we would like it to be. The ground rule for traditional software development is that the requirements should be specified well. Although, this has been relaxed over the years, the ground rule that says the better we specify the requirements, the better the software architecture will be, is still valid. Traditional software development does not consume changes as well as we would like.

- Due to the semantic gap between business processes and software architecture, changes in business processes may require large changes in the software architecture. The more times such changes are made, the worse the overall software architecture gets. This brings us to a position where the software can no longer accommodate new changes.

- Platforms used for traditional approaches including Java and .NET focus on applications. There is no support for monitoring and executing business processes. To implement end-to-end support for business processes including process execution, control, and monitoring, a lot of "infrastructure" work has to be done manually, because the traditional platforms do not provide support out of the box.

Standardized ERP Solutions

Business processes should be unique for each company, and should present a competitive advantage. This is particularly true for core business processes. Each company, however, has many support processes that are not as business-critical. To provide IT support for these processes, implementing a standardized ERP solution can be a good choice.

ERPs, such as Oracle or SAP, provide built-in business processes. Implementing such ERPs can be an opportunity for a company to optimize existing processes, if the existing processes are not as good as those implemented in the ERPs. This can be true for support processes, but will vary depending on the process quality of each individual company.

The cost of implementing ERP can sometimes be lower than the cost of individual software development. It can also be an opportunity to standardize business processes between departments, particularly if mergers and acquisitions have taken place.

Processes built into ERP systems are best practices in the industry. However, it is reasonable to asses them in detail before taking the decision as to how these processes will influence the company.

It is also true that in most cases, built-in processes in ERPs can be adapted to suit the company's actual needs. The rationale for ERP modification, rather than development of custom application, and the cost involved, will depend upon the level of adoption.

It is also important to understand that ERP systems cannot fulfill all of the requirements a company has. Therefore, sooner or later, it will be necessary to integrate ERPs with other applications, particularly with custom-developed applications. Research has shown that ERPs can cover approximately 40% of the company's requirements. A chosen ERP system, therefore, should provide good integration interfaces. Recently, all of the major ERP providers have started to incorporate SOA concepts into their solutions. This means that ERP and SOA will provide a "perfect fit" in the future. Therefore, let us now discuss the benefits of the SOA approach.

Service Oriented Architecture

SOA has been designed from the ground up with the focus on business process support. Therefore, one of the key elements of SOA is the process server, which enables direct execution of business processes in BPEL. Another important SOA element is the business rules management system, and the third element is business activity monitoring. As we can see, SOA provides out-of-the-box support for major elements that are important for BPM.

Another important SOA aspect is that it dramatically changes the development cycle. Instead of requirements gathering, analysis, design, implementation, and testing, SOA introduces phases that are better-aligned with process modeling:

- **Modeling**, where we design processes, ideally using BPMN
- **Composition**, where we compose services to support process execution in BPEL
- **Testing**, where we test the process
- **Execution and Monitoring**, where we execute the process and monitor the execution parameters

SOA enables much tighter integration between business processes and software architecture. Many tools on the market today provide bidirectional lifecycle support. This means that changes made to the model (BPMN) are automatically propagated to implementation (BPEL), and vice versa. This means that the model and the code should not become discordant.

Because of this tighter integration, SOA makes maintenance much faster and more flexible. Applications developed on SOA concepts can be modified quicker and with less effort. Therefore, they can reflect changes faster, making the IT (and the whole company) more flexible.

[Efficient BPM is the basis for successful SOA implementation.]

Using SOA, business processes can start dictating the business requirements, which are decomposed to services that provide the actual implementation. Services can be developed in different ways:

- They can be developed in-house
- They can be developed by external software companies
- They can be exposed from existing software
- They can be bought (off the shelf)
- They can be used as remote services from other providers

SOA also provides a more natural separation of work between the IT department of the company and external software vendors that develop custom applications for the company. Usually the process management should stay in the domain of the IT department, while services development should be outsourced. This gives more control and prevents situations where the outsourcing partner controls to the company the application.

Process Implementation Phase with BPEL

In the process implementation phase, the key technology of SOA is BPEL. This language minimizes the semantic gap between the process model and the actual execution code. BPEL enables business processes to be executed directly. Process models, preferably developed in BPMN, can manually, semi-automatically, or automatically be translated into BPEL.

With BPEL, various activities, called partner links, are performed by services. Therefore, an important aspect is the decomposition of the business process and its mapping to the services. Services are the central artifacts of SOA architecture. We use services to model automated business activities or human tasks.

Developing SOA-compliant applications requires architects and developers to perform a proper mapping of services, where the following choices are available:

- The service needs to be developed from scratch, because the required functionality does not exist yet.
- The service needs to be exposed from existing applications, because such functionality exists in the legacy applications.
- The service already exists and can be re-used. Re-use can occur:
    - Without modifications of exiting service
    - With minimal modifications of existing service
    - With larger modifications of existing service

Certain process activities can be modeled as human tasks. They can be process tasks, which are by nature human tasks, and require human intervention. They can also be tasks that have not yet been developed as automated services, and will be replaced by automated activities (services) in the future.

 Developing a sound SOA architecture is a task, that is out of the scope of this book. Please refer to *SOA Approach to Integration*, Packt Publishing, 2007, and *Business Process Execution Language for Web Services*, Packt Publishing, 2006 for more information.

Process Execution and Control

According to ancient wisdom,*'if you can't measure it, you can't manage it'*. This is particularly true for business processes. Measuring different aspects of a business process, such as activity duration, resource utilization, total execution time, average execution time, and so on, is crucial to understanding how the processes performs in the real-world. We can only understand the process if we have numbers, and we can get numbers from measuring the process execution.

 Measuring process execution is a valuable source of information, which is used to understand and control process execution, and to identify possibilities for process optimization.

SOA provides sophisticated support for process execution and control. Process execution relates to the supervision of several hundred or even thousand process instances, which can be active for anything from a few seconds up to several days or even weeks. In the latter case we are talking about long-running processes.

Processes usually include human interactions. On the other hand, things can go wrong while executing processes. We cannot simply restart a process that failed because of a hardware or software failure, particularly for long-running processes and for processes that include human interactions. Therefore, it is important for us to have powerful tools that help us in such scenarios. SOA process servers provide such support.

The process control phase is about measuring and monitoring the efficiency of the process. This means that we control whether the processes are running as defined in the process design, or not. We also measure process efficiency and compare it with the KPIs. Such measurements identify opportunities for process optimization. Continuous monitoring of actual business processes bridges the gap between corporate strategy and its operational implementation.

SOA for the Process Execution and Control Phase

SOA also plays a crucial role in the process execution and control phase. SOA applications consist of BPEL processes, and such processes are executed on process servers. Process servers are the centerpieces of the SOA platform. They enable us to execute processes in a managed environment and follow the execution of processes regardless of the duration of the process (be it short-running, or long-running).

Process servers provide valuable information for process supervisors. They enable us to monitor specific process instances, follow the execution of activities, find out the current activity for a process, and identify possible exceptions. Examples of possible exceptions in process execution include service failures, or the unavailability of employees in human tasks.

Process servers also provide elementary control over processes, such as, how many process instances have been started, how long has it taken to execute a certain process activity, the average execution time of process instances over a period of time, and so on. This information can be valuable to process supervisors and process analysts.

In addition to process servers, SOA platforms also provide means for more sophisticated process monitoring such as **Business Activity Monitoring (BAM)**. BAM provides quantitative metrics on process execution and helps us to measure those aspects of processes that are related to key performance indicators. In this way, we can obtain valuable data that we can use to optimize the processes.

The role of SOA in the process execution and control phase is immense, as SOA platforms today offer out-of the-box execution and monitoring capabilities, which means that the developers do not have to put huge effort into gathering and presenting this data.

Business Activity Monitoring

One of the key elements for process control is BAM. The key objective of BAM is to provide a complete overview of business process execution within the company. Management, and other people who are responsible for development and operations of the company, use this data. The most important component of BAM is **time**. Time is crucial, because BAM shows actual, near real-time information on process execution. This allows the company to react quickly and efficiently to changes reflected through process execution.

[Business activity monitoring is real-time observation of key performance indicators.]

`Whatis.com` defines BAM as follows:

> *BAM, also called business activity management, is the use of technology to proactively define and analyze critical opportunities and risks in an enterprise to maximize profitability and optimize efficiency. The BAM paradigm can be used to evaluate external as well as internal factors.*
>
> *Three main steps compose effective implementation of BAM. First, relevant data is gathered in an efficient and timely manner and in sufficient quantities to provide meaningful results. Second, the data is processed to identify and categorize factors relevant to specific concerns. Finally, the data is analyzed and the results displayed in a clear, user-friendly interface so personnel can take appropriate actions.*

To provide information for decision-making, BAM first has to gather data. This data is gathered from business processes and is related to process activities, resources utilized in these activities, such as employees, and so on. The more the data that is gathered the better and the more statistically relevant the derived information will be. The BAM tools have to gather the data and calculate interesting information that can help in decision-making. BAM can process the gathered data in different ways:

- Data can be processed immediately. In this way, the related KPIs will be calculated immediately and shown to the supervisors or sent to a decision-support application. Such KPIs can then be recalculated in near real-time.
- Data can be used to notify supervisors and other people involved in the process that something important has happened. For example, if a KPI value is too high or too low, certain action can be triggered. A supervisor can be alerted (by email, SMS, or voice call), or some automatic action can be executed.
- BAM can also be used to identify patterns in the incoming data and notify or even react to them. Because BAM gathers data from different, independent business processes, BAM can identify certain patterns between the processes, and can react to such patterns. This gives an additional level of control and flexibility to the information system.

BAM is not only a system that displays interesting information about processes; it consolidates data gathered from different, often independent sources also. Connecting this data with past data enables BAM to identify critical situations in process execution, or even automatically or semi-automatically solve some frequent critical solutions.

 The ultimate goal of each BAM user is to optimize the process execution, to improve the process efficiency, and to sense and react to important events.

The BAM user interface should be simple and present information and data in an easily- understandable manner. It should hide all of the complexity that takes place behind the scenes. A typical BAM user interface uses graphical elements such as graphs, and colors to present the data. The following figure shows an example BAM screen shot:

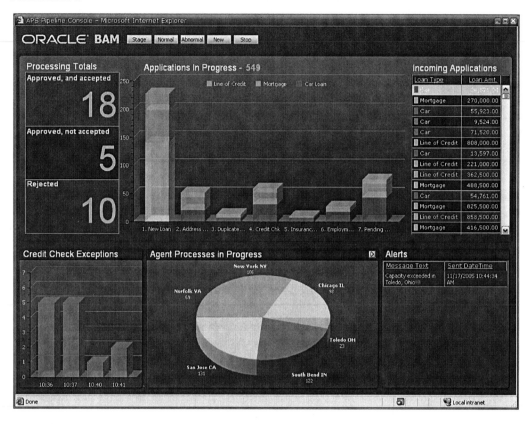

In the figure above, we can see the BAM dashboard showing various important information for decision-makers. In addition to the dashboard, another important part of BAM is the decision-support module. This module can use decision methods, business intelligence, or simulations for support, and can help decision-makers take the right decision at the right time, which can improve business efficiency.

Process Optimization

Process optimization offers huge opportunities for each company to distinguish itself from its competitors and focus more closely on customer wishes and requirements. Customers assess the whole shopping experience, not just the product or service. Therefore, it makes sense to optimize processes at all levels, from handling a sales inquiry, to processing an order, product or service, production, delivery, and support.

Process optimization can increase revenue and profits considerably, if done the right way.

A systematic approach to process optimization, which should include all end-to-end processes, has multiple positive effects on a company. It can help increase the competitive advantage of a company in several ways. The following are some of the most important effects of process optimization:

- **Increased sales** of products or services through of better service, better and faster production, increased flexibility, better customer experience, the ability to better -sense customer requirements, and so on.

- **Cost savings** are the most obvious benefits, and are directly related to optimizing activity execution times, and people and resource utilization. Simplifying business processes also saves costs. Sometimes, process optimization helps in identifying processes or parts of processes that can be outsourced or shared.

- **Improved efficiency in business operations** is another important aspect. Process optimization is not only about minimizing process activity times. It is also about coordinating private processes (those processes that a company executes internally) with public processes (processes that involve business partners). Just-in-time delivery and manufacturing are just two examples of highly-coordinated business processes between several partners. Such processes save money, and allow for more efficient business operations.

- **Increased customer satisfaction** can be achieved through process optimization. Better support for customers, faster response times, and higher visibility into processes (for example ordering process where the customer can monitor on-line what happens with his or her order) are directly related to customer satisfaction. Integrating customer on-line support with a problem ticketing system is another example, and we could identify more.

- **Improved exception handling** can also be achieved. Exceptions are the most undesirable events in business processes, because they interrupt or even stop the usual process execution. The fact is that when exceptions occur, they take up considerable time and resources. Optimizing and automating exception handling can be very useful.

From a technical perspective, process optimization is about developing optimized process models, which we will look at in the next section.

The To-be Process Model

Process optimization is the final phase in the BPM cycle. The objective of this phase is to develop the optimized process models, called to-be models.

Developing the to-be process model is a challenging task, because we must balance different factors. First, we have to define the objectives that we want to realize through process optimization. The most obvious objective can be that the process performs faster, with less utilization of resources and people. The other objective can be to improve visibility into the process execution. Knowing the stage at which the process execution currently is can be helpful for management as well as for the customers, which might even be able to track the process online. The objective of optimization can also result in improvements in the quality of products/services, better working conditions for employees, reduced impact on the environment, and so on.

Then, we have to identify where to start the optimization. To identify this, we use the data gathered in the process execution and control phases. Data, gathered by BAM tools can be very helpful in identifying process bottlenecks in real time, and in identifying activities or sets of activities that would be suitable for optimization.

Another way of identifying process optimization points is process simulation, which we mentioned earlier in this chapter. It is important to understand that SOA provides tools that propagate the data from BAM (process execution and control) into the process modeling tool, where this real data can be used for process simulation. This is important because the tedious work of estimating process runtime parameters (activity execution, resource utilization, number of requests in a given time, and so on) is eliminated. At the same time, data gathered through BAM is much more accurate that estimates.

An important aspect of process optimization is new ideas. In closed organizational structures, the people involved in process optimization may be blinkered, and may lack the ability to look at the process from a broader perspective. It would therefore be useful to recruit external consultants or other people from outside the organization, who can generate fresh ideas. .Only in this way can we realize the full potential of process optimization.

However, when we gather new ideas, we should be careful to assess each new idea and find out if it is realizable. We have to find a balance between new ideas and the level of changes a company's existing organizational structure can accommodate.

[Optimizing business processes means changes. People, however, do not like changes.]

As employees do not like changes, we have to be careful in deciding how much change we want to introduce at one go. Ideally, we could change the process model considerably, and try to implement changes in one large step. However, in many organizations this has proved to be a failure, because employees could not accommodate such changes overnight. If we do not invest enough time in communication with employees, they could start showing resistance to the changes. Therefore, it is often better to optimize in smaller steps, and reach complete optimization over several stages.

On the other hand, we also have to be aware that process optimizations require modifications in the applications. Software modifications can be costly, and they require time and resources. Therefore, from the IT perspective, it might be better to modify the applications at one go, that is, to optimize all at once.

SOA is particularly helpful here. As SOA reduces the effort required for application modifications, and because it is more closely aligned with business processes, SOA-enabled applications are much easier to change. Therefore, we can adopt a systematic approach and optimize more easily in small steps. This can considerably increase our chances of success.

Process optimizations often require changes in a company's organizational structure. We have to think about these changes too, and obtain the necessary support from top-management. Otherwise, we will not be able to change the organizational structure.

Finally, we have to verify whether the optimizations have been successful and whether we have achieved our goals. We do this by process simulation, before it goes into production, and after the process has been deployed to production, through process control and monitoring.

Key Performance Indicators

Monitoring the processes closely is essential, and we use KPIs to specify what we wish to monitor. KPIs are financial and non-financial metrics used to help an organization define and measure process efficiency. Monitoring KPIs in real-time is nothing but BAM. KPIs should be related to the strategy of a company.

[KPIs should not be confused with critical success factors.]

Examples of a KPI are: Average revenue per customer, Average time for response to a customer call, Average order amount, and so on. KPIs differ from company to company. Therefore, the first step in using KPIs is to identify them.

We identify KPIs for a selected business process, which has to be specified well. We must also have clear goals and performance requirements for that process. When we define KPIs, we should follow these SMART rules:

- Specific
- Measurable
- Achievable
- Result-oriented, or Relevant
- Time-bound

When identifying KPIs, we should apply considerable thought to them, because in practice KPIs have a very long lifespan. After we have defined them, it is difficult to change them, because, if we change them we lose the comparisons to performance in the previous years or periods.

KPIs should also be defined in a way that will enable comparison with other similar companies. Therefore, KPIs should not be unduly confined to a company's internal specifics.

In the real world, measuring KPIs efficiently and accurately is a major challenge. SOA, together with BPM, offers huge advantages over previous IT architectures, because most SOA platforms provide KPI measurements as a built-in function of process monitoring and control.

Typical Problems in Process Optimization

Process optimization is not an easy task. The following are some common problems that you might face during optimization:

- **Too little imagination:** When optimizing processes, we should not only improve bottlenecks in existing processes, but also include innovations and new approaches.

- **Noncritical experience consideration of other companies:** Although it is good to consider the experiences of other companies in process optimization, we have to be critical while comparing their experiences with ours, and the facts related to our company. Therefore, before adopting them, we should assess if these experiences are really best practices, and if they are, we should adapt them to our specifics.

- **Too much focus on IT:** When modeling or optimizing processes, we should not focus only on end-to-end support by IT. This may generate unrealistically high expectations. IT cannot solve all problems.

- **Praxis-relevance:** An optimized process model might seem perfect, but this does not guarantee that the process model will work perfectly in the real world. Therefore, we should put enough effort in process implementation, otherwise we might end up with a failure.
- **Process metrics:** We should measure process related metrics such as KPIs, to be able to assess if the process works efficiently. Without metrics, we will not be able to optimize processes, because we will not be able to identify where the real problems are hiding.

Summary

In this chapter, we had an overview of the role of business process modeling for SOA. We outlined the importance of BPM. We saw that IT and business processes are closely related. SOA along with BPM provides a huge opportunity to align business processes with IT better, and make the whole company more efficient and successful.

We had an overview of the BPM life cycle, which consists of business process design, process implementation, process execution and control, and process optimization. We focused on process design, where we explained the methodologies and notations. We discussed ARIS methodology and BPMN notation. We also explained what the results of business process design should be, such as process map, roles, relations, etc. We also discussed process simulation in brief.

Further, we discussed business process modeling principles. We learned that modeling business processes is not an easy task, and it can consume a lot of time and generate poor results if not handled the right way. Therefore, it is particularly important that we understand the principles, know the best practices, and be aware of possible problems and mistakes.

We also discussed the process implementation phase, where we compared the traditional software development approach, implementation of ERP systems, and SOA approach. We saw that SOA approach provides numerous advantages and the best choice for providing end-to-end support for processes using IT.

We also had an overview of the process execution and control phase, where we discussed the advantages of process servers. We introduced BAM and explained why it is useful for decision-makers.

Finally, we discussed process optimization, which is the final phase of the overall BPM life cycle. We identified the opportunities, discussed the approach to optimization, explained KPIs, and also identified some typical problems in process optimization.

3
BPMN for Business Process Modeling

This chapter will introduce the foundations of business process modeling using a standards-based approach. In this chapter, we will discuss the concepts of using BPMN, a standard developed by the **Object Management Group** (OMG), especially from a practitioner's perspective.

The Need for Standards in Business Process Modeling

When we look at a business process, it's always from a certain perspective, a view of how a series of activities are performed in an organization. A picture is worth a thousand words, and when it comes to process elicitation, nothing beats a neat graphical representation.

Business communities have been using different techniques to graphically represent processes, mostly flowcharts. The critical problem, however, has been the explosion in multiple methods of representing a process, with business analysts and organizations both tweaking existing representations to suit their needs. This makes it difficult from an understanding and common approach perspective, especially when we look at processes as being key assets for an organization.

Another issue with some of the incumbent process modeling techniques and tools has been their inability to bridge the gap between the business and technology communities. At the business level, there is a need for creating process models in order to graphically visualize the process. Also, before the process is executed, the business analyst requires enough information to carry out an analysis of the process before sending it for execution or change in the production environment.

So a business user will look for a process modeling approach to carry out mapping and analysis of a business process. A technical user will look for the best way to interpret the processes, that is, whether process models have enough information to be prepared for execution. Most techniques only perform one or two elements of the process-modeling requirement, leading to a lack of common understanding and duplication of efforts. With increasing need for business IT alignment, there is a need for a standards-based approach to mapping, describing and assisting the execution of business process.

The BPMN specification is becoming increasingly popular as a standard approach to process modeling. The capability of BPMN to graphically express a process, and enable a common approach to its modeling greatly enhances the value it provides to any enterprise.

Business Process Classification and BPMN

As we know, Business Process Modeling is aimed at capturing a range of information pertaining to how a business works, and making this information available to a wide variety of stakeholders. This means that processes mapped in BPMN should easily be comprehensible across the organizational hierarchy. BPMN is therefore designed to cover a wide array of usage in its notation, and allows its modeling of end-to-end business processes.

BPMN is also a standard notation designed for mapping most kinds of processes used in an organization. Today, most organizations are using BPMN to create a process repository for all of their processes. Hence, the range of processes mapped by BPMN can be categorized depending on the business usage as described in the following sections.

Strategic or Operational

Based on the level of a given business process, it could be categorized as strategic or operational. Typically, an organization will define high-level strategies, which will be decomposed to lower levels until a representation that can be implemented is reached.

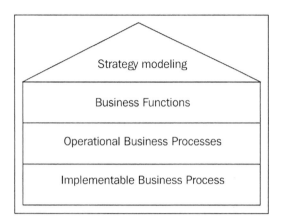

Strategy modeling is usually a textual or a simple block representation of an organization's strategic intent. For example, gaining leadership status in online retail in UK could be a strategic intent of an organization. These business strategies are further decomposed to a set of goals which, if fulfilled, will help achieve the strategy. For example, reducing item delivery time can be one of the goals.

At the next level, we usually define the main business functions of an organization, that are instrumental in the achievement of the goals. These business functions are typically represented using block diagrams. For example, to reduce item delivery time, the main business function to focus on would be 'supply chain department' and other functions such as marketing and sales, which are part of the end–to-end order to cash process.

At this level, we can also have very high-level business process diagrams to provide an abstract view of the end-to-end operational process. One example of a sample process at this level of abstraction could be as follows. In this case, the BPMN is used in an informal way to represent the end-to-end operational process.

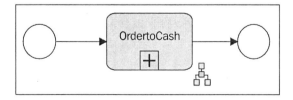

This process will typically go through a series of decomposition before it reaches an implementable stage. For example, the order-to cash process could be further decomposed into another business process diagram that divides the end-to-end process into two main activities: process order and process payments.

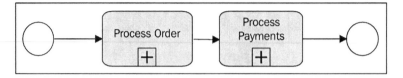

These activities will again be further decomposed to add more details to the business process diagrams utill we reach a stage where we can expose these business process diagrams to a BPM for implementation.

Process Type

A business process can also be classified based on its type and the extent of the requirement for automation. In the BPM world, a process can be divided into human-centric processes that mainly require human intervention for the process to move from one state to another. An example of such a process could be an underwriting process in insurance, where the underwriter needs to gather customer information before deciding on the insurance coverage and premiums. Similarly, there could be processes that are more automated, say a financial trading process, where the trade settlements between parties could be automated by integrating multiple systems to ensure minimal human intervention. Processes can also be categorized according to some other factors such as how document-centric the process is, or whether the process requires ad-hoc case management. The categorization of the process in this manner is typically done during the initiation of a BPM project, as the choice of the technology platform will depend on the process types (technology providers are still consolidating their offerings to cover all aspects of process automation). In BPMN, we can use attributes to differentiate activity levels, whether manual, or automated. Tools such as Oracle BPA architect provide extensions to the BPMN stencil to graphically represent a manual or an automated process. An example of how tools provide extensions to graphically enrich the process models is a simple premium approval process. The premium approval activity in this case is manual activity involving a series of approvals that are performed in order to arrive at a premium percentage. Once the premium is decided, an automated task updates customer status, and also updates the customer information system. Then the customer is notified of these changes via phone or email, which is again an extension of the BPMN stencil.

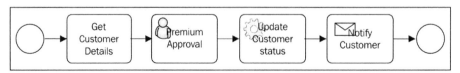

These extensions are important to better describe processes and allow tighter integration with the implementation engines. However, care should be taken to ensure that the BPMN specifications are followed to a large extent, ensuring consistency in understanding and usage.

Process Scope

Typically, the business process scope could either be limited to the organization, or could be a collaboration process that involves interfacing with external parties such as customers, suppliers, partners, and so on.

In case of internal or private processes, the scope is to map out the operational processes for process improvement and implementation. Examples of private processes are explained employee performance appraisal process, or the ordering process that we explained earlier. In this example, managing the order by the retailer is a private process, as shown in the following diagram:

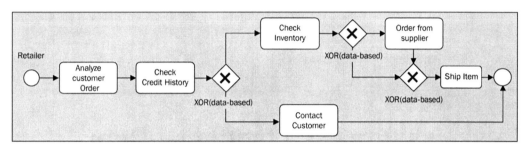

In the case of collaboration processes where external parties are interacting with the organization process, the scope becomes larger, and this will require careful thinking about how the process choreography will happen across various external entities. In this case, all of them will have their own application infrastructure, which in turn will pose its own interoperability challenges. In BPMN, a collaboration process represents these interactions or sequence of activities by message flows, and highlights the touch points between the entities involved. Typically, standards such as RosettaNet, ebXML and so on would be mapped to a collaboration process defined in BPMN. However, the mapping of BPMN to these standards is a future development objective for OMG. As an example, the same ordering process can be represented as a collaboration process by introducing a buyer in to the ordering process, where the buyer selects a product and places an order, and this is followed by a series of message flows between the two pools.

In BPMN, swim lanes are represented by using pools and lanes to group organization and role-based interactions. Any interaction between two pools can be done only using a message flow represented by a dotted line with a small circle at its origin, as shown in the following diagram. These elements will be discussed further in this chapter.

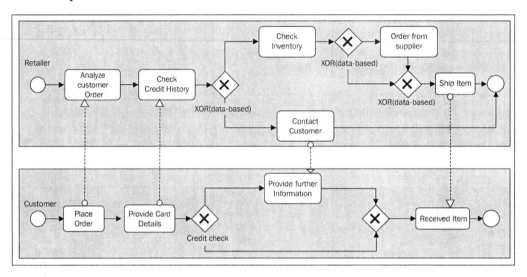

Business Process Diagrams—Core Elements

As we discussed, within a **Business Process Diagram (BPD)** elements are categorized allowing users to easily understand the diagrams. There are a set of *core elements* that have been defined in a BPD allowing users to start creating the essential gist of a process. These core elements can be further elaborated to take care of the complexities, while still maintaining the standard look and feel of the diagrams. These core elements are subdivided into four categories, each of which contains a specific set of elements, as shown in the following figure.

Flow objects consist of the backbone elements in a business process diagram, and are used to represent the basic behaviour of any process. These elements are events, activities and gateways. Events represent the various states relevant for the business process, such as the start of the process, wait time in a process, the termination of a process, and so on. Activities denote the work conducted as the part of the business process. Gateways are used to represent the decisions points where a split or join takes place in the flow of control.

Swimlanes represent the organizational relationships within a BPD. In BPMN version 1.0, they are restricted to a two level hierarchy of pools and lanes. BPMN 1.1 supports representation of nested lanes. Pools usually represent the organizations that interact in a business process, while lanes denote the various departments within an organization. Although one may see pools representing the departments, and lanes representing individual roles performing the process in lower-level BPDs, BPMN does not specify how we use the pools and lanes to represent the type of hierarchy.

Artifacts are used to show additional information about a business process. These elements include data objects, text annotations and groups. Data objects are used by business analysts to denote the use of specific data points as part of the flow, for example, the use of a document, or data from an information source, can be represented using data objects. Text annotations, as the name suggests, are used to add textual information within a BPD, and are typically associated to a specific element for elicitation purposes. Groups are used to group a set of elements in a process. They are purely for documentation purposes, and help highlight sections of a process.

Connecting objects connect various elements in a BPD. A sequence flow is used to represent the order of flow objects, while message flows represent the flow of objects between different business partners, who are represented by pools. An association is a connecting object used specifically to link artifacts to different elements.

For modelers who want to create an overview business process for their readers, use of the core elements of BPMN should be enough. Let us illustrate our understanding of the core elements of a BPD using our simplified order processing example. The following diagram has been created using the **Oracle BPA architect tool** to represent the core elements of a business process diagram. The process is depicted using sequence and message flows. The process has two main participants, retailer and customer, who have been represented using the pool element to denote the swimlanes. The process starts with a start event, which triggers the start of the process. As we can see, Start events are represented as circles, which can contain different markers depending on the type of event. A customer will start the process by placing the order, which will send message flow to the retailer pool where someone will analyze the order. The process continues with a set of logical activities and decisions represented by rectangles and diamond symbols respectively.

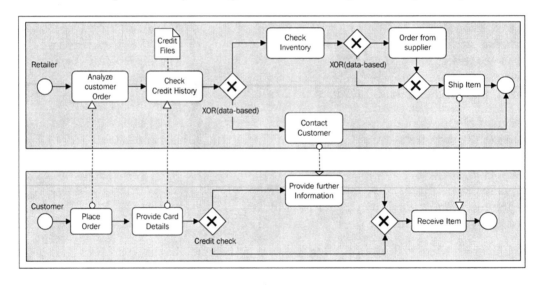

In the case of the **Check Credit History** activity there is an associated data object called **Credit files** that represents performing the customer's credit file which is used for verification, when required. As we discussed earlier, you will also note the use of gateways to decide whether to split the sequence flow based on certain conditions. For example, after the credit check, we use an exclusive OR gateway to choose one path based on whether the customer's credit was approved or not. Similarly, we can use the gateways to join multiple incoming flows.

Business Process Diagrams—A Deeper Analysis of the Key Elements of BPMN

Having looked at the core elements of BPMN from an understanding perspective, it is now essential to understand the various elements in detail, and see what extensions BPMN provides for each of the elements to create truly illustrative and complete BPDs. Business Analysts will realize that BPMN, apart from allowing easy process building, also provides sufficient detail and variety to allow a modeler capture the complexities of real life processes. It is also essential to understand how understanding these elements in detail will help the designers of business process and respective IT teams later on to provide enough detail in a process to allow for successful mapping from the process design to its execution in a BPM engine.

Let us understand in some detail the main BPMN elements within the categories that make a BPD.

Events

Events play a vital role in modeling with BPMN. The comprehensive coverage of events makes BPMN more appropriate as a business modeling language than its counterparts. Events, as we have discussed, define how an organization will respond to a situation through its business processes. Events will usually trigger a flow, or will generate a result. Events can trigger-start a particular process for example, the 'Customer Application Form Received', event starts the 'Opening a Bank Account' process. Alternatively, it could be an intermediate event used to delay the execution of the process, for example an event of 'Wait five Seconds' prior to the 'Send Response to Customer' activity. Finally, it could be end event say 'Account Open Complete' which completes, a given process. So, depending upon where an event occurs in a process we can divide them into three types:

- **Start:** Indicates the start of a process
- **Intermediate:** Events that occur in between a process
- **End**: Event An event signifying the end of a process

Events are further represented by types (basic, message, timer, rule, exception, cancellation, compensation, link, multiple, and terminate).

The following figure shows the event types in BPMN, OMG Version 1.0. The shape of an event is a small circle; a start event has a thin border, an end event a thick border, and an intermediate event has a double border. For each event, the type of event is indicated by an icon inside the circle.

As we can see, not all event types are applicable to each event. For example, we can start a process using a message event type, but we cannot start a process using cancel event type. For intermediate events, all types are possible except terminate, which is only used to end a process.

Let's understand what each event type does at each stage in a process:

Type	Description	Start	Intermediate	End
None	Modeler does not use any event type; just signifies an occurrence	Depicts an occurrence that is more of a placeholder; also used to depict start of a sub process	Used by modelers to denote a change of state in a process any time without highlighting the type of event	Used by modelers to denote end of the process without describing an event type; also used to end a sub process and transfer flow to parent process
Message	Used to denote how a message-based event is handled across the process	Indicates start of a process after receiving a message (for example, receipt of a credit card application form)	Event dependent on the receipt of a message from other participants, or sending a message to another participant (for example, waiting for an approve claim message from underwriter)	Event denotes sending a message to a participant after completion of the process (for example, send a response to a customer)
Timer	Time-based event	Denotes start of a process depending on a schedule, or specific instance (e.g. start the claims pending process every day at 9:00 a.m.)	Can be set for an event to start based on a specific time or schedule. Also used to introduce a delay in the main process flow. (for example, wait for ten minutes before sending the escalation mail)	Process will not end using a timer event
Error	Denotes an exception that occurs during normal process flow	Process cannot start with an error event	Used to throw and catch an error midway through a process flow	Based on the error caught by an intermediate event, this will end the process by generation of the error

Type	Description	Start	Intermediate	End
Cancel	Used in a transaction process to denote cancellation of a set of activities, that are part of a particular transaction	Process cannot start with a cancel event	Gets triggered when a cancel end event has occurred within the transaction sub process, or a cancel message is received while a transaction is running	Will trigger inside a transaction sub-process to initiate the cancel intermediate event attached to its boundary; also sends a cancel message to all activities that are part of a given transaction
Compensation	Used to start a compensation activity that is used to roll back a set of activities (for example, ATM transaction)	Process cannot start with a compensation event	Initiate and handle compensation; it calls for compensation if the event occurs during a normal process flow; it works on compensation when attached to an activity boundary	Indicates requirement for compensation at the end of a process; will initiate an intermediate event to take care of rolling back
Rule	Condition-based event	Starts a process based on a condition for a rule being met (for example, bullion price has moved up 5% intra-day)	Typically, used for exception handling in a process when a rule condition is met.	Process will not end with a rule event
Link	Allows two processes to be connected together; end of one process can be a link to another	Will be a link from another process, typically another sub process of a common parent process	Link from end of one process to an intermediate event in another process	Initiate a link to another process, typically a sibling

Type	Description	Start	Intermediate	End
Terminate	Results in the abrupt end of a process; it is like killing the process, with no exception handling			Termination of all instances of process activities; no exception handling or compensation is performed
Multiple	Suggests multiple ways of triggering the event	Multiple triggers can start a process; they can be a message, timer, rule or a link	Denotes that a trigger can happen based on multiple event types; only one of them is required to trigger the event	More than one result expected from the end event; all of them will occur

Activities

Simply put, an activity denotes a unit of work that is performed. In a BPD, activities act as the major components. A series of activities undertaken in order to achieve an objective having clear starting and stopping points is a process. From a process perspective, any activity can be categorized as atomic, or compound. 'Enter Name' would be an atomic activity or task, if it cannot be further decomposed, and performs a single atomic action. On the other hand, 'Conduct Interview' would be a compound activity or a sub process if it involves several subactivities, for example 'Analyze Resume', 'Ask Questions', 'Analyze Answers', 'Decide Next Steps', and so on, to get the work done. The following figure shows the notation of an activity:

In a BPD, the representation of a process is hierarchical in nature, that is, a given process can have multiple sub-processes. This also allows the process modeller to organize complex business processes in a decomposed fashion affording easy maintenance and navigation. Any given BPD can contain three types of activities: **Process**, **Sub Process**, and **Task**. In BPMN, Sub Process and Task are represented as rounded rectangles. The activity notation changes with the type of activity and what happens within that particular activity.

Sub-Process

In a parent process, a given sub process will be represented with a plus sign inside the rectangle. This is also called the 'Collapsed Process', with a plus sign denoting that the given activity is further elaborated in a separate diagram. This can be seen in the following figure:

The collapsed process could be represented as an 'Expanded Process', which requires the details of the sub-process to be made available inside the given activity rectangle. Typically, depending on how a modeling tool implements this feature, it is either initiated by clicking on the plus sign, or navigating to the sub-process.

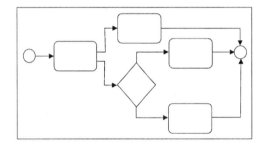

The Expanded Sub-Process can be seen in the figure above. In BPMN, this feature can be used to flatten the process diagram to show the details for a process in a single diagram. This makes it easier to visualize the complete process. However, in some practical scenarios, a large BPD could be too cluttered if represented by expanding all sub processes. The use of expanded sub-process is also beneficial while visualizing exception flows, and provides context to a set of activities inside a sub-process. The Expanded Sub-Process with time-based exception flow can be seen in the following figure:

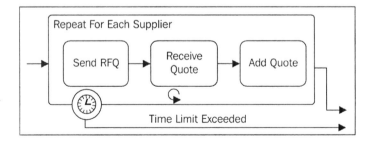

Expanded sub-processes are also used for representing a set of parallel activities in a manageable way, as we can see in the following figure:

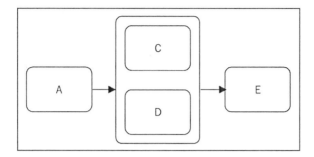

Further, a Sub-Process can have five markers, which are illustrated in the figure below the explanation:

1. **Collapsed Sub-Process:** This is represented with a plus sign. The collapsed sub-process marker can be used in conjunction with any of the four other markers.

2. **Loop Marker:** A sub-process with a loop is represented using a curled line with an arrowhead.

3. **Multiple Instances Marker:** A sub-process with multiple instances is represented using two parallel lines. This marker cannot be used in conjunction with Loop marker.

4. **Ad Hoc Process:** An ad hoc sub process is represented using a tilde (sometimes referred to as the 'ad hoc' marker) marker. It means that the activities in the sub process can occur in any order. It can be used in conjunction with any other marker.

5. **Compensation:** This marker suggests that the sub-process has a set of compensation activities.

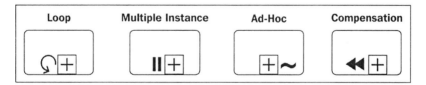

Let's take an example. In the following figure, you can see that Check Inventory is an activity that will require a sequence of activities to be performed, if we go to the next level. This can be represented by using a collapsed sub-process, with the details being embedded in the expanded sub-process. Another way to represent sub-processes is by using the tools to link the higher-level activity to the lower-level BPDs, allowing the creation of a hierarchical representation of the business process. This is very helpful in cases where it's impossible to represent all of the process details in a single diagram. We have all seen situations where process printouts fill out the whole wall of a meeting room. Use of proper decomposition provides a clean and efficient method of business process modeling.

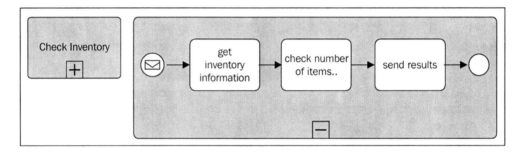

A sub-process can also be divided into two types:

1. **Dependent or Embedded Sub-Process:** A sub-process is said to be embedded when the parent process spawns the sub-process. In this case, the sub-process is dependent on the parent process for initiation. The embedded sub-process will usually contain basic BPMN constructs such as activities, flow control and gateways.

2. **Independent Sub-Process:** In this case, the sub-process is, a complete BPD in its own right. The called process is independent of the calling process, and hence can be called by any process.

Task

A task is the atomic unit used to represent an activity. We use a task when we cannot break down a process activity into a lower level of detail. Typically, a Task is a piece of work done by either an application or a user during execution of the process. In BPMN, a Task is represented as rounded rectangle, by a can be seen in the following figure:

Similar to Sub-Processes, Tasks also use markers. In the case of Tasks, the markers you can use are Loop, Multiple Instance and Compensation, which are shown in the following figure:

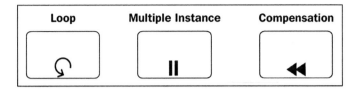

Based on the kind of work involved, a task can be further divided into various types. BPMN has not specified any specific marker to differentiate a task type. Typically, the type information will be stored as an attribute value generally provided by the modeling tool.

The task types are:

1. **Service:** A Task providing some kind of service; it could be a web service or an application.
2. **Receive:** A Task expecting to receive some message from an external participant in a process.
3. **Send:** A Task that sends a message to an external participant.
4. **User:** A workflow-type task, where a user is supposed to perform an activity using an application. It can be also called a semi-automated task.
5. **Script:** Meant for running a specific script by the execution engine. This kind of task will allow an implementer to specify a script to be run when the task is executed. The Task is considered complete when the script has been run.
6. **Manual:** Typical manual activities such as 'Agent shreds the document'. These tasks are performed without any help from an application or a BPM engine.
7. **Reference:** Tasks that refer to a similar task available to the modeler.

Gateways

Gateways are used to control how flows interact as they converge and diverge within processes. In basic terms, gateways are like decision junctions where a particular flow decides to fork into multiple activities, or join/merge back into an activity. Depending on the kind of behavior we want to control at a gateway, BPMN allows their representation as an open diamond with options to use markers to differentiate between various gateway types. Gateways can also be interpreted as 'if-then' or 'switch' constructs, typically used in programming control structures. The gateway notation is as follows:

Depending on the kind of decision to be made at a particular gateway, gateways can be divided into multiple types as shown in the following figure:

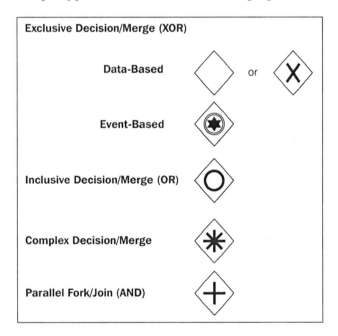

Gateway type markers would generally be placed inside the diamonds.

The exclusive decision/merge (OR) has two types of gateways: Data Mode and Event Mode. In the case of Data Mode, the gateway will evaluate each sequence flow linking to the gateway and evaluate the same like a switch for each of its outgoing paths. It will only let through the first path it finds with a true condition. Because the behavior of this gateway is exclusive, the other paths will be ignored by default. Exactly one condition must be true. We can also define a default branch in case none of the conditions fall true. In merge/join mode, the gateway lets through the first of its multiple incoming branches and discards all others.

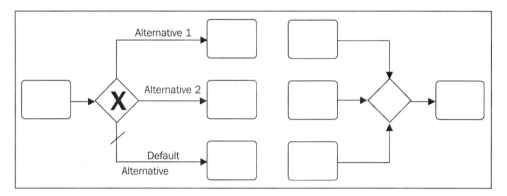

As we can see in the above figure, in case of Exclusive OR (event-based), the gateway will have inputs coming in that are similar to those in the data-based XOR gateway, and outgoing branches that are event-based. These gateways are similar to 'pick' in BPEL. The basic difference in the data-based gateway is that, the gateway will be based on a specific event; for example, receipt of a message decides the path to be taken. The gateway will let through the branch having the first triggered event, and ignore all others.

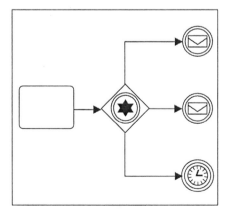

Inclusive OR is similar to exclusive OR, but unlike the exclusivity of selecting only one path, the gateway lets through each outgoing path whose condition is true. In the case of a merger situation, the gateway will block passage until each expected incoming path is received. The merge Inclusive OR gateway knows in advance how many active inputs to expect. This can be seen in the following figure:

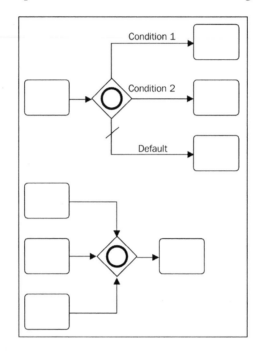

A Complex gateway is quite unique to BPMN and provides the capability for allowing a path analysis based on expressions defined by the users. It is used when other gateways cannot provide the desired results. The expression defined is evaluated during the decision and merging stage, to evaluate which path to choose. The key point to keep in mind is to ensure that, the expression should lead to at least one path being chosen.

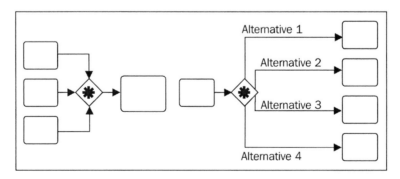

Parallel or AND gateways are used to create and synchronize parallel flows. This gateway, although not really required to create a parallel flow in a BPD, is normally used as a good practice to balance the creation and synchronization of parallel flows. The merge or join gateway will wait for all input activities to complete before going forward with the next set of activities.

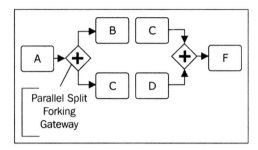

Sequence Flow

The sequence flow represents the order in which activities are performed in a process. It can be seen in the following figure:

If you use a sequence flow to evaluate a condition before moving on to the next activity, then you use a conditional sequence flow. These are represented by a diamond at the start of the sequence flow, as can be seen in the following figure:

If you want to represent a default path among a set of options, especially in case of decision gateways, a default sequence flow should be used. The marker used is a back slash at the beginning of the line, as follows:

Message Flow

We represent message flows between two participants in a business process by using a Message Flow element. In BPMN, two pools or swimlanes represent two participants involved in a process. For example, Finance Department and Human Resources Department are participants in a process. Interaction between these departments would be depicted using message flows. A Message Flow must connect two pools or swimlanes, or connect flow objects in one pool to flow objects in another. You cannot have a message flow connecting two objects in the same pool.

Message flow is denoted by a dashed line with an empty arrowhead, and beginning with a small open circle, as follows:

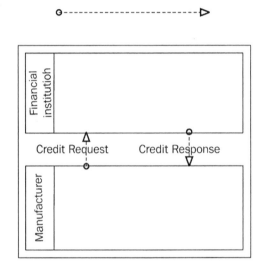

Message flow can be from a flow object within one pool to a flow object in another pool. This is important mostly when depicting how the activities will send to and receive messages from participants. During the execution of these processes, the flow can be similar to a service call between partner links in BPEL. The message flows between pool boundaries as can be seen in the above figure. The ordering process example also demonstrates the use of a message flow between two pools, as can be seen here:

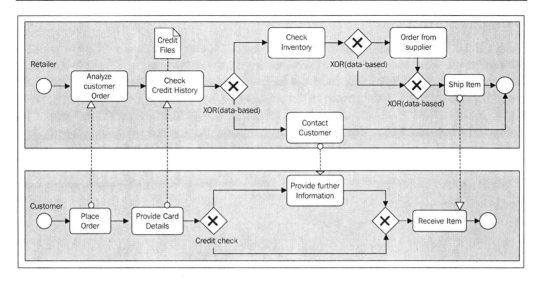

Association

Association provides a link between information and flow objects. General artifacts such as Text and graphical non-flow objects can be linked directly to a flow object by using an Association. For example, if you want to show additional text information for an activity for the sake of clarity, the text and the activity can be associated using an Association flow object. Association is represented with a dashed line, with or without an arrowhead, as shown in the following figure:

------------------------------>

An association is widely used to represent the related data objects in a flow, or to add text annotations to an object.

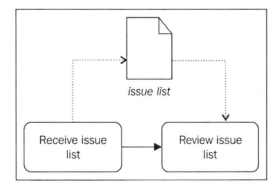

Pool

A Pool depicts the participants in a given process. It allows the 'swimlane' concept to be used in the diagram. The participants in an organization can be different internal departments. In a B2B process, they can be two organizations themselves, or from an SOA point of view, they can be different service providers or consumers. We will typically use a Pool in our process diagrams to group various activities performed by different participants in a process. To show any flow between a pool and its activities to another pool, a message flow is used as shown in the following figure:

Lanes

In a given pool for a process, you might require demarcation of various activities, allowing for further organization and categorization, to provide greater clarity to the process users. A Lane is used to do just that. It is used to subdivide a Pool into multiple sections. For example, you might divide a Pool representing a 'Loan Department' into activities performed by the various roles within the department, such as Customer Service Representative, Underwriter and so on. Or Alternatively, if the pool represents a company in a collaboration process, lanes can be used to represent various departments within the company as shown in the following figure:

Data Object

A Data Object, which can be seen in the following figure, is a widely used artifact in BPMN. We use Data Objects to provide information about what a process does. This can be details of documents, data and objects used by or created for a process activity. Data objects do not have any direct effect on the sequence and message flow in a BPD.

Name
[State]

Data Objects are usually used to provide details of data that goes to and from a particular Flow Object. Association flows are used to show the relationship between a Data Object and a Flow Object, as follows:

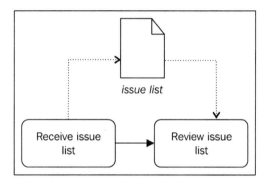

Group

Group artifacts, as the name suggests, are generally used to group a sequence of activities for the purpose of documentation and analysis. They are represented by rounded corner rectangles with dashed lines. Business Analysts also use groups when a set of activities that falls across pools, needs to be represented as a part of a single distributed transaction.

Text Annotation

A Text Annotation is a simple graphical aid for the reader of a BPD. It allows a modeler to provide further textual information on a diagram to make it easier for the users to understand. You can use an association to relate a text annotation to any object on a BPD, as follows:

Text Annotation Allows
a Modeler to provide
additional information

Introduction to Oracle Business Process Analysis Suite

As we are discussing BPMN in detail and looking at how it fits into the overall SOA vision of an organization, it is fair to say that the mere modeling of a business process as a graphical object is not of much value to an organization. Any organization looking to map processes as part of an overall SOA implementation, should look into the tools that provide at least the following basic capabilities:

- Standards-based process modeling
- Process Simulation for As-Is and To-Be analysis
- A Process Repository for centralization of all process modeling activities
- Process Model Execution—support for creating execution models from process diagrams
- Process Communication—an approach for allowing multiple stakeholders to view the most recent and complete process data

Most of the tools we see around the market for business process modeling and analysis come from a history of either being case tools for systems modeling, such as UML, or model repository tools. This differentiation results in these tools providing different sets of features to support process modeling and related standards, such as BPMN.

Typically, the tools available in the market can be divided into different levels depending upon the capabilities they offer:

- **Basic diagramming tools**: These are static tools with the capability to create diagrams and store these as files, for example, vision. Mostly, these tools will provide standard support for BPMN as a template or stencil that users can use for modeling. These tools will have no, or limited support for business process simulation. They will also have no, or limited capability for converting a BPMN diagram into a BPEL model.

- **Enterprise Architecture Tools**: These tools are more focussed on the IT-oriented approach to overall enterprise modeling. These tools will have process modeling as a subset of their overall support for modeling all aspects of an organization. Primarily, the Enterprise Architecture tools will have a combination of framework support such as Zachman, TOGAF and so on, and will divide the enterprise modeling primarily into categories of organizational architecture, and then further into business architecture, process architecture, application architecture, and information or data architecture. Most of the tool vendors in this market provide support for BPMN as part of their process architecture. Some example tools are Telelogic System Architect, and Casewise Corporate Modeller. You would be looking at these tools if you are working as an Enterprise Architect with process modeling being a subcomponent of your overall enterprise modeling requirements. Typically in an organization, the enterprise architecture teams make use of these tools to manage the high-level architecture, and logically these architectures should drive the BPM/SOA roadmaps and projects to allow them to be incorporated into the bigger picture of an enterprise.

- **Business Process Analysis Tools**: These tools are primarily focussed around business processes. Most of the sophisticated tools in this market have been providing support for process modeling using either their own methodologies or known standards. Almost all tools of this type have extensive support for BPMN, and are getting better. Largely, BPA tools provide support for process modeling using BPMN, setting up analysis attributes and KPIs for process simulation, allowing As-Is to To-Be process analysis, and process reporting. Most of them also have added support for integrating these tools with known **Business Process Management Systems (BPMS)** by creating conversion utilities for BPMN to BPEL, which then becomes the entry point for the BPM tools. Some of the better-known BPA tools are IDS Scheer Aris, which is actually used by Oracle as its choice for business process modeling, Metastorm Provision, and iGrafx. We are also looking at most of the BPA and EA tools providing overlapping features with respect to process modeling an analysis. Hence, you would find mention of common tools in specific analyst reports out in the market. Mostly, BPA tools selection would be with objectives of maintaining a common process repository, performing a thorough process analysis using simulation, six sigma, impact analysis, reporting, and so on.

- **Business Modeling Module of a larger BPM Suite**: As the industry is focussing more on automation and management of business processes and the implementation of SOA, vehicles for driving this strategy, such as the BPM systems, are gaining a lot of popularity. A BPM system, as we have discussed earlier, provides a platform for modeling, analysis, design, orchestration, monitoring, and optimization of an organization's end-to-end business processes. In terms of technology, any BPMS tool will provide ways to model, analyse, execute, measure, and monitor a business process on a continuous basis, to enable constant control, cost-effective process changes, and flexible process improvements. Process Modeling using standards such as BPMN, and its close relationship to the underlying execution environment, is very crucial to achieve the real benefits of BPM and SOA. Today most of these tool either provide their own process modeling tools, or integrate with larger BPA suites to reduce the gap. For example, Oracle has partnered with IDS Scheer's Aris to provide Oracle BPA Suite as an addition to its overall suite of products for BPM and SOA. This addition allows a user to model and simulate processes in BPMN within the Oracle BPA Suite, and then later take the information into Oracle's BPEL Process server for execution (using Rules for enforcing policies), Business Activity Monitoring for monitoring, and Enterprise Service Bus for creating the standards-based service integration layer.

As we go into the details of BPM, and delivery of SOA, Process Modeling and Analysis becomes a major component.

As mentioned earlier, for this chapter, we will be focusing on the business process architecture tool from Oracle Business Process Analysis Suite 10g (version 10.1.3.4) –Oracle BPA Suite, in short. The trial version of this tool can be downloaded from `http://www.oracle.com/technology/software/products/bpa/index.html`. You will need an Oracle technology network username and password to access this resource.

This suite provides a platform for users to model business processes using BPMN, and to analyze and optimize the developed business processes using simulation techniques to identify the potential bottlenecks, before creating an execution model for these processes, to be implemented inside SOA-based Orchestration engines. The reason for choosing Oracle BPA Suite is to demonstrate the complete life cycle of BPM and SOA, and the core concepts of how BPMN-based process models fit into the overall SOA strategy of an organization. Tools such as Oracle BPA suite, by allowing support for these standards, facilitate centralization of all process modeling activities of an organization, and allow for further automation. Integration of the BPA Suite with other Oracle products, such as SOA Suite, BPEL Process manager, and BAM, allows the business community to align the process analysis work with the implementation of these processes at technical levels, thereby allowing organizations to implement closed-loop BPM.

The various components of Oracle BPA suite are as follows:

1. **Business Process Architect**: This is the modeling and simulation platform for creation and analysis of various types of process models using standard techniques and methodologies. The tool provides a user friendly and intuitive interface to enable business users to start modeling at a rapid pace. The platform is not restricted to process modeling using only standards such as BPMN, or specific methodologies such as "Event Process Chain diagrams". The tool also allows the creation of other models and objects necessary to provide an overall architecture view of an enterprise with processes as a core element. Therefore, it also provides support for modeling of Functional diagrams, organizational charts, UML-based diagrams, and so on. Business Process Architect, hence, provides a dynamic platform to not only create process diagrams, but also add to necessary information as attributes for these process models, in a single repository. Business Process Analysis will involve mapping the current process, that is the"As-Is" process, and then analyzing the process using techniques such as simulation.

   The Business Process Simulator provides the capability for a process to be simulated based on discrete events. The simulation capability of Business Process Architect allows business users to perform gap analysis between the current state and the as-is process, to arrive at target state, or to-be processes. It can allow users to evaluate critical paths of the process, and isolate resource bottlenecks and other process improvement opportunities. This allows analysts to remove potential bottlenecks in a process before sending the process out to the technical teams for automation purposes.

2. **Business Process Publisher**: The publisher component allows the various process models created by the teams to be shared with all relevant stakeholders. This is done by exporting the process model and attribute information to a centralized portal that can be accessed by the relevant stakeholders. This access is secure, role–based, and allows the non-modeling community to get up-to-date information on the processes and their attributes. The publisher, therefore, becomes more of a communication platform, allowing updated process information to be made readily available to all applicable parties. This is one of the major benefits of using a BPA tool, as it allows a collaborative environment to be built around business processes and information by using a centralized process repository that is accessible over the network by the user community.

3. **Business Process Repository and Oracle Business Process Repository Server**: These allows the centralized process models to be shared across users in a multiuser environment. Typically, the users working on process architecture are from cross-functional sections of an organization. The availability of these process models to the core team allows efficient collaboration, unlike any basic design tools available today. Using the server, the repository provides a central location for storing all metadata information about the processes, and enables concurrent usage, role-based access, and check-in or check-out of business processes by multiple users.

The evaluation version of Oracle BPA suite we are using in this book provides 90 days access to Business Process Architect and Business Process Publisher. The Business Process Repository server does not come as part of the evaluation version. We will be focussing primarily on business process architect throughout the chapters for modeling using BPMN, analysis, and integration with SOA components.

Developing an Example Process Using BPMN and the Selected Tool

Let us illustrate the features and use of Oracle Business Process Architect using our order processing example. We will be using different examples to demonstrate the use of the BPMN standard during the course of this book.

Assuming that you have downloaded and installed the Oracle BPA Suite, let us start by opening the tool. The following figure shows how the first screen looks. This screen provides an introductory dashboard to the user. The left vertical panes provide various options that can be used to open the designer workspace, or explore current process databases and so on. The middle section allows the user to jumpstart the creation of new models using some quick links. This view is customizable, and you can set it up to suit your individual requirements.

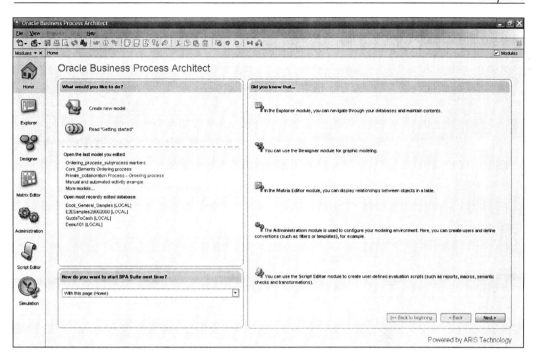

Let's start by exploring the databases of existing models. The tree shows the hierarchy in which models are stored in Oracle BPA. You can have any number of databases, within which you can set up groups to logically structure the models, for example, Organization Models, Process Models, IT models, and so on. Within a group, you can create new models of different types as supported by Oracle BPA.

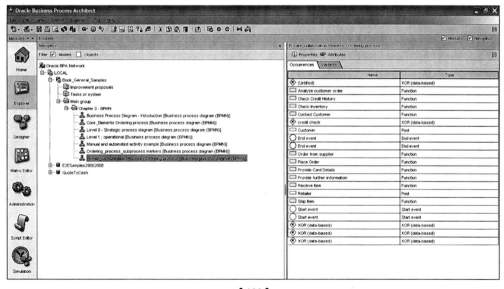

Using this explorer, you can open an existing model in the list, or you can create a new model as follows:

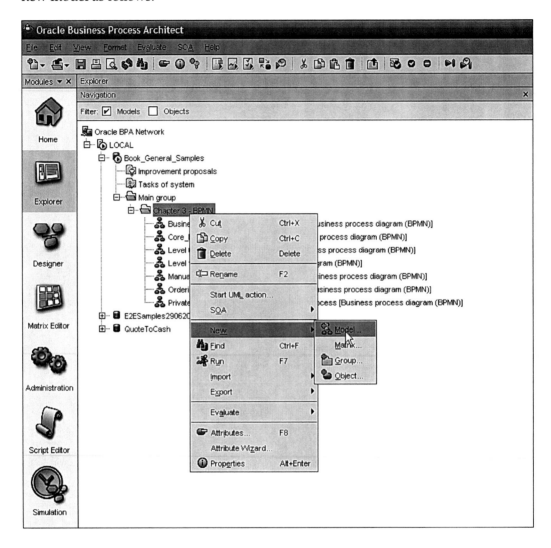

We will select the BPD from the list of available options. Let us call this process, **Online_Order_Processing**.

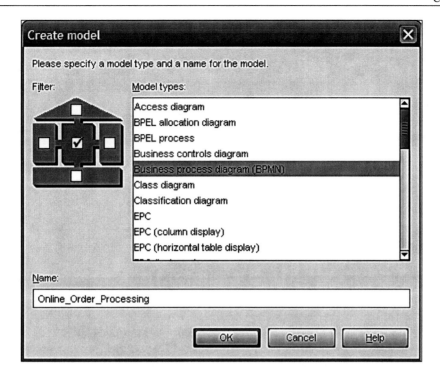

Click **OK**, and the modeling workspace is opened, shown in the following figure,
Initially, this will be blank workspace, which is the canvas on which we will draw
the business process model. On the right, you will see a list of available BPMN
elements including events, gateways, annotations and connectors that can be used to
model the diagram.

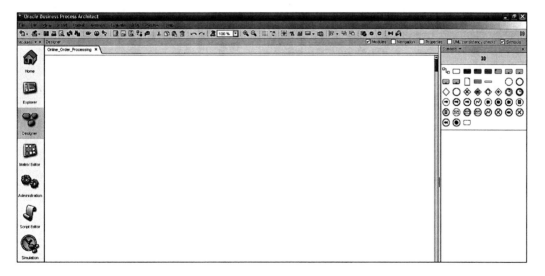

You can now start modeling simply by dragging and dropping the symbols from the stencil to the canvas. This is how your canvas looks when the process model is a work-in-progress.

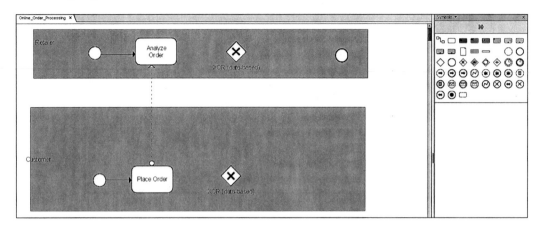

As an example, the finished product would look something similar to the following figure. The aim here is to understand the use of core elements of BPMN to represent a business process. A lot of complexity can, and will be added in a normal business scenario. We will be covering more examples and further usage of the tool in subsequent chapters.

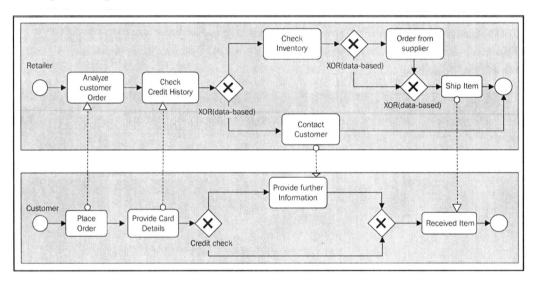

Summary

We have covered the key concepts of business process modeling, and the use of BPMN as a standard in providing a consistent, process vocabulary to any business. We have also covered the essential components of BPMN, using some examples, which should enable you to start creating BPDs. We also had an introduction to the Oracle Business Process Analysis Suite. In subsequent chapters, we will focus on some of the detailed concepts of BPMN, especially with regard to various workflow patterns that can be modeled in BPMN. Our focus will also shift to how a BPD can feed the requirements of the IT teams in carrying out process execution.

BPMN—Advance Constructs

The chapter will go into the details of using events and other main BPMN elements, and how they fit together to represent a business process. This section will define how the common BPMN patterns are to be used by analysts to represent scenarios typically seen in an organization.

Business Process Modeling General Guidelines

Before we move further, it's really important to understand some of the rules that are helpful while modeling and designing our business processes. In this section, we will look into some main modeling rules from the perspective of modeling a process, and the instructions specified by BPMN and supported by Oracle BPA.

Rule #1: Process Models Should Provide Aid in Process Understanding

A good process model should allow the overall process flow to be visible at one glance, either from left to right, or from top to bottom. To achieve that, a modeler can follow these basic rules:

- Aim for a minimum of four, and a maximum of fifteen tasks in a process

- Aim for a maximum of three or four levels in a hierarchy

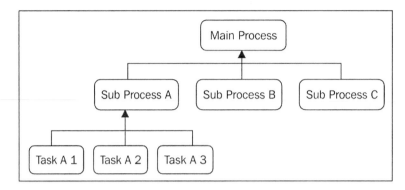

A good model gives you an intuitive and easy to understand overview of how a business process works, as this is the main purpose of a graphic model. A model with a large number of tasks may be correct and unambiguous, but becomes difficult to understand and, therefore, less useful. You can improve this diagrammatically by grouping tasks into a sub process. In other words, by creating a hierarchy of processes, sub-processes, and tasks. Depending on the complexity of the process, several levels of nested sub-processes are allowed. However, in terms of best practices, it's always better to keep the nesting to a maximum of four levels. This also ensures that the number of activities represented in a process is reduced to a maximum of 10 to 15, which can make the process more readable.

Rule # 2: Match Each Split with a Join

In the following figure, the process shows a common mistake with parallel tasks, where an AND split is not properly closed by an AND join.

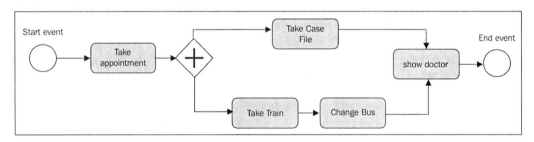

This mistake can cause a serious problem. Visually, if **Take Case File** is completed, then users might think that the process is ending, while it might be possible that the patient has still not reached the doctor. Therefore, it is wise to close the path by using an AND-join to provide the process with a clear checkpoint. This will allow us to check whether all parallel tasks have been completed before the process can continue. The following figure is an example of using an AND-join to ensure that the process can move forward with any further activities. only after both the case file and patient arrive.

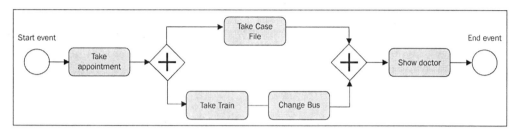

In addition, it is nice to use gateway symbols while modeling the process as this improves readability and understanding while reading or creating business process diagrams.

Another issue, especially with the use of AND Join, is the possibility of a deadlock situation in a process. Consider the following process:

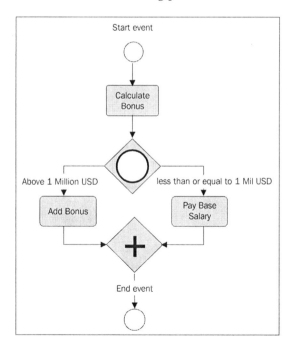

In this example, an employee's bonus is calculated based on sales targets achieved. The inclusive OR gateway ensures that only one option is taken. However, if you notice, the join gateway used is of type AND, and hence will wait for all parallel processes to complete. Now we have a deadlock situation as the process will never take one of the paths. To avoid this situation, use an OR Join instead of the AND join. The basic rule of thumb to avoid deadlocks is to ensure that every path in a process reaches the end state, especially when working with parallel or AND gateways.

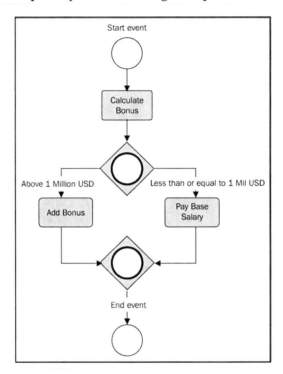

Another technique to avoid possible process deadlock is always to ensure there is at least one outgoing task for every possible condition at the gateway. Consider the following example:

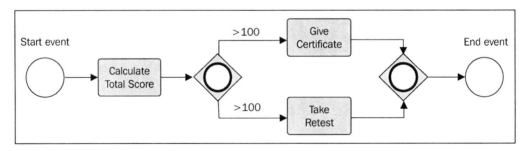

In this case, the conditions for both processes are either greater than, or less than 100. Therefore, in a situation with an expression value of 100, there will be no output path. Hence, it could result in a deadlock. This is a simple example, and in some business scenarios, it may be overlooked by an analyst and can be misinterpreted as we go down the implementation route. To avoid this situation, it would be appropriate to use the Default flow provided in BPMN, or ensure that there is always at least one path out of the gateway.

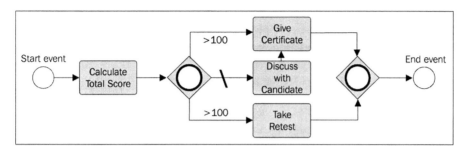

The notation used for Default flow in BPMN is a sequence flow with a tilde at its origin. In this case, if the candidate scores 100, he or she will be called in for a discussion before being given a certificate. This was just an example, but in normal process flows, care should be taken to provide default flows to prevent deadlocks.

Rule #3: Have a Well-Defined Start and End Event

Though not mandatory, it's a good idea to start the process using the start event, and end the process using an end event. This keeps the process elegant, and also gives motivation to designers to ensure that all paths are closed, and linked from the start event, or to the end event, either directly or indirectly.

Rule #4: Look Out for Orphan Tasks

Consider the following example:

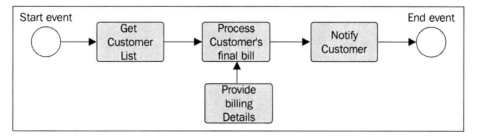

The activity **Provide Billing Details** will never be executed, as it does not have an input sequence flow to this task. As this is a simple process, it looks like an obvious mistake, but in a complex process, such a case can sometimes be overlooked. All efforts should be made to link every activity from the start event, and have at least one incoming sequence flow to maintain consistency.

The BPMN standard also places a number of conditions on the representation of a process flow. The aim of this is to ensure consistency in diagram display and interpretation. These rules help in ensuring that BPMN maintains a degree of control on how a diagram is created, and at the same time, allows a bit of flexibility for a modeler and modeling tool vendors to work around the notation. Most of the modeling tool vendors are still maturing, and we will see further compliance to the standards and adherence to modeling rules as specified by BPMN.

BPMN Attributes and Tools Support

Most Business Process Analysis Tools, such as Oracle Business Process Architect, provide an object model for every entity modeled within the tool. This means that apart from just providing a diagramming capability for the various models including BPMN, each entity created, say a process or a service, can have variables or properties. These variables can have values defined by the user, which could be used for various analysis needs. The use of these variables allows a lot of rich information to be stored for a BPMN object when creating the model.

BPMN provides details, as per its specification, of the various attributes that can be used when modeling, especially for facilitating mapping to BPEL. Apart from that, Oracle Business Architect provides more variables for objects for reporting purposes, which is an essential requirement to enable optimal process analysis and management.

To access the properties and attributes of any element or diagram in Oracle BPA, right-click on any element or object, and select **Attributes,** or select **Edit** from the menu bar, and select **Attributes** as shown in the following figure. The **Attributes** window can also be opened by pressing *F8* for a selected object.

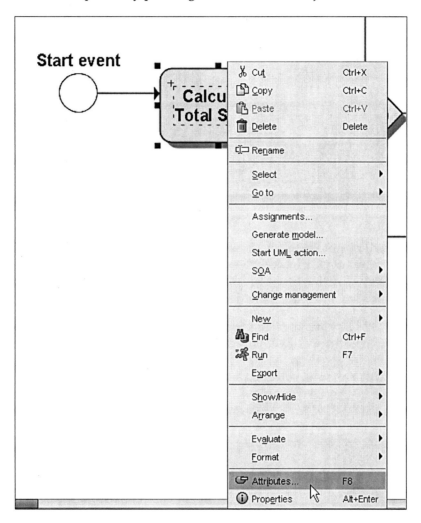

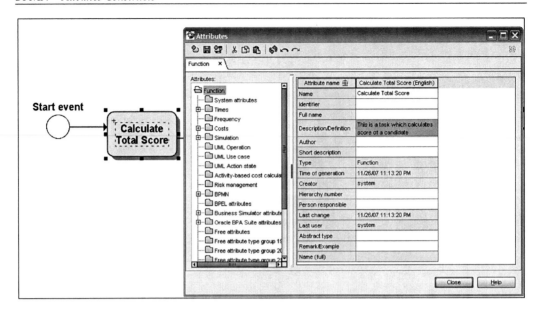

Oracle Business Process Architect allows a user to maintain and manage existing pre-defined attributes, which are generic to any object and specific to BPMN. Apart from that, a user can define his or her own set of attributes, depending on the kind of information required by the organization for a process artifact.

Within Oracle BPA, the tool provides a common section for maintaining attributes. However, it also maintains substantial information on the various models and objects as system information that can be used with respect to BPMN-specification requirements. For example, object ID is maintained for all objects in Oracle BPA as GUID, which is a unique identifier. Every element in BPMN has its own set of attributes defined by BPMN. To elaborate on how to access and use attributes, let us go through some of the common BPMN attributes maintained within Oracle Business Process Architect for the main diagrams and elements.

Business Process Diagram

By right-clicking on a **Business Process Diagram** (BPD) from the explorer view, you can access the various attributes provided by the tool.

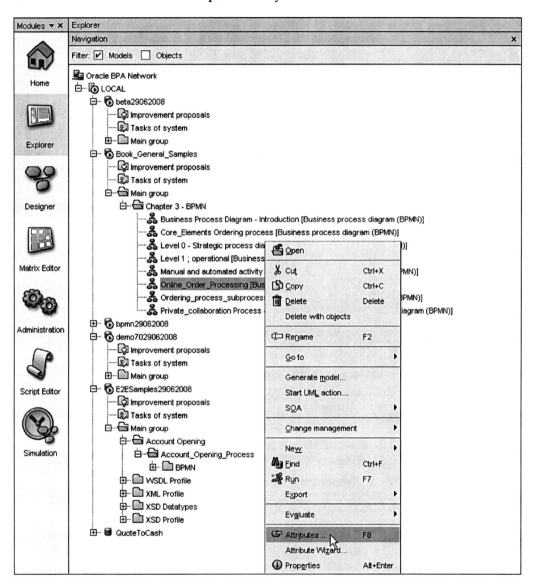

Common attributes of a BPD are shown in the following figure:

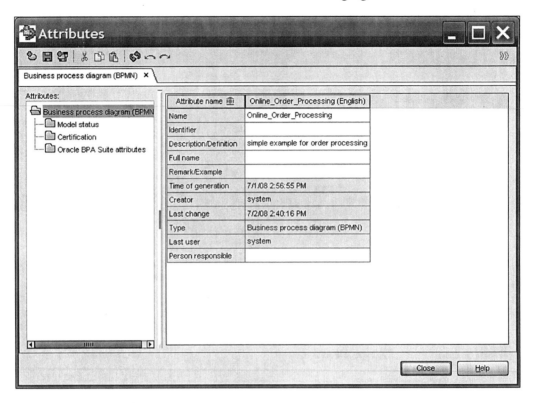

Some of the common attributes of a BPD are:

Attribute Name	Description
ID	Unique ID for the diagram. This is system-generated, and is maintained by the tool as GUID.
Name	Name of the BPD.
Author/Creator	This attribute holds the author details for the diagram.
CreationDate/Time of Generation	Date of creation of the diagram. This is system-generated.
ModificationDate/Last Change	Date when the diagram was last modified, BPMN refers to this as the Modification Date, and Oracle BPA refers to it as Last Change. This attribute is system-generated.

Process

In Oracle BPA, the **Function** object has been used as the base object for defining BPMN graphical objects, extending to process, sub process, and tasks. In BPMN, each has specific attributes that need to be defined, some of which have been covered in Oracle BPA. The following figure shows common attributes for the **Function** Object

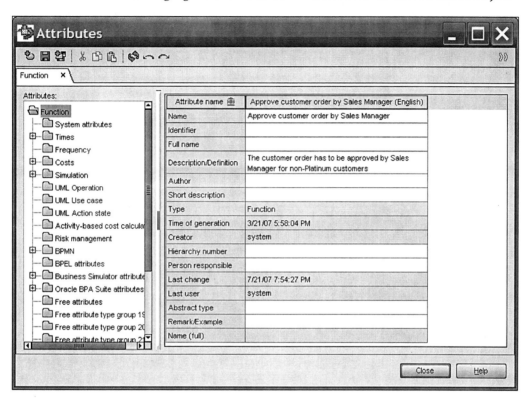

The **Process** and **Subprocess** attributes in Oracle BPA are maintained together in one group under BPMN attributes. The following figure shows the specific attributes for the **Process** Object:

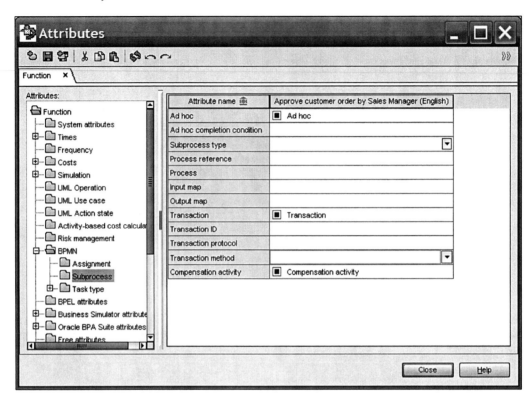

Some of the common attributes for **Process** Object are:

Attribute Name	Description
ID	Unique ID for the diagram. This is system-generated and maintained by the tool as GUID.
Name	Name of the Process.
Ad Hoc	Boolean Property, with a default value of false. Ad-hoc processes contain activities that are not under control, or sequenced in any particular order. The performance of these activities is determined by the performers.
Completion Condition	If the Ad Hoc property is true, the users need to provide an expression defining the completion condition for the process. This will allow the condition under which the process will end to be determined.

Sub-Process

A Sub-process is an activity that is part of the larger process flow, and can either be embedded or independent. There are many attributes that can be specified for extending the sub-process activity, and some of them have been defined in this section. The following figure shows the common attributes for **Subprocess:**

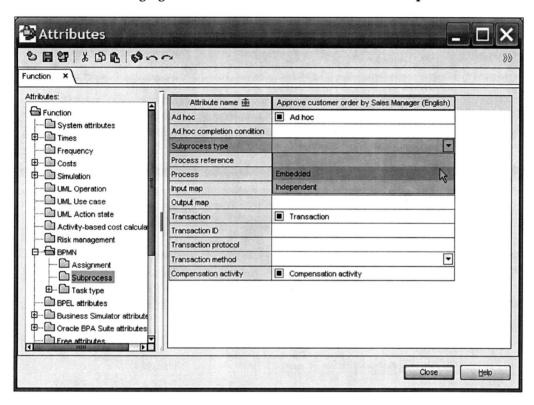

Figure:

Some of the common attributes used in a Sub Process are:

Attribute Name	Description
Sub Process Type (Embedded | Independent)	Sub Process Type defines whether the Sub-Process details are embedded in the higher level Process, or whether the Sub-Process links up to other re-usable Processes.
**Process Reference	ProcessRef**	This attribute contains the identifier of the referenced process for an independent sub process. This attribute must be maintained if a value of **Independent** is set for the Sub Process Type attribute.

Attribute Name	Description
Process	This attribute contains the name of the re-usable process that is referenced by the sub-process. This attribute may be maintained if a value of Independent is set for the Sub Process Type attribute.
Input Map	This attribute describes the mapping of inputs in the parent process to inputs in the referenced process. This assignment is made using expressions. This attribute may be maintained if a value of Independent is set for the Sub Process Type attribute.
Output Map	This attribute describes the mapping of outputs in the parent process to outputs in the referenced process. This assignment is made using expressions. This attribute may be maintained if a value of Independent is set for the Sub Process Type attribute.
Transaction	If the activity is a transaction, then this Boolean attribute needs to be set to True.

As we know, a sub-process can be either embedded or independent and, based on this, certain attributes need to be used.

As we can see, there is a lot of information that can be captured for a BPD and its elements using attributes provided by BPMN, and extensible attributes provided by the BPA tool. For a detailed study, I urge readers to go through the comprehensive list provided by the BPMN specification. Some of the key attributes for events are also covered in detail in subsequent sections of this book.

Events in Detail

As we have discussed in the earlier chapters, events play a vital role in business process modeling and management, allowing an analyst to represent and analyse business situations and scenarios, and see how a business process will work within its constraints. In BPMN, events can be divided into three types: start, intermediate, and end. This section takes a deep dive into events and their use while designing a BPD.

Start Events

Looking in detail at **start** events, we can look at the scenarios in which they can be used. As discussed, there are six possible ways of starting a process. These are shown in the following figure:

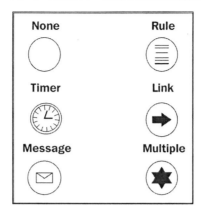

None

Sometimes, the process designer may not be aware of the reasons for triggering a process, or the way a process starts is not dependent on any trigger, and has no bearing on the way process is performed. In such a case, we should be able to start a process using no specific symbol that is, **None**. This is also used when starting a sub-process that is initiated by a parent process.

Consider the following process flow:

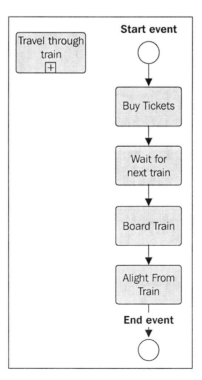

In this case, we can choose to keep the **Start** event as **None,** as this would typically be a sub process of a parent process, which is **Travel through Train**. I also feel that it is not essential to use a trigger to define how this process will go forward. However, you can always consider using a **Message** event as well, in case the process starts based on instructions from a process participant.

Timer

Use of the **Timer** events is for cases where the process is based on a time schedule, or is dependent on a certain time. Consider the following process flow:

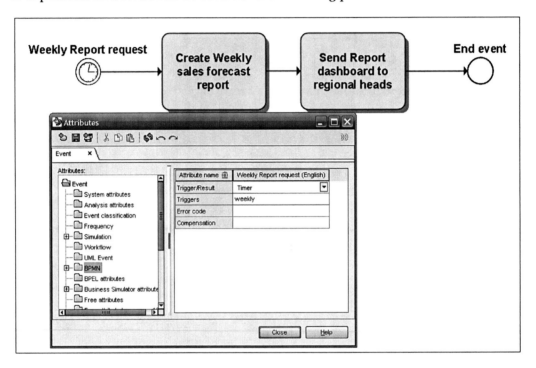

In this case, the timer event is used to start a weekly request for a sales report. Notice the attributes "Time Date" and "Time Cycle", which can be used to define a particular time, or frequency of occurrence, of this event respectively.

Message

Message events are used for starting an event when an external influence is involved. The message must be supplied to initiate the process. As per BPMN, a message event trigger uses two attributes to elaborate the message.

1. **Message**: An attribute of the type message to define the variable being sent or requested.

2. **Implementation**: This attribute can have one of the three values: Web service, Others, or Unspecified. These are the technologies used for sending the message. Usually, it is web services in the context of Business Process Management and SOA.

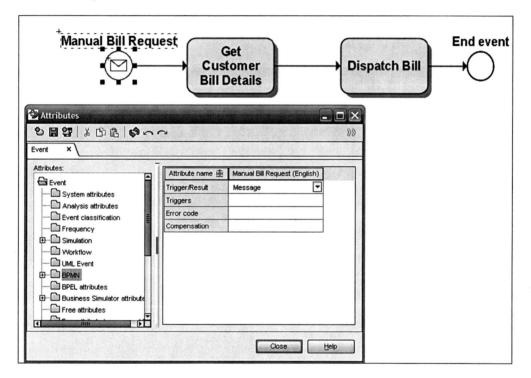

In this scenario, a customer sends a request for sending his or her mobile phone bills to the customer's home address manually, instead of sending an electronic bill. The message for this request is routed to the billing department, which takes the necessary actions to dispatch the bill accordingly. This message can be communicated in any manner, including the implementation of a web service to automate the process, which is specified in the event parameters.

Rule

Most of the time, Business Analysts will encounter the need for starting a process based on the outcome of a condition, or a rule. This can be implemented using the **Rule** event at the start of the process. **Rule name** is the attribute that can be supplied for the rule trigger event.

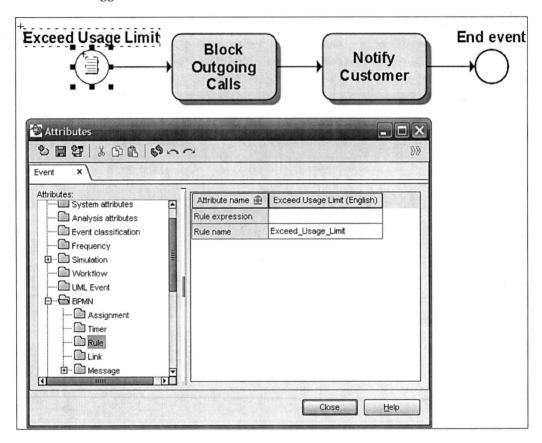

There can be many examples where a **Rule** event can be used. For example, if a customer's age exceeds 70, this will initiate the Insurance Maturity Notification Process. In the previous example, there is a rule event that evaluates whether the mobile phone user has exceeded his or her monthly acceptable outgoing calls. In the event of that rule condition becoming true, a process to block the user's outgoing calls, and issue of a notification to the user for bill payment is initiated.

Link

The **Link** event is used to create a link between the end of one process and the start of another process. This is used in practical scenarios when the drawing canvas of the modeling tool is not large enough, or if it's not elegant to draw a very large or complex BPD on a single sheet. It is also used when linking two sub-processes that are siblings of the same parent process. When using the Link event, we also need to provide information for the Process Reference, which is available as an attribute for the Link trigger.

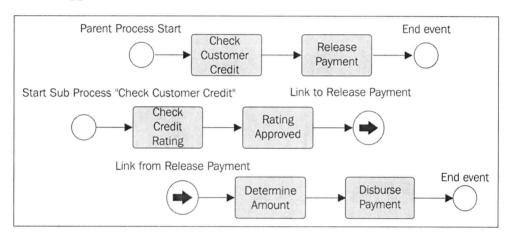

The example above shows a parent process that defines a simple customer loan disbursement process based on a credit check. Both **Check Customer Credit** and **Release Payment** have sub processes, as shown. With the **Check Customer Credit** activity, the sub-process is carried out after the credit check is done, and the rating is approved by the bank. We have created an end event, which is of type **Link**, and named this as **Link to Release Payment**.

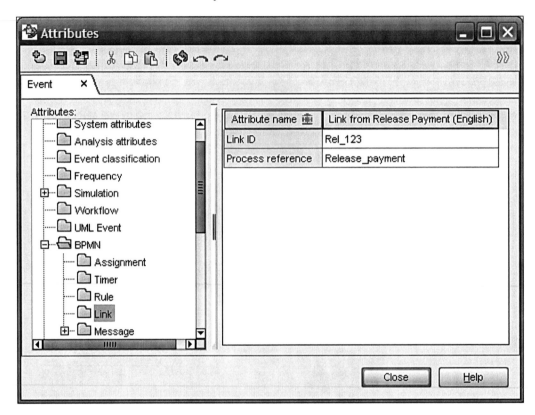

The **Link ID** and **Process reference** attribute value is provided for specifying the common Link ID, which each of the linked events should have in common. The process that is to be linked by the end event and the same **Link ID (Rel_123)**, are used in the start event of the next sub process. Now this link is available from one sub process, and the link is the trigger for starting the linked sub process for **Release_payment**, as shown in the figure. This way, the end of one sub process links to the start of another.

Multiple

Multiple events are used to start a process in which there is more than one way to trigger the process, which means that the process could be started by a timer event or a message event. The number of events that can start the process depends on the attribute values filled for the given event.

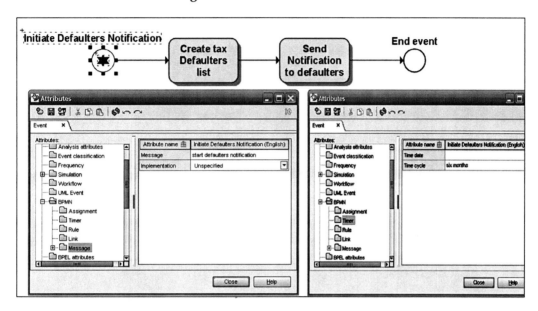

In the preceding example, the tax department creates a defaulter list every six months, and sends a notice to each defaulter. The same process should be followed if there is a directive from the senior management, and can be initiated any time of the year. So in this case, the event **Initiate Defaulters Notification** has been set with a **Timer** event with a cycle of six months, and a **Message** event for initiating the process based on a management directive.

End Events

As suggested, **End** events indicate the end of the process. This means that all the sequence flows ultimately terminate at the end event, and there can be no flow originating from an end event. From the perspective of creating elegant, well-balanced BPDs, it's advisable to have start and end events depicting the start and end of the process; otherwise it's an optional requirement. If you do not use the end event in a process, any task in a diagram with out an outgoing sequence flow will be the process end. In case of multiple tasks of the same nature, all of them must be completed before a process can be considered to have reached its end.

None

This is the event most commonly used by the process designers to depict the end of a process. It is also used in a sub-process to signify the end of the process, and to pass control back to the parent process.

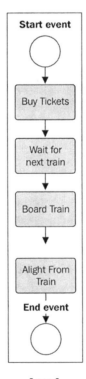

The preceding example simply demonstrates the use of end event with **None**, without additional information.

Message

This type of end will signify that a message has to be sent after completion of this process. As suggested earlier, the implementation is similar to that of a start event. However, in this case, the result is the generation of a message, which will either be used as a notification to external parties, or to trigger another process in the organization.

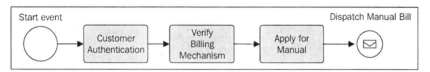

In this case, to make it simple, the customer is checking the billing status of his mobile phone online, and is applying for a manual bill. The end event, which is a message, will send the request to another process in the organization, most probably within the billing department, to work on this request and take the necessary actions. In this case as well, we will fill the **Message** and **Implementation** variables to elaborate on the message to be sent, and the mechanism of its implementation, as shown in the following figure. Also note that this could result in a start event for the annual bill dispatch, as in the example we have covered earlier.

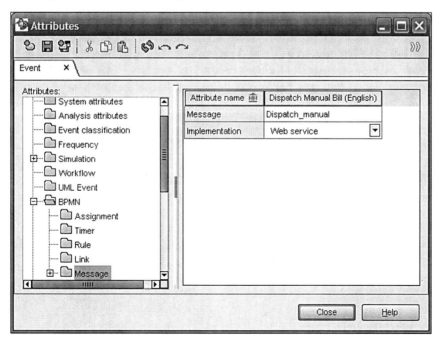

Link

For end events, **Link** provides the mechanism for joining two processes, for reasons mentioned earlier. We can refer to the same scenario to refresh the concept.

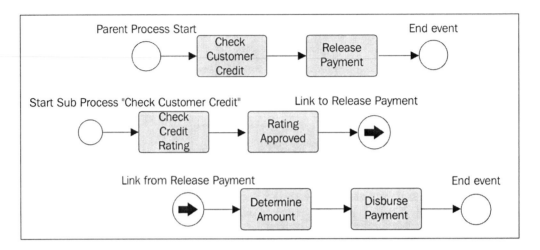

In the above figure, the sub process **Check Customer Credit** uses the **Link End event** to link the process with the next sub-process.

Cancel

The cancel event for ending a process can be used only for a Transaction sub process. The main aim of the cancel event is to indicate that the transaction has gone wrong for some reason, and needs to be cancelled. This will further trigger Cancel Intermediate Events attached to the sub process boundary. This will also result in a cancel message being sent to all activities involved in the transaction.

Error

The **error** end event is used in a similar way to the Cancel end event, as the exception handling is used by the programming community for throwing and catching exceptions. If the process is ending with an error condition, it will call an error message, which should be received or caught by an error intermediate event.

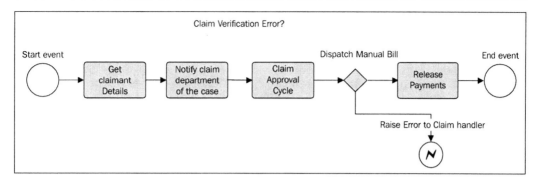

To demonstrate this scenario, let's consider a simplistic representation of the claim process shown in the preceding figure. In this case, once the claim details reach the claim approval cycle, some checks are performed to verify and detect any errors in the case file. In case of an error, the error is raised using an error event to the claim handler, to take necessary actions for this exception. If there is no issue, the process moves forward with releasing the payment.

Terminate

As the name suggests, the **Terminate** end event is used in scenarios where everything happening in the process should stop immediately. This includes all parallel activities in the process, and any multi-instance processes in progress. The termination also means that no compensation or any event handling is possible.

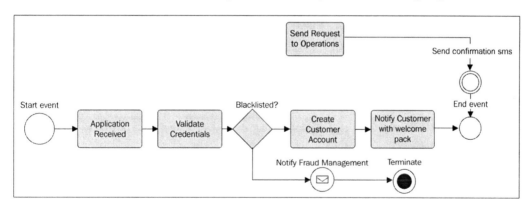

In this scenario, a customer had applied for a mobile phone connection, and the application is now going through the process of fulfilment by the telecom provider. The process, apart from many other checks and validations, also checks whether the applicant is in a group of blacklisted people who are not allowed to get a mobile connection for various reasons. In a normal case, if the customer is not on that list, the process will move forward to sending his mobile number creation request to the operations team, and also notifying the customer of the this by sending a welcome pack through post. However, if the customer is found to be on the black list, then, a notification with customer details will immediately go to the fraud department, and the process will terminate. At this point, all processes that were underway will be cancelled, and the process instance will cease to exist.

Compensation

This type of event suggests that compensation is required, and will raise a request for an intermediate event to start the process of rolling back the activities, that need to be compensated.

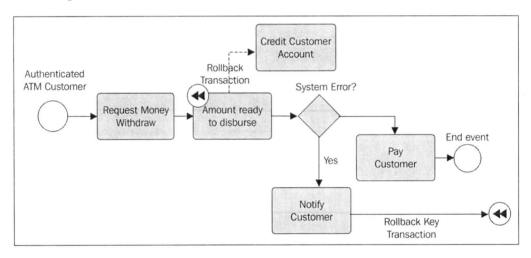

In this case, the customer is performing an ATM transaction in which he or she has been authenticated, and is now selecting the amount to withdraw and receiving the money from the ATM machine. Let us assume that before the money is disbursed, a system error is identified and validated by a system check, depicted using a gateway. If it is not a system failure, the counted money is paid by the ATM machine. Otherwise, it reaches the compensation end state that triggers the **Rollback Transaction,** which is the intermediate compensation event for **Amount ready to disburse** activity. This is required, as the ATM has already sent a request to the bank for debiting the money from the customer's account and so the same amount will need to be credited back to the customer's account.

The above scenario is just a demonstration of how a **compensation** end event can be used. However, in real life, the same process will definitely have more complex flows, which have been removed from this example for the sake of simplicity.

Multiple

Similar to the multiple start event, with a **Multiple** end event, there might be multiple results or triggers that can be expected at the end of the process, for example, sending out multiple messages.

Intermediate Events

Any event occurring between the start of the process and before its end is depicted using **Intermediate** events. The main aim of an intermediate event is to help users understand and depict the messages that are being sent to or received by activities within a process, represent any delays and time dependencies that are occurring before or after an activity, link various intermediate activities, create exception paths for a process in case of any errors in normal flow, and initiate work to compensate activities.

There are, in total, nine intermediate events that can be used while working on a BPD, as follows:

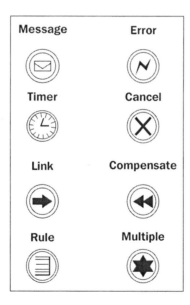

Intermediate events have two ways of representation: either as part of the normal flow, or on the boundary of the process. When used over the boundary of the process, intermediate can be used to handle exception and compensation.

Message

As mentioned earlier, a **Message** intermediate event can be used either in the normal sequence flow, or on the boundary for managing exceptions. In case of a message event, the process is triggered through a message that causes the process to continue, based on the receipt of the message event.

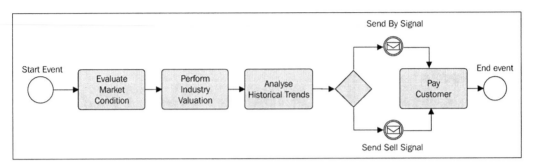

The preceding scenario depicts the use of message intermediate events for a normal flow. It shows how a trader analyzes the financial market in terms of the market, industry, and a particular stock's history, before he makes the 'Buy' or 'Sell' call for the trade. The message for sell and buy are the intermediate messages that are sent out as triggers to perform the trade.

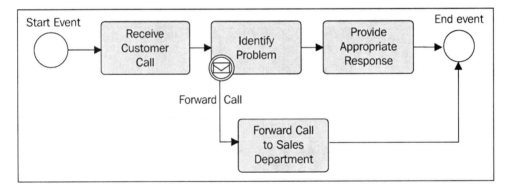

In this case, the message intermediate event would convert the normal flow to an exception flow. Consider the preceding figure. The call center executive receives a call from the customer, the executive identifies the problem, and, in a normal flow, would provide the response to tackle the issue. However, there can also be an exception where the customer might be experiencing an issue that only another department can solve. Hence, the call center executive sends the message to the appropriate department.

Timer

The use of a **Timer** intermediate event in a normal flow signifies a delay in the process, and its use in a process boundary demonstrates an exception from normal flow.

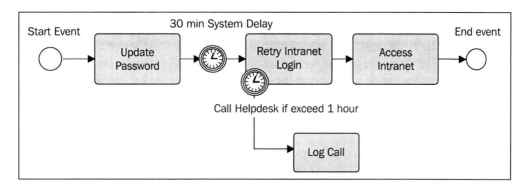

In the preceding example, both the scenarios for using timers have been highlighted. In the case of a user accessing his or her company's intranet portal after resetting his or her password, the usual system delay to provide him with his **Single Sign On (SSO)** password is 30 minutes. This delay is represented by using a timer in the normal flow. After waiting for 30 minutes, the user can retry to log in to the intranet. In a normal flow, the user will be able to login and access the intranet. But in case the login is not working for more than an hour, then the user is advised to log the call with the helpdesk, which is triggered using the timer event on the process boundary.

Link

Link, as already explained before, provides a mechanism for linking the end of one process to the start or intermediate link event of another. Also, two intermediate link events can be used as a GOTO mechanism within a process. Consider the following example:

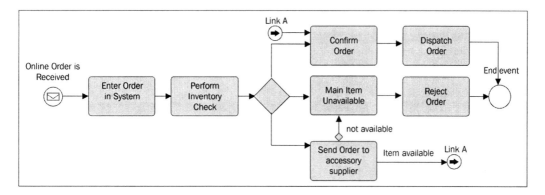

In this scenario, an order is received from a third-party site for a specialized electronic item, for example, a laptop. The typical process of order entry and inventory check is performed, and a gateway is used to decide whether the item is unavailable, or if there is a need to procure some additional accessories from the company's suppliers before the order can be executed. The order confirmation that is to be dispatched to the customer will require both the main item as well as the accessories to be available. The link intermediate event **Link A** is used in the bottom right of the process diagram to provide a link to the process step above so that the customer order can be confirmed and dispatched. This could have also been achieved by just creating a sequence flow between the **Send order to accessory supplier** and **Confirm Order**, but using a link intermediate makes the overall process more elegant and readable, especially when we are designing a considerably complex processes.

Rule

A **Rule** intermediate event will provide a rule condition that triggers the linked activity. Typically, a rule event linked to a normal flow will convert it to an exception flow for the outgoing activity.

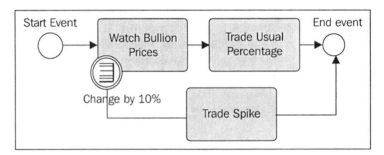

If you look at the preceding scenario, a trader in gold normally watches the market and usually trades 2-3% of his portfolio to buy or sell gold, depending on the market movement. However, a rule has been set which notifies the trader of a change in gold price of more than 10% (this is a dummy scenario) and hence, he moves to an exception path of either selling or buying larger quantities then usual. The main thing to note here is the use of a rule intermediate event will always create an exception path.

Error

Error events in BPMN 1.0 are used both for throwing and catching of errors. If used as part of the normal flow, the error event triggers a Throw, which can be caught by an error event placed on the boundary of any activity.

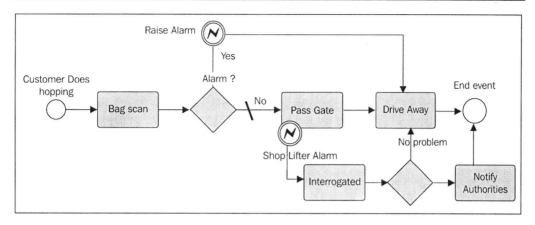

In this case, the scenario shown is from a department store where the customer has completed his or her shopping, and is now moving out of the store. The **Bag Scan** process is an automatic process that scans for any item that is not meant to be taken out of the without being charged for. Now, most of the time, this process will be smooth represented by a default flow for customer to pass the gate, but there may be times when an alarm goes off. In this case, the **Raise Alarm** error event throws an alarm trigger which should immediately be caught by the **Shop Lifter Alarm** error event. Now, this alarm can cause various activities, depending on the kind of facilities the store has. Typically, a security guard will ask the customer to get the bags checked for any mistakes and so on, by going through the till receipts. If the alarm is valid, the security guard will take the necessary legal actions. Otherwise, the security guard will apologize to the customer, and ask them to walk out of the store, avoiding further embarrassment. It is vital that the response to the error event is fast enough and accurate enough to catch the error every time. Otherwise, the customer or shop lifter can just walk away. The error events can help depict this scenario, but the way the process is implemented will also determine the efficiency of the exception handling.

Cancel

As mentioned earlier, a **Cancel** event is only to be used for a transaction process. It is usually triggered by a cancel end event inside a transaction, which calls the transaction intermediate event on the boundary of the transaction process.

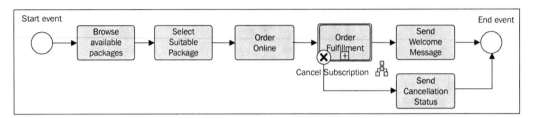

The preceding process map is for a user applying for an entertainment package consisting of TV, Internet Broadband, and phone from his service provider. We have created the **Order Fulfillment** process as the transaction that is represented as a rectangle with double boundary lines. We have also shown the output of the **Transaction** variable to show that it's a transaction, for users to understand. The figure also shows the variables for **Transaction** to be completed by designers to provide details, as required.

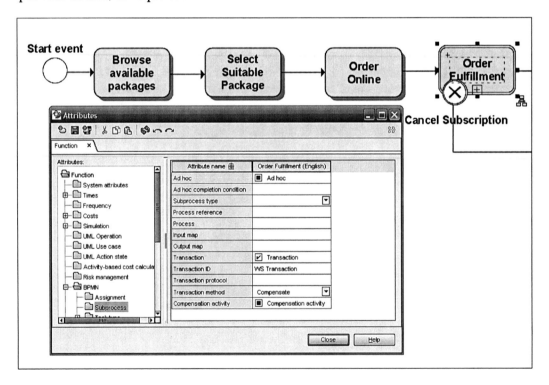

You will also notice that **Order Fulfillment** process has a sub-process (represented by a plus sign in the rectangle and small icon next to the lower right corner), which provides further details for this transaction. The sub process can be opened by double-clicking on this icon. The **Order Fulfillment** process also has an intermediate cancel event called **Cancel Subscription,** which represents the path to follow in case of a cancelled transaction.

The transaction details are as follows:

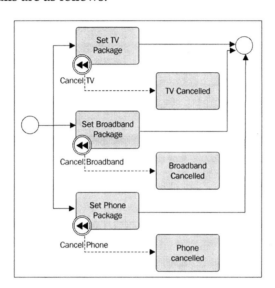

The transaction for **Order Fulfillment** contains details for setting up all three services to complete the package. In a transaction, the process will wait for all three services to be set up before it sends control back to its parent process. This is done to ensure that all of the activities in a transaction are complete and correct, as there could be a chance of a cancellation or error any time in between. In case of a cancellation, which can be either through a cancel end event or through a **Cancel** message using a Transaction protocol supporting this transaction, the control is passed to the cancel intermediate event, that is, **Cancel Subscription** which in this case is a parent transaction process. This intermediate event will wait until all of the compensation activities are complete for each service, before it sends the trigger for notification of the status to the customer. If there are no cancellations, in the normal process flow, the customer is sent a welcome pack with details of the services, and other information.

OMG is still trying to figure out the best mechanism for representing transactions and cancel events that cover all scenarios. Therefore, in my opinion, we should eventually see ratifications to the specifications in BPMN 2.0 to cover them in more detail.

Compensation

The **compensation** intermediate event, as elaborated upon earlier, will call for compensation to be used in a normal sequence flow, and will catch a compensation to perform that is attached to the boundary of any activity.

Multiple

For **Multiple** intermediate events, the implementation is similar to the way it works for start and end events, and is based on the attributes you provide for the multiple event. This will decide the way a particular event can be triggered. Hence, it could be a combination of a rule, timer, or message that could trigger a process mid-way through execution.

Process Modeling Patterns and BPMN

While working on a process model, we will notice the use of several repeatable and re-usable steps that are commonly used. These are referred to as business process patterns, and are important for us to understand and keep in mind while developing a BPD using BPMN. These patterns began as developmental work by Wil van der Aalst, Arthur ter Hofstede, Bartek Kiepuszewski, and Alistair Barros who together identified many workflow patterns that could be used to describe a process behavior, and be considered for execution by a BPM system later on. We will be discussing some of the main business process patterns in subsequent sections of this chapter.

For ease of understanding, we can divide these patterns into the following categories:

- Basic Control and Sequence Patterns
- Branching and Synchronization Patterns
- Iteration-based Patterns
- Termination
- Multi Instance
- State-based patterns

Basic Control Patterns

In this section, we would be describing some basic control patterns, which are need while modeling business processes.

Simple Sequence

This is a common pattern that a modeler and reader of the process model will notice. The following pattern will represent a series of process steps executed one after another in sequence. In the following (figure), **Activity B** will start only after **Activity A** is completed.

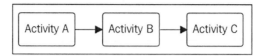

This pattern can be better understood by examining a sample BPMN diagram. Notice the shaded area in the following diagram, which represents the use of a simple sequence pattern inside a BPD.

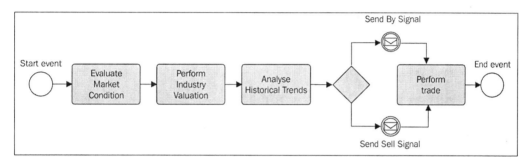

In this example, as a simplification, we are assuming that a trader will go for industry valuation of the stock only after he has done a market evaluation of that sector. In other cases, it could be a parallel activity, but in this scenario, it's a sequence of steps that are dependent on the earlier activity ending.

Other examples for sequence patterns are:

- Print of receipt after the purchase of groceries
- Elevator doors open after pressing the elevator buttons
- Creditworthiness check after loan application forms are received

Parallel Split Sequence or Forking

Type 1: Uncontrolled Flow

This pattern is used where a process needs to be divided into multiple activities for the next steps to take place. This kind of flow is also called an uncontrolled flow, as **Activity A** in the following diagram can fork out to both **Activity B** and **Activity C** without any conditions or dependencies. A Fork in a process is initiated from either a task, a sub-process, or a start event.

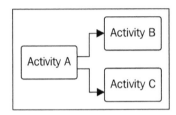

Type 2: Controlled Flow

If you notice, in the previous fork pattern, the flow of process was uncontrolled. A second mechanism, considered a 'good practice', is to use a parallel split or gateway between the sequence flows for control. By using the gateway, multiple threads will be executed in parallel, as shown here:

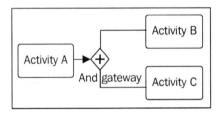

Type 3: Parallel Box

Another way of representing parallelism in BPMN is through the use of expanded sub-processes. In this method, a modeler can put the task elements inside a bigger process box to group the activities to be performed in parallel, as shown in the following diagram. Again, this is an uncontrolled flow as Activity A will fork into Activity B and C with no dependencies or conditions. Typically, BPMN process diagrams should have a start and end event. However, in this case, it's not necessary for the embedded sub-processes inside the main process box to have them.

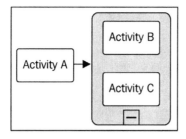

To demonstrate the parallel controlled flow, we can use the following example, where the highlighted portion is where a parallel gateway is used, signifying that both **Take Case File** and **Take Train** are activities to be performed concurrently.

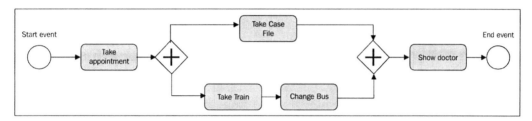

Some other forking pattern examples are:

- When a customer query is received, send an acknowledgement mail and enter the details into the sales automation system
- On receipt of an online payment, provide a receipt mail to the customer and ship the goods

Synchronization or Joining Flow

This pattern would be used to model the join or convergence of one or more parallel flows into a single flow. If we look at it from a Token terminology perspective, during the forking of a process flow, one token would be split into one or more tokens based on the number of flows that span out. During the joining of these flows, multiple tokens will converge and become one again before continuing forward.

Synchronization also has multiple ways of representation in BPMN:

Type 1: Use of Parallel (AND) Gateway

The parallel, or AND, gateway is used to represent the convergence of two or more concurrent paths to produce a single output path. In this case, **Activity A** and **Activity B** will converge using the AND gateway to create a single sequence flow to "Activity C".

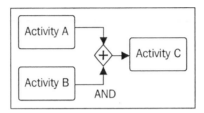

Type 2: Sub Process Completion

In this mechanism, the synchronization is achieved by completion of activities within a sub-process. As soon as all activities within the sub process are completed, the sub process will reach its end state, and control is given back to the higher-level process. This aspect of the sub-process makes it a convergence point.

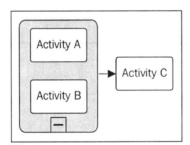

An example of using the synchronization pattern can be taken from the previous example of a visit to a doctor. In this case, **Take Case File** and **Change Bus** converge and cease to exist as separate paths. After that, one thread emerges, which, **Show Doctor**.

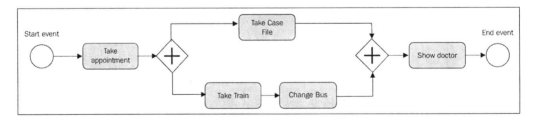

Some more joining flow example scenarios are:

- Online Tickets Dispatched after completion of the **address verification** and **credit card verification** processes.

Branching and Synchronization Patterns

In this section, we will describe more advanced branching and synchronization patterns, which we will need when modeling business processes.

Multi Choice

Sometimes also referred to as conditional routing or OR-Switches, the multi choice pattern allows a particular thread of a process execution to be divided into multiple branches based on a selection criterion. This decision, to send the thread of execution to a particular branch or set of branches, is made during run time. The choice can be based on a variety of factors such as outcome, or on results from preceding tasks, the value of data elements in the process, or the output of a calculated expression.

In BPMN, multi choice can be implemented either through the use of an OR gateway, or a complex gateway. It can also be implemented using conditional routing on the sequence flow. It is important to use a default path in a Multi Choice scenario, as it can otherwise lead to a deadlock situation. There should always be at least one path that the process can take if no other condition is applicable.

In the following example, once the customer's order is dispatched, the process involves sending some form of notification to the customer via mail, fax, or email. So the process based on the gateway could be to choose mail, fax, or email, combination of these choices, or all of them.

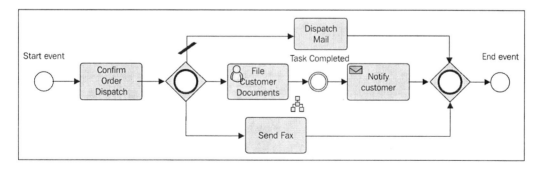

Some other multi choice example scenarios are:

- Based on nature of the issue, the helpdesk creates a severity ticket, and sends a message to one or all of: the network specialists, the application management team, and the data center management.

- Depending on the product selection on the new account application form for a portfolio management service, send action tasks to one or all of: the equity advisory, the mutual fund, and the insurance teams.

Structured Synchronizing Merge

This pattern is used in conjunction with multiple choice constructs to merge all of the branches coming out of a multiple choice. The flow of control is passed forward to a single branch only when each incoming branch, which had been created earlier by an OR gateway, is complete.

In BPMN, Structured Synchronizing Merge is supported by using an OR-join gateway. We can use the same preceding example to show the join.

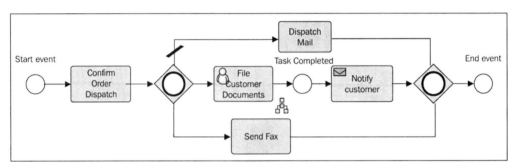

There is, however, one thing to note about this pattern, which can be a problem when modeling and understanding the process flow. As the OR join flow is waiting for the incoming threads, it has no way to decide how many threads are enabled by the OR split gateway. So, if a fax and a hardcopy mail have both been sent to the customer, what should the OR join gateway do once it knows about the fax? Should it wait for the mail path to arrive or move on to the next step? This is a classic example of where it's difficult to model the waiting time, as it could be possible that the second thread never occurred, which would create a deadlock situation.

This problem can be solved on the modeling side by providing additional information on chosen scenarios and preferred wait times, to reduce the chances of deadlocks, especially during implementation.

Some more examples for structured synchronizing merge scenarios are:

- Based on the nature of a helpdesk ticket, the request is sent to both the hardware and application service groups; only after receiving feedback from both departments, can the **close ticket** activity starts
- Depending on the product selection on the new account application form for portfolio management services, send action tasks to equity advisory, mutual fund, and insurance teams; only on receiving inputs from each team can the response be sent to the customer

Multi Merge

The Multi Merge pattern is used to represent the convergence of a two or more branches of process flow into a single ongoing branch, so that each incoming branch flows without restriction to the continuing branch. This is different from a simple merge where, at the point of the merge, only one branch can be active. In the case of multi merge, it does not require such safety during merging, and allows multiple branches to pass through at once. So in BPMN, it's like an uncontrolled flow. Multi Merge is generally used in the context of the Multi Choice Pattern.

In the following example, any of the threads comings out of the OR split, such as **Dispatch Mail**, or **Send Fax**, will immediately be sent for notification activity. This is actually asking for a customer response for each communication with the customer.

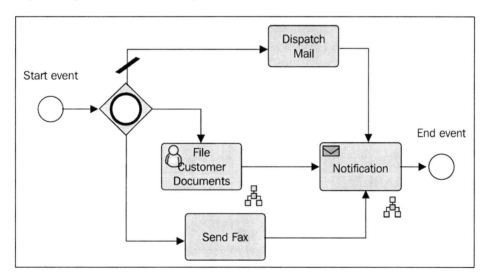

More multi merge scenarios are:

- **Send_Email** and **Send_Fax** can be parallel processes and different process branches. After each task is performed, it goes through a **Get_feedback** task from the customer.

- The **create_design_document**, **update_project_plan** and **create_test_plan** tasks occur in parallel in different branches. After completion of each task, they need to complete the **artefact_quality_check** before that particular branch of the process ends.

One thing to note here is that although this particular construct can be represented in BPMN, it is not to be used while designing particular lower-level business processes that need to be executed using BPEL as BPL is block-structured. It is not possible for two branches or threads of execution to run through the same path in a single process instance.

Iteration Based Patterns

These sets of pattern are aimed at depicting repetitive behaviour in a business process model.

Arbitrary Cycles

This is a looping pattern that allows sections of a process to be repeated. This pattern allows looping that is either unstructured or is not block-structured. This means that it has the ability to represent loops in a process model that have more than one entry or exit point. It must also be possible for individual entry and exit points to be associated with distinct branches.

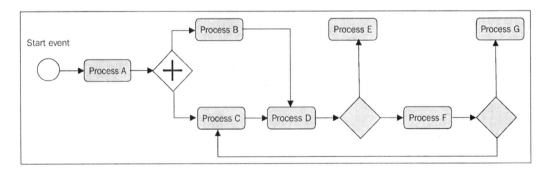

In BPMN, it is possible to create an Arbitrary Cycle pattern within a BPD by connecting the Sequence Flow to any upstream activity.

Structured Loop

This is a looping pattern used to depict repeatable tasks or sub processes. The loop will have a pre-test or post-test condition that is evaluated either at the beginning or at the end of the loop, similar to the familiar 'while-do' or 'repeat-until' programming language constructs.

In a while-do construct, a pre-test condition is evaluated before the loop starts, and allows for repeated sequential execution of a specified task or sub-process zero or more times, while the evaluated condition holds true. Once the pre-test condition evaluates to false, the thread of control passes to the task immediately following the loop.

In case of the repeat-until loop, a post-test condition is evaluated after the first iteration of the loop, which then allows for the execution of a task or sub-process one or more times, continuing with the execution as long as the condition is true. Once the post-test condition evaluates to false, the thread of control passes to the task immediately following the loop.

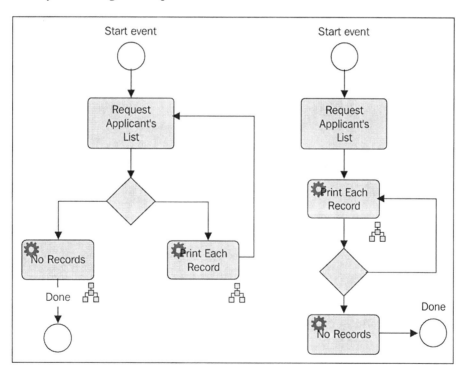

The preceding figure shows a structured loop using **While-Do** and **Repeat-Until** scenarios. It explains how each looping scenario can be represented. In the first case, the applicant list is printed based on the condition at the gateway. In the next case as well, the print loop is repeated until the conditions are satisfied.

BPMN also allows both pre-tested and post-tested loops to be captured through the loop task construct by using a loop attribute for each activity. In the following figure, the loop conditions for **Print Each Record** process are shown. In BPMN, there is no restriction on the expression language to define the conditions. So we can use **English** or, as we go into detailed modeling, we can use exact mathematical expressions to facilitate ease of understanding during implementation.

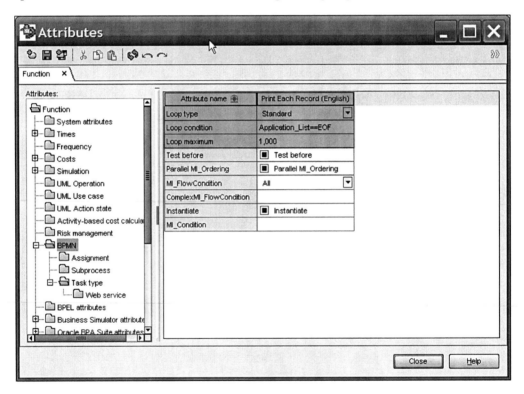

There is also a recursion-based pattern suggested as a typical workflow scenario, allowing a recursive loop to be defined for a process. Recursion-based iterative patterns, however, are not supported in the current version of BPMN.

Termination

These are patterns used to determine completion of a process. They are typically divided into two types.

Implicit Termination

Implicit termination provides a pattern of where a process should terminate when there is nothing else to be done. Mostly, in BPMN, we use explicit termination where there is one end event for a process instance. However, there could be situations where a process could be in more than one state, and where it could terminate.

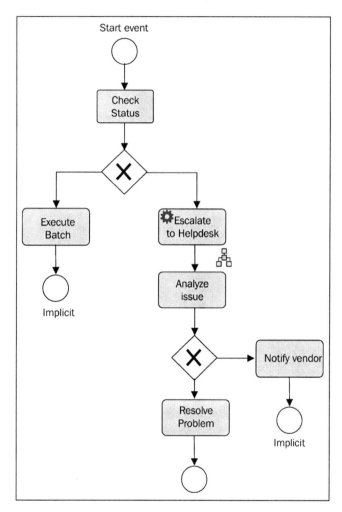

To elaborate on the scenario after the **Check Status** activity, the gateway will route the flow based on the status of the error, and we can either directly execute the batch, or escalate to the helpdesk department. The helpdesk can further notify the vendor as part of its action. In any of the three scenarios, it will reach its end, and the process will terminate as soon as the activity is complete. There is no other activity happening in parallel.

Explicit Termination

In this case, there is an explicit end node which, if reached by any branch in a process, will lead to the process being considered complete and any remaining tasks in the process being ignored and rendered cancelled.

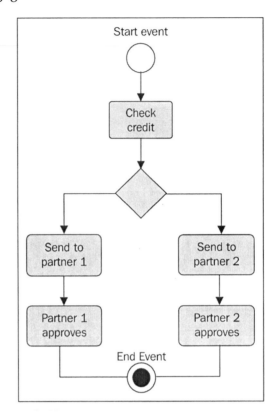

To explain this scenario hypothetically, if the **Check Credit** is approved by any of the partners for a customer, the bank will ignore inputs from the other partners, and the process will terminate. The terminate end event is used in this case to implement the explicit pattern.

Multiple Instance Pattern

Multiple Instance Patterns are used to define scenarios in which a given activity creates or instantiates multiple threads of execution. Typically, this scenario is seen where one activity, once triggered, creates multiple instances of itself.

Multiple Instances without Synchronization

In this scenario, for a given process, multiple instances of a task are triggered. For this specific pattern, the instances created are independent of each other and require no need for synchronization at the end of the process. In BPMN, this is achieved by using a Multi Instance task with 'Loop Flow condition' equal to 'none', signifying an uncontrolled flow. This means that all tokens created by the instances from this activity will move forward when completed. Oracle BPA does not depict the task with the Multi Instance mark graphically, and the user will need to check the BPMN attributes for the sub process or task to determine if the process has the Multi Instance parameter set.

To explain the scenario, the **Issue tickets** task will trigger several instances for each income tax defaulter. Hence, it's a multi instance task. The window provides details of the task BPMN attributes, where **Loop type** is set to Multi-Instance, and Loop Flow condition is left unchanged, signifying "none". The **parallel instance generation** check-box is also selected to signify the creation of multiple parallel tasks.

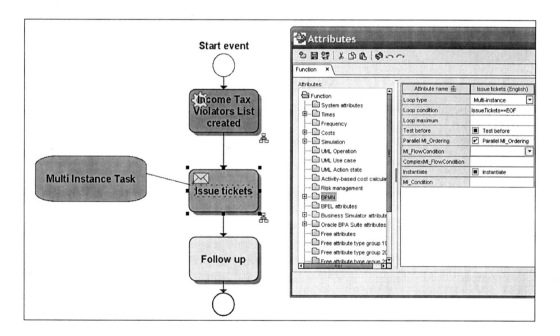

Multiple Instances with a Priori Design-Time Knowledge

In this case, multiple instances of a task can be created with a prior understanding of the number of instances required. The instances created run in concurrence and, post completion, will need to be synchronized before moving to the next activity.

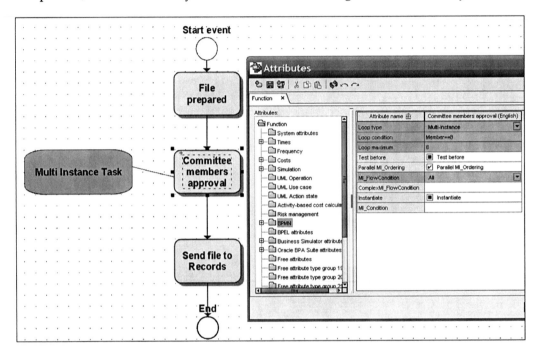

In this scenario, the Multi Instance task **Committee members approval** will create eight parallel instances for approvals from each committee member before the file can be sent forward. In BPMN, this is achieved by modifying the **Loop Type** to **Multi-Instance**, with **Loop Condition** set to eight, signifying the number of committee members, **Parallel Instance Generation** selected, and **Loop Flow Condition** set to **All**. The **All** value for **Loop Flow Condition** acts as a parallel gateway ensuring that next activity takes place only after all instances have completed, that is, all of the committee members, approvals have been received.

Multiple Instances with a Priori Run-Time Knowledge

In this case, similar to the design time multiple instance pattern, multiple instances of a task can be created for a given process. However, the number of these instances are not known to the modeler during design time. The number of instances can depend on various factors during run time, but it is known before the task instance is set to be triggered. Similarly, post initiation, the instances run independent of each other and, once initiated, these instances are independent of each other and run concurrently. It is also necessary to synchronize the instances before they move to subsequent activities. In this example, we would like to have the system perform some checks based on the type of tickets received and the list of errors generated based on unique error identifiers. Depending on the kind of ticket and the indication of the list of issues, the system can choose to perform a number of checks and controls.

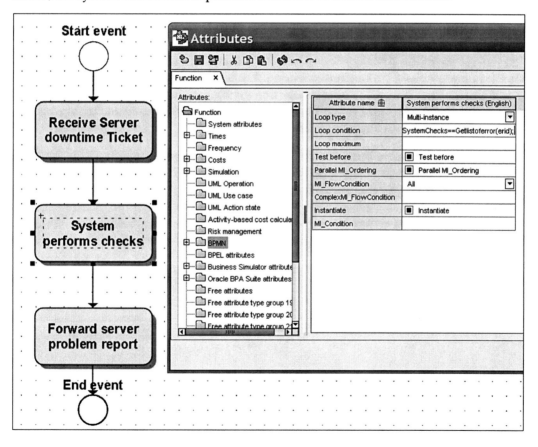

The run time instance can be determined by using an expression for the **Loop Condition** attribute instead of a constant value, as we did for design time. This expression, in this case, will check for the number of server checks, depending on the value calculated by the expression at run time. Also, the **Loop Flow Condition** is set to **All**, to represent synchronization of the instances before it moves on to the next activity.

State-Based Patterns

These patterns are used to model scenarios for processes that are affected by reasons outside the control of process engines. Most of these scenarios require process designers to consider the state of the process, which can be determined based on numerous considerations including process-specific data used for the process execution. BPMN is not well-suited to state-based modelling, but there are ways to implement some of these patterns using the specification.

Deferred Choice

As the name suggests, this pattern assumes that before a decision is made, all available branches are valid courses of action for the process. With pattern, based on a decision, one of the branches will be chosen. Once the decision is made, then all the alternate options are no longer available as options for this particular decision.

A BPD uses an Exclusive Data-Based Gateway to implement this pattern, and makes the decision of which alternative path to take. This acts as the branching point, and is followed by intermediate events linked to the sequence flows for each decision branch. When a token arrives at this gateway, it will wait there for an event to occur, which usually is the receipt of a message. This event determines the next course of action, and other alternates will be ignored. Instead of an intermediate event, a task of type *receive* can also be used, with similar results.

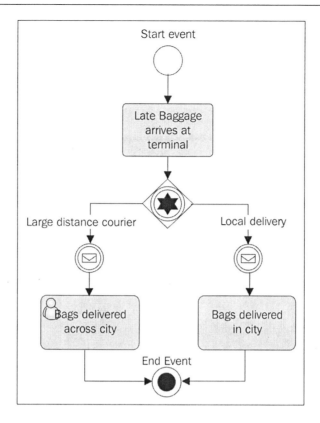

In the scenario of late baggage arrival, as shown here, an airline can have the option to use a long-distance courier company or local delivery companies, depending on the distance of the customer from the airport. So upon the arrival of the baggage at the terminal, and the receipt of a message of the customer location, the bags can be sent by the appropriate means. Once the decision is made, only one route will be taken, and the other is ignored.

Summary

In this chapter, we addressed some general guidelines for process modeling before taking a deep dive into some complex constructs of BPMN, especially the length and breadth of Events, and the role they play in creating and visualizing BPDs. We also covered support for workflow patterns in BPMN, which will be important in understanding and designing elegant and consistent BPDs by the analysts' community, in order to re-use BPMN process patterns to model processes, and further use these patterns during process execution using BPEL.

5
Process Analysis and Transformation—From BPMN to BPEL

We have seen how BPMN can be used by business analysts primarily to model business processes. The notation allows a user to represent the business processes graphically, which is easily comprehensible, and allows a consistent representation of the organization's business processes.

This chapter will discuss two important aspects that help in realizing a process from being just a diagram to something that is implementable. We can divide our discussion into:

1. **Business Process Analysis (BPA) using Simulation**: We will cover BPA using the Oracle BPA tool for simulation in order to analyze business processes for process improvement. This activity allows for deriving the most optimum process model before its implementation cycle.

2. **Business Process Transformation—BPMN to BPEL mapping**: While we design the business processes at the abstract level, we decompose the business processes into details using multiple process levels with increased information and granularity at each stage. At a certain decomposed level, the process it will reach an atomic state that can be executed manually or by using IT. This is where BPMN provides graphical properties in the notation which allow mapping of BPMN objects and attributes to generate executable BPEL.

We will cover the capabilities provided by BPMN and the Oracle BPA tool to map the process models for creating BPEL code for IT implementation.

This section will also look at the current gaps in how the OMG's BPMN specification visualizes the generation of BPEL from BPMN, and will also look at some tweaks incorporated by the Oracle BPA tool to provide comprehensive BPEL output.

Business Process Analysis Using Simulation

So far, we have understood the use of BPMN for modeling a business process. Modeling is followed by an analysis phase to identify bottlenecks and areas of potential improvement in a process. Generally, BPA tools, such as Oracle BPA, provide capabilities for simulating business processes before they are sent to the IT teams for execution.

Simulation helps business analysts in understanding, analyzing, designing, and improving business processes. It allows users to study the impact of various business scenarios over an existing business process and to understand the areas where improvements can be made.

We can study business process simulation by understanding various steps involved in the analysis phase as shown in the following figure:

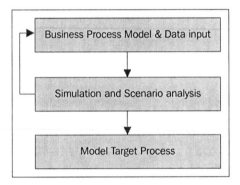

The Business Process Model and Data input

Business process simulation starts by having a graphical business process model in place, which you will analyze through simulation.

Let us start by taking a simple example of the ordering process to represent our current model.

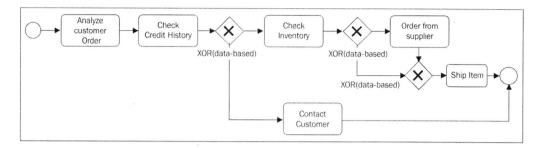

The process, at the moment, is just a graphical representation, with no additional information in the activities and events that would allow us to carry out a meaningful simulation.

After we have mapped the process, we will need to finalize the data regarding costs, cycle times, and resource allocation for activities in the process that can be entered into a model. Once we have done this the process is ready for its first simulation run.

We will use Oracle's **Business Process Simulator**, which comes with the BPA suite, to demonstrate the simulation concepts. The details for simulation are managed as attributes in this tool. An example of these attributes is provided in the following figure:

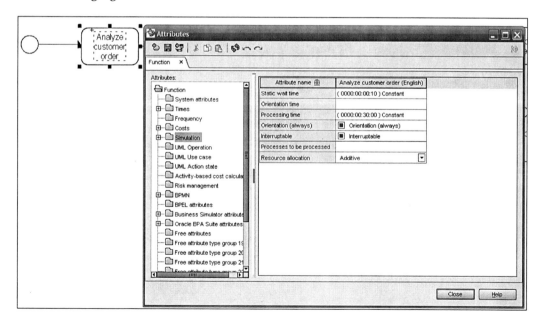

The main attributes we should consider for a process simulation are:

- **Processing Time**: This indicates the actual time spent in doing an activity. This can be a constant value, or can be based on a distribution.
- **Wait Time**: This indicates the waiting time before a particular activity can commence after the previous activity has completed its task. This can be a constant value, or can be based on a distribution.
- **Orientation Time**: This indicates the time required for an employee to orient themselves before carrying out an activity. If the **Orientation (always)** check box is selected, this time will be considered for every process instance during simulation.
- **Resource Allocation**: This specifies whether designated human resources are required for carrying out the activity (Additive attribute value), or any person from the pool of designated human resources can be selected to carry out the activity (Alternative attribute value).

For our example, let us take the following values for the various activities:

Activity Name	Processing Time	Wait Time
Analyze customer Order	20 min	5 min
Check Credit History	5 min	1 min
Check Inventory	5 min	
Contact Customer	10 min	10 min
Order from supplier	1 day	10 min
Ship Item	2 day	5 min

Let us start by adding values to all the activities. To modify the simulation attributes for all activities, select any activity, right-click, and choose **Select all of this type** option.

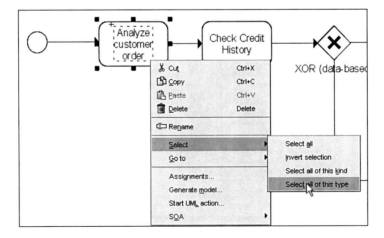

Now press *F8* to bring up the **Attributes** window and navigate to **Business Simulator attributes,** as shown in the following figure.

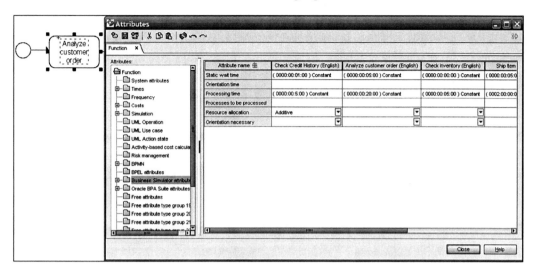

Enter the values of the simulation attributes for each activity as per the table. We can also set the value to a non-constant distribution. There is a choice of seven mathematical distributions we can use, as follows:

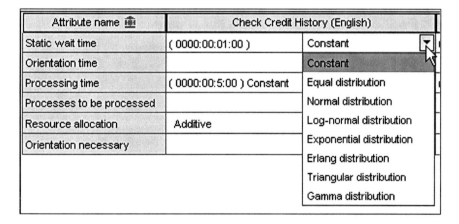

For the simulation to work at the decision points, for example, after the **Check Credit History** activity, we will need to specify the probability of the process taking any given one of the paths after the gateway. This is done by specifying the probability values of the sequence flows coming out of the gateway. In this case, we have opened the attribute window for the sequence flow activating **Check Inventory**, and have set the **Probability** to **0.9**, as shown in the following figure. Similarly, we have set the probability of the exception sequence flow to **0.1,** to take the total to **1**.

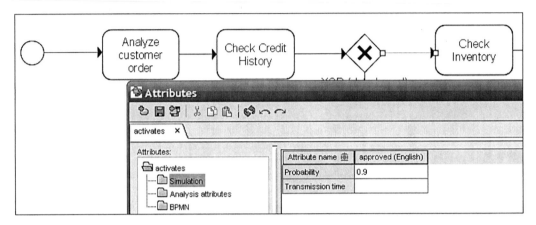

You can also modify simulation parameters just before starting the simulation. These parameters can be accessed from the main window, via menu option **View | Options**.

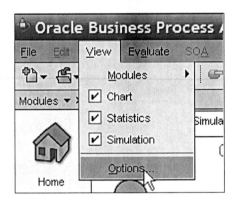

The simulation options window allows us to modify various parameters for a simulation, such as the **Duration** of the overall simulation. In this case, the simulation will run for a hundred days (simulation days, not elapsed days).

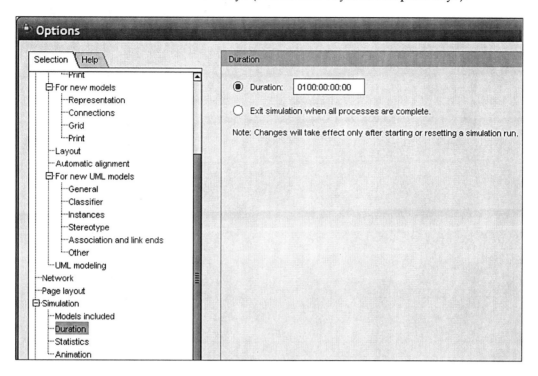

Simulation and Scenario Analysis

At this moment, the model is ready to conduct a test simulation run to demonstrate the capabilities of this feature. However, in real life situations, you will need to provide a greater level of detail to the process model, such as resource allocation information and detailed time and cost attributes, to get meaningful results that can be used for making any improvements.

To start the simulation, right-click on the diagram, select **Evaluate,** and choose the **Start simulation** option. You can also access the simulation screen by using the *Ctrl + Backspace* keyboard combination, or from the main menu, under **Evaluate.** This will initialize the simulation for this process, and the process is now ready to start.

The highlighted section in the following screenshot is the simulation toolbar, from where you can control the simulation instance. You can play, pause, reset, stop, and select many more options from this toolbar. You can also toggle the animation feature on and off, which can help you see the simulation flow using color-coded animation. The boxes on the right display the simulation data during the simulation.

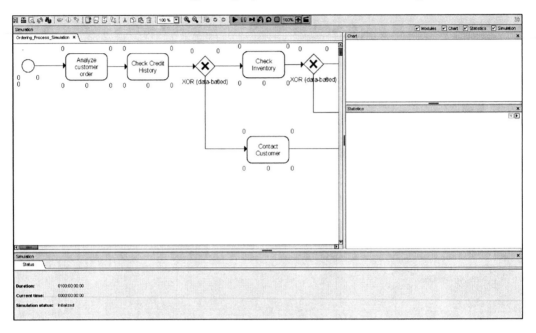

Let us start the simulation by pressing the play button in the simulation toolbar.

The following simulation window shows the animated simulation flow, with grey blocks representing active tasks (I think - strictly tasks or sub-processes). The box on the right shows various metrics regarding the process. We can see information about events, activities, gateways and so on. We can also analyze the cost and resource information based on values specified for the process attributes.

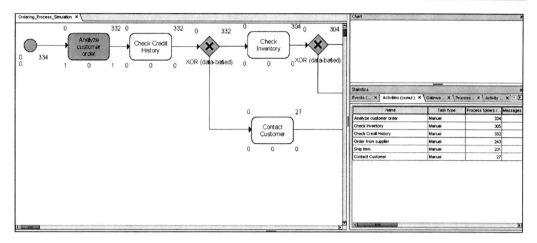

The process simulation stops once it completes its specified duration. You can also pause or stop the simulation at any time by clicking the following two icons, respectively.

Once the simulation has stopped, we can conduct various kinds of data analysis on the process model. The data generated from the simulation will be used by the business analysts to conduct analysis such as:

- Processing with extraordinary processing time
- Processing bottlenecks and steps where significant backlogs are building up
- Typical wait time analysis between tasks {again, I think} and its impact on the process
- End-to-end process completion time
- Cost Analysis to analyze expensive process steps
- Resource under-utilization or over-utilization

Oracle Business Process Simulator provides users with the simulation data that can be used to do detailed analysis. This data can be used to perform spreadsheet analysis, or create various charts. In this example, we are looking at a chart calculated on the basis of the **Processing time** attribute in simulation for the process.

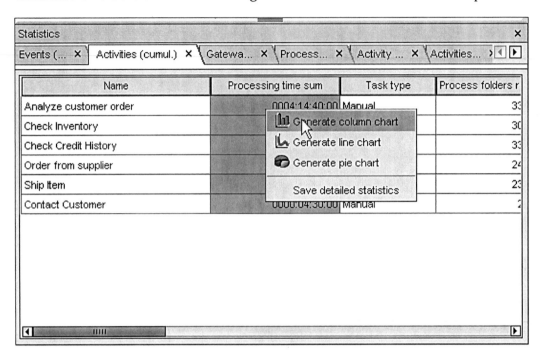

The chart is created by selecting the values in the activities column represented in the **Statistics** block. Right-click on the selection and select and **Generate column chart**.

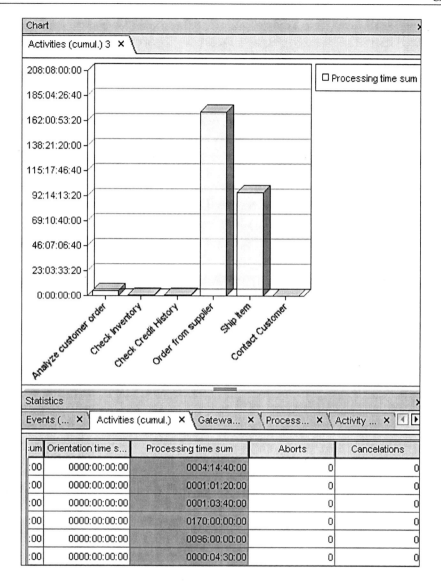

This example shows that the maximum time spent in this process is in ordering the process between the retailer and its suppliers, which could be a good opportunity for improvement–for example, automating the information flow between the retailer and the supplier. For our current example, we realize that the maximum time is taken when the retailer has to source the item from the supplier. In this case, one way we can introduce some improvement is by automating the internal ordering process to reduce the processing time from the current two days to something lower. We can also achieve some improvements in how we ship the items to the customer, perhaps by opening some local warehouses to stock popular items and reduce delivery time.

It can take several simulation runs, considering the multiple scenarios, to arrive at more optimal (Some are more optimal than others-the most optimal is the optimum) versions of the process models, before we can identify the target process to be taken for the implementation stage.

As we can see, the most crucial aspect of simulation analysis is the data we enter for the process steps and other objects that represent the real world. This step of gathering data and entering it for activities and events is a very crucial step, but can sometimes be difficult for process projects. For the simulation to reflect the real life, it needs information about the process that is accurate enough. Unfortunately, most of the time, business analysts will face difficulty in getting sufficient information about a process to create relevant simulation models. Therefore, it is worthwhile investing in some time by business analysts to carefully analyze and dig out any existing data available for the process, and use this for simulating different business scenarios during simulation.

Model Target Process

Analysis of the simulation metrics on the basis of time, resource, and cost will help identify areas where process bottlenecks exist. Also, as the simulation provides us with an end-to end process duration, we are in a good position to understand which improvements would lead to the maximum impact. As in this example, it is not essential that these improvements lead to visible change in the process, and could be more attribute-level changes. However, in real life, we will see processes improved with new activities, refined workflow patterns, discarded activities and so on, to arrive at the new to-be, or target, business process. Hence, the iterative results of simulation and process analysis will be a modified process model that is more efficient and optimal, for use in the next stage.

One of the greatest benefits of using simulation is our capability to identify process improvements that do not require significant changes to the process, which could be disruptive to the organization. These changes can be iterative in nature. Efforts should be made to tweak the process rather than go for radical changes to the process, to allow a smooth transition during implementation and execution of the to-be process. The flexibility of BPM allows the business and IT teams to introduce these changes iteratively during the course of process implementation and usage.

Business Process Transition: Bridging the Business—IT divide

There have been many discussions around traditional approaches to IT projects, with the fundamental issue being that business and IT are not aligned to each other during the course of a project. There have been several experiences where business requirements set out by the business stakeholders have been misinterpreted by IT, and the resultant solution had half of the core requirements missing. In a process-oriented project, this problem can be further escalated due to the project's dynamic nature. Also, the use of standard tools such as Word, Visio and so on, for documenting process flows and their associated static requirements, is not a preferred mechanism of communication for solutions that are changing on a daily basis.

For a BPM project to be successful, there needs to be a high degree of participation from both the business teams and the IT teams to work collaboratively and share responsibilities. The business should own the job of business process modeling and analysis, while IT should own activities around the design and execution of the process models. This process can be made simpler by following these common guidelines:

- The use of standards across the BPM project, such as BPMN for process modeling, BPEL for process orchestration, and various web services standards for service implementation

- The use of appropriate tools to allow greater integration between modeling and execution

- The use of governance and shared responsibilities for process and IT artefacts, allowing control over changes and the communication of these changes to stakeholders

Keeping these points in mind, the main areas (areas where or reasons why) where BPMN scores over any other modeling standard is its vision and outlook on the alignment of business processes, and its technical implementation going downstream. Also, being a standard specification, it allows some level of consistency by allowing the business users to document and analyse the business processes, and then having the technical teams implement these processes using the IT capabilities and infrastructure available, by exposing existing and new services provided by various systems in the organization. This ability of BPMN to map to BPEL helps organizations move closer to their SOA objective and BPM, and is a very important vehicle to achieve this handshake.

It is not essential that following BPMN as a standard is mandatory for achieving BPM and SOA, but it does introduce a degree of control and predictability, which is essential for managing processes and services in a complex business set-up.

BPMN to BPEL—Key Considerations

When we try to analyse ways of mapping BPMN to BPEL, we need to conceptually address and understand the following two areas:

1. What is prescribed by the BPMN Specification for BPEL mapping?
2. How does the tool vendor implement the specification for BPMN to BPEL mapping?

BPMN Specification for BPEL Mapping

The way BPMN goes about mapping BPEL is via the transformation of object types and the use of properties or attributes for the BPD and its objects to similar BPEL counterparts. Every object in a BPD, such as a process, event, or gateway has attributes that the user can specify, and can use during transformation to BPEL. For example, the Start Event of a type *message* will become a *receive* element in BPEL with the createInstance property set to **yes**. The end event of the type *message* will be translated into Reply or Invoke. Similarly, there are other mappings for processes, flows, and gateways, which have been explained as a section in BPMN specifications, to which we can refer. We should also note that different BPM tool vendors implement the transformation of BPMN and BPEL differently. For example, Oracle uses some of its own extensions to elaborate BPDs further before generating BPEL, instead of using only the BPMN attributes for conversion.

It is also evident, considering the details involved in the BPMN attributes for mapping, that a business analyst will not be inclined to specify or understand these properties. This will require either a technical team at the BPMN model level, or completion of the generated BPEL once the skeleton code is generated, by a business analyst.

Tools to Support BPMN-BPEL Transformations

OMG and **The Organization for the Advancement of Structured Information Standards (OASIS)**, another standards organization, have defined a BPEL standard, which describes how business processes can be executed. As these are separate organizations, the chances of gaps occurring in interoperability between these standards can be an issue to consider, especially the way they are interpreted by the existing tools.

BPMN, for example, has tried to cover various attributes and rules to provide a detailed transformation of a business process model in BPMN to BPEL, which is a good step forward. BPM tool vendors are continuously working to bridge gaps between these standards as the standards are maturing themselves.

BPMN and BPEL are currently in the process of being largely accepted as standards of choice, which is evident from a wide range of products and tools providing support for BPMN and BPEL. As these standards are maturing, this is still an area where a tool vendor needs to use work arounds or extensions to allow production-level implementations. Oracle BPA, for example, has provided constructs in BPMN today that are helpful in representing human tasks and automated tasks separately.

The fundamental difference between BPMN and BPEL is also the reason why some tools have started providing extensible features to allow this transformation to happen seamlessly to a large extent, and to allow a round-trip feedback loop between the business users working in BPMN and technical teams developing in BPEL, and vice versa. Also, some of the complexities can be avoided by modeling the business processes to be more structured, and to not use too many arbitrary loops in BPMN diagrams that are difficult to export to BPEL. This is a topic of debate, as we are asking our business community to think like a programmer and model business processes to create consistent technical output in the form of BPEL, which is unfair.

So we need to work out a good balance between the available choices, and as we speak, the vendor's tool developers are working hard to make the transition from BPMN to execution environment tighter, and enable a one-click deploy of business processes, hopefully in the near future. Specifically, the vendors supporting BPEL for process execution are working very closely to see tighter integration between the upcoming version 2.0 of BPMN and BPEL.

Oracle BPM Suite: Oracle BPA and SOA Suite for BPMN-BPEL Mapping

Before we start discussing the BPMN to BPEL mapping process, let us discuss some of the tools we will be using to demonstrate these capabilities.

So far, we have used Oracle BPA Suite to model business processes in BPMN and allow process analysis. For the purpose of showing end-to-end Business Process Management and SOA, we can also integrate Oracle BPA Suite with Oracle SOA Suite, Oracle BPEL Process Manager, and BAM to demonstrate end-to-end Business Process Management in a closed loop. We will use Oracle BPA, Oracle BPEL Process Manager, Oracle BAM, Oracle BAM, Oracle Business Rules, and Oracle SOA Suite in combinations to represent the Oracle Business Process Management or BPM

Suite. You can download the Oracle SOA suite from `http://www.oracle.com/technology/software/tech/soa/index.html`. You will need to have an Oracle Technology Network account to download this software. Oracle has also announced the BPM suite, which is a combination of tools. We will be covering it in later chapters. The details of BPM Suite can be found at `http://www.oracle.com/technologies/bpm/bpm-suite.html`

Before we discuss the Oracle BPM suite in detail, let us go through a typical BPM lifecycle and map the capabilities to the tools we will discuss subsequently.

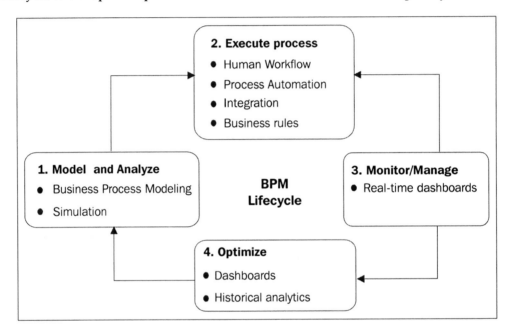

Let us quickly map the BPM life cycle to each of the product components that we will use further in our examples and demonstration scenarios. The Oracle BPM solution also allows a closed-loop implementation of BPM and SOA, comprising the following key components in terms of functionality:

1. **Model and Analyze**: Oracle Business Process Architect is used for modeling and analyzing the models being developed. This component can not only be used for modeling processes using BPMN, but also for modeling a variety of other dimensions of an organization such as business strategy, data models, UML models, organizational structures, IT system design, and so on. It provides support for over 50 model types, including BPMN and **Event Process Chain Model (EPC)**.

The processes being modeled in the modeling component can be simulated using Oracle Business Process Simulator. Process modelers can simulate various scenarios using this component to identify potential bottlenecks with regard to time, cost, and resources. This provides a very effective mechanism for analyzing the suitability of a process before a decision to execute or implement it can be taken. The purpose of modeling business processes in these components is not just for implementation, but also for communicating the consistent representation of these processes to various stakeholders. Oracle Business Process Publisher is used for publishing Business Process Models. It also provides a role-based and target group oriented access to process content.

2. **Implement and Execute**: For implementation of the process, we use **Oracle JDeveloper** which is an **Integrated Development Environment (IDE)** for developing executable BPEL-based processes. It is used to develop services and orchestrate services into composite applications and business processes.

    To implement security, we can use **Oracle Web Services Manager (OWSM)** to secure and manage authentication, authorization, and encryption policies for services that are separated from your service logic.

    Oracle BPEL Process Manager allows an enterprise to orchestrate disparate applications and services as per the organization's business processes. It provides the ability to quickly build and deploy these processes in a standards-based manner, which is critical in achieving successful Business Process Automation and SOA. It is used for orchestrating both automated and human tasks.

    For integrating multiple disparate systems into an existing integration environment of an enterprise as per their SOA roadmap, we can use the **Oracle Service Bus**.

    Business rules play an important part in implementing business logic and policies for any business. Most of the time, these rules are embedded in an application's code, making it complex and time-consuming to implement changes. One of the key components, which works collaboratively with a BPM system, is a **Business Rules Management System,** which allows centralized management of key business rules, and achieves considerable flexibility and adds value to any business. Business rules are implemented by the **Oracle Business Rules** component, which can be used for executing dynamic decisions at run time, the logic of which can be managed by business stakeholders and analysts. We will be covering business rules in detail in the next chapter.

3. **Manage, Monitor, and Optimize**: **Oracle Application Server Control** can be used for managing services, processes and systems.

   Oracle Business Activity Monitoring is a component available for building interactive, real-time dashboards, and proactive alerts for monitoring business processes and services. Oracle BAM provides business stakeholders and operation teams with the information they need to make better business decisions and take corrective action for current process bottlenecks. Information available from BAM is an important source for business analysts in identifying potential process improvements. This activity allows business analysts to rework the current business process and work out changes that can make the process more efficient and optimal. This capability, when properly used and implemented, allows us to achieve closed-loop BPM, which can result in an agile process of process improvement and its execution on a continuous basis.

Tool Approach for Process Transformation

The process of transformation from BPMN to BPEL and information sharing among Oracle BPA suite, Oracle JDeveloper, and BPEL Process Manager can be explained by the following diagram.

Oracle BPA will mostly be used by the business analysts and business process architects to model and analyze the process. Once the process is selected for implementation, more details are added to the process model to allow IT teams to get a comprehensive BPEL output that they can work on. Oracle BPA then provides capability to generate a Business Process Blueprint that combines all information available for a process into a file and stores it in the business process repository.

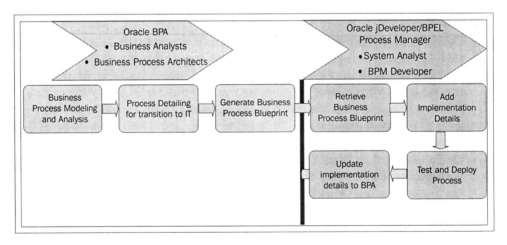

At this juncture, the business process is ready to be picked up by the IT teams. This area is usually covered initially by JDeveloper as JDeveloper it provides a link to Oracle BPA through which IT teams can retrieve the business process blueprint. Once the IT teams have an access to the skeleton BPEL output, and associated information from the business teams such as process descriptions and so on, the IT teams can start the work of adding implementation details to the BPEL code. The process can then be deployed into the BPEL process manager for testing or production. This process of information exchange is not one-time, and is iterative in nature as changes made to the process by the business users can be notified to IT teams as they work on the implementation. These changes can then be merged by the IT teams without affecting their existing work. Similarly, IT teams can suggest changes to the business process, which translates to a changed proposal in Oracle BPA, allowing the business users to decide on the suggestions and take action. We will discuss this process in detail next.

Let us cover some of the main concepts provided by the tools for transformation from Oracle BPA to JDeveloper, in detail.

Modeling and Analysis Process

In this case, as we explained, a business analyst will create the process model in BPMN to represent the abstract process, which will then act as the business requirement for the IT teams in case the model needs to be implemented. The business analysts will also use simulation and other analysis techniques to further refine the process before they set the process for implementation.

When the business process needs to be implemented, we can add further details in a process model, which can make the process more comprehensive and result in a detailed BPEL generation. Some of these details are added using extensions over and above BPMN provided by Oracle BPA. These details and extensions, which are helpful during transition from BPMN to BPEL, are covered in the next section.

Process Detailing for Transition—A Look into Oracle Extensions for BPMN and BPEL

Although we have seen that the BPMN specification provides a number of attributes and features that allow a business analyst to embed implementation-level details into the business process, it is still far from being 100% compliant in currently-available tools, including Oracle BPA. One of the fundamental reasons is the current mediocre level of maturity, in the adoption of BPMN by both the user community and the tools. Also, BPEL has its own shortcomings when it comes to managing human tasks and sub processes, which has forced tools such as Oracle BPA and BPEL Process Manager to provide extensions over and above the BPMN and BPEL specifications to support these important implementation artifacts.

In addition, tools have different ways of mapping BPMN to implementation using BPEL. For example, Oracle BPA does not translate the attribute details in the BPMN diagram to use for BPEL transformation, but relies on a method of understanding the BPMN objects used, and details are provided in a special diagram called a 'Function Allocation Diagram'. These diagrams are usually created automatically for the activities based on the specific attributes we provide for Oracle extensions, for example, in the case of representing a human task. We can manually link a functional allocation diagram to an object as well. These diagrams are used along with BPDs to generate the blueprint, which results in detailed BPEL output for IT teams. We will cover these diagrams in detail as part of our sample example.

To ensure that the modeling performed in Oracle BPA is comprehensive, and is well integrated with the Oracle SOA suite, Oracle has extended the modeling objects present in the underlying product. The BPMN modeling types and stencils have been extended with objects and attributes to cover enhanced features. Some of these extensions are:

Automated Activity

Automated activity represents interaction with a system and refers to a Business Service. These are activities that are performed automatically by the systems. In terms of BPMN, where we use **Automated activity**, it can be interpreted as a call/ invocation to a business service, or a receipt of a business event from a business service. Automated activities are converted to a Business Scope upon BPEL transformation.

The properties of the automated activities can be accessed by pressing *Alt-Enter* for the activity. The standard properties for **Automated activities** can be seen in the following screenshot:

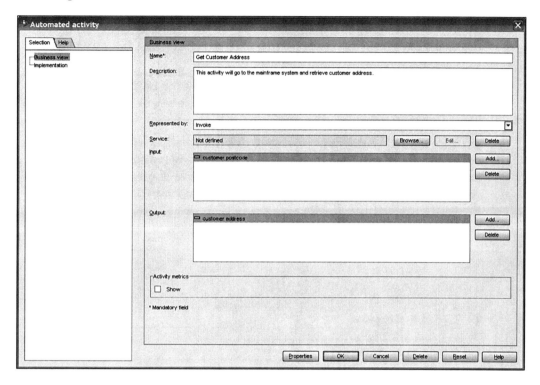

- **Name**: Unique Name for the activity.
- **Represented by**: Drop-down for how you want to represent this activity.
  - **Empty**: No details specified for the activity.
  - **Abstract BPEL activity**: In case the user is not sure whether the type of activity is an 'invoke service' or a 'receive event'.
  - **Invoke**: Select this if you want the activity to invoke a business service.
  - **Receive**: Select this if the activity receives an event from a business service.

- **Service**: In this field, either enter the name of the business service, or select an existing business service. Existing business services are available in the IT system models, and a user can browse and select the required business service.

- **Input**: Input represents the input message of the business service. It is business data. Enter the input (as free text) or select items from a list of technical terms used to signify an input.

- **Output**: Output represents the output message of the business service. Output is business data. Enter the output (as free text), or select items from a list of technical terms used to signify an output.

- **Activity metrics**: After being checked, this information will be used as BPEL sensors to allow real time monitoring of the activity (variables being passed, faults, and so on) using BAM dashboards. They are like probes that are constantly evaluating this activity and sending relevant data to BAM when they notice something of relevance as per their properties. These metrics are converted to sensors value on BPEL transformation.

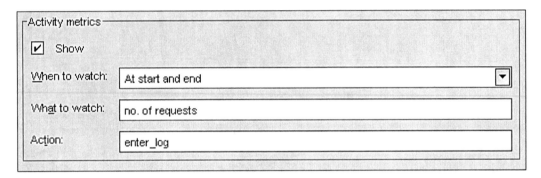

- ○ **When to watch**: Select a monitoring period from **At Activity Start, At Activity end, At Fault, At start and at end**, or **At Compensation.**

- ○ **What to watch**: These are the variables to watch, which you can specify using commas.

- ○ **Action**: A free-form text field that can be used to describe what to do when the watch conditions are met by the BPEL Sensors. This will be implemented by the IT teams based on the information received.

The following screenshot is a sample from the transformed BPEL scope in JDeveloper for this automated activity.

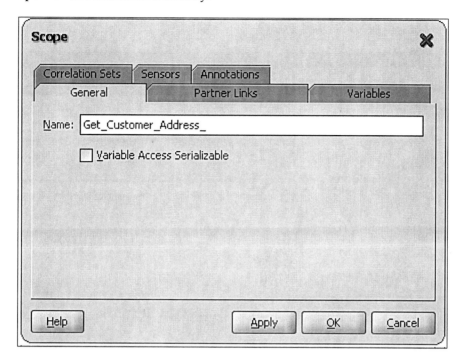

Human Workflow Activity

You cannot model a business process just by having automated activities, as human interactions are also required to carry out an end-to-end process. The users who participate in the business process have roles and privileges to perform tasks in the business process. The Human workflow activity represents the human/manual tasks as follows:

- **Name**: This is the name of the human task.
- **Description**: This is a free-form text field and appears as an annotation in the BPEL diagram after transformation.
- **Priority**: Here, we enter the priority of the task. Priority can be **1** through **5**, with **1** being the highest. By default, the priority of a task is **1**.

- **Duration before expiration**: Typically, every task in a process should have an expiration duration that can be entered in this field. If the assigned user does not complete the task within this duration, the task will be escalated to the manager for further action.

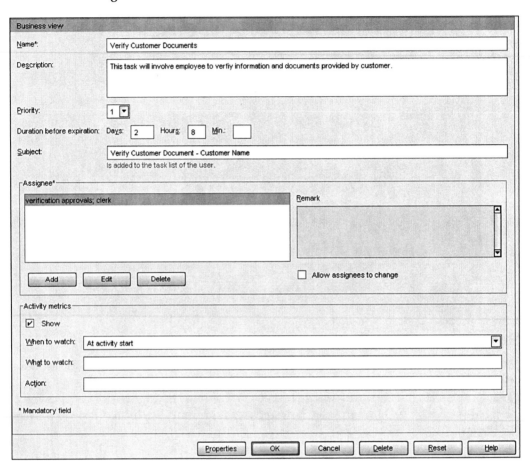

- **Subject**: Enter the subject.

- **Assignee**: In this section, you provide details about the person who will be working on the task.

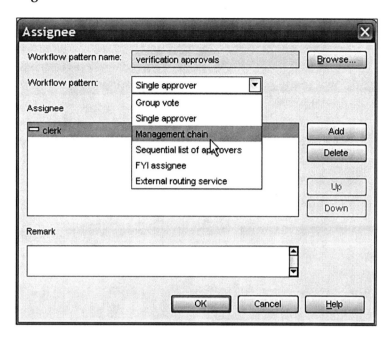

- **Add**: Click this button to enter a new assignee, say **clerk**, or you can select an existing assignee to edit in the **Assignees** dialog. In this dialog box, you can set the following:

    ○ **Workflow pattern**: There are various kinds of human task patterns that you can select for the assignee or assignees as follows:

      ○ **Single approver**: A single user is allocated to the task to be fulfilled.

      ○ **Group vote**: This option is used when multiple users who are working in parallel must take action simultaneously; for example, voting to select or reject a feature for the next product release. In this case, you can specify the voting percentage that is needed for the outcome to take effect.

      ○ **Management chain**: Based on a management hierarchy, the task is routed for a series of approvals. This is specified as a list of users who represent the management chain.

- Sequential list of approvers: This is similar to the management chain participant type, except that with that type, the users are part of an organization hierarchy. In this case, they can be a series, or a user or groups required for the approvals.

- FYI assignee: This is more of a need-to-know-basis task, where the process is not waiting for the assignee to send a response.

- External routing service: This is used to configure an external routing service that can decide on the kind of pattern to use, at run time.

- Remark: Enter a comment (in free text) to describe this assignment.

Some of the extended properties for the Human Task activity are:

- **Owner**: This indicates the owner of the task that can be browsed and selected.

- **Notification instructions**: Enter instructions for the notification to be sent to the business user's as well as reminders before the start of the task or before its expiry.

- **Parameters**: Enter business data items to be used as the task parameters.

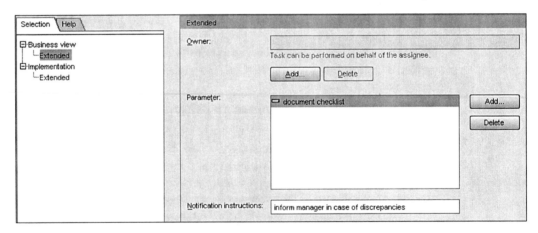

Human tasks are converted to a human task activity upon BPEL transformation. The task service for the human task also gets automatically generated. The BPEL artifacts for invoking these task services are also generated. Most of the attribute details, such as priority, workflow pattern, notification instruction and so, on get translated to business annotations to be referred to by the IT teams. Task parameters transform the attribute of **Human Task**. A sample from JDeveloper for this transformed human task can be seen in the following screenshot:

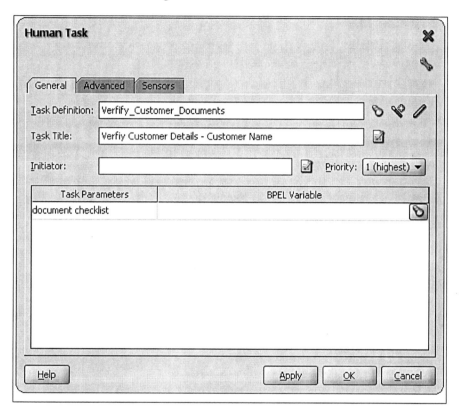

Notification Activity

Notifications are sent to users to alert them of changes to the state of a task. Notifications can be sent through any of the following channels: email, telephone voice message, fax, pager, or SMS. This is captured by the Notification Activity as follows:

- **Name**: Enter the name of the notification activity.
- **Description**: Enter a description for the notification activity.
- **Channel**: Select from **Email, Fax, Pager, SMS,** or **Voice**.
- **Subject**: Enter the subject line to be used in the notification.
- **Text**: Enter the message text to be used in the notification.
- **Receiver**: Enter or select the name of the receiver who will receive the notification.
- **Activity metrics**: This will be used as BPEL sensor for monitoring purposes to be used in real time business activity monitoring.
- **When to watch**: This could be set to **At Activity Start, At Activity end, At Fault, At start and at end,** or **At Compensation**.
- **What to Watch**: These are the variables to watch, which you can specify using commas.
- **Action**: A free-form text field to describe what to do when the watch conditions are met by the BPEL Sensors. This will be implemented by the IT teams based on the information received.

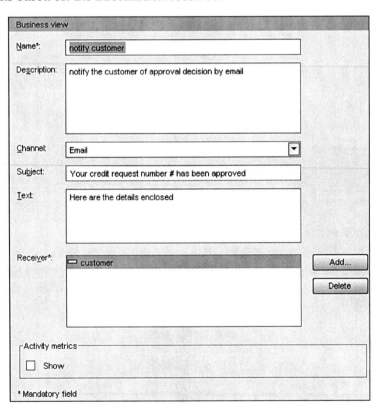

Notification Services are converted into a Business Scope upon BPEL transformation. A Notification service, as well as artifacts for invoking the Notification service, is created within this business scope. Based on the channel for notification, the invoke service's operation call changes. For example, for email, the transformed operation will be 'sendEmailNotification' to the notification service.

Business Rules Activity

Information supplied in this section will be used by a business rules engine to execute a business rule. Business rules are statements that describe the policies and decisions in a process. The Business Rule activity in the Oracle BPA Modeling tool is used to point to the Business Rule defined using the Rules Editor of a Rules Engine. Business Rules should be converted into a Decision Service during transformation to BPEL. At the moment, this conversion is not supported in its current version.

The text attributes of the Rules activity are converted into annotations for the IT teams to refer to and implement.

Some of the properties for a business rules activity are:

- **Name**: Enter the name for the business rule.
- **Repository**: Enter the name of the repository that contains your data models.
- **Catalog**: Enter the name of the rules catalogue.
- **Business rule function specification**: Enter the description that defines the Business Rules set.
- **Input**: Enter a technical term to define inputs to the rule.

- **Output**: Enter a technical term to define outputs to the rule.

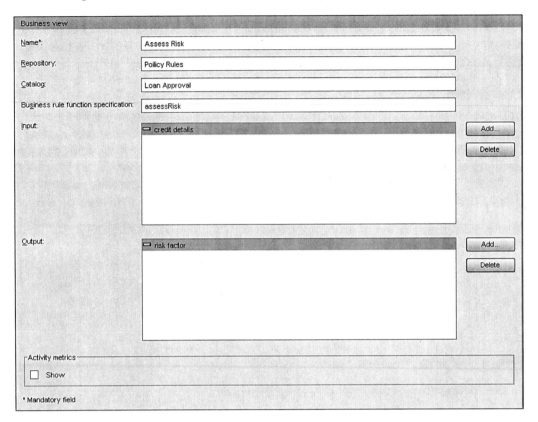

Business- IT Synchronization using Process Blueprint

The greatest difficulty, when it comes to tools support for BPMN to BPEL conversion, is the synchronization of changes made by the business teams to the business models and technical modifications made by the IT teams to the BPEL code. Due to this reason, most of the time organizations preferred to create their process models in isolation with IT teams, and IT teams preferred to take the bundle of process models or business requirements, and create BPEL code directly in the IDE. This resulted in information silos, which in turn meant wasted effort and "lost in translation" problems.

To provide a solution to this problem and provide a tighter coupling of our BPMN models and BPEL, the Oracle BPA provides a mechanism for sharing a common metadata format, which is called a 'process blueprint'. The metadata, or process blueprint, which is basically an abstract level BPEL process is shared with IT. At this stage, the first handshake between business and IT can take place to agree upon the specifications for executing the business process. Though I will not call it a panacea for all problems, it's a major step toward providing common metadata that can be shared between the business and IT teams, and allowing for an iterative, closed-loop feedback process during process implementation.

When any process is shared with IT for implementation using Oracle BPA, a process blueprint is published.

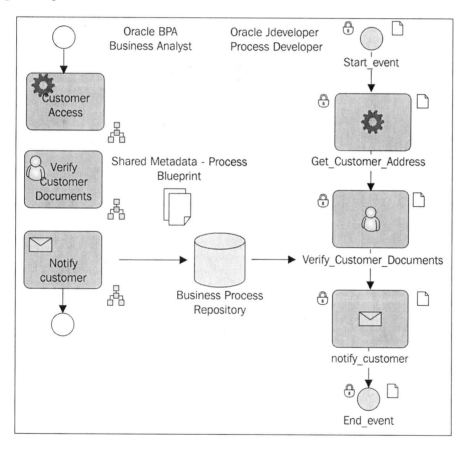

Let us take a very simple example to demonstrate the concept of sharing metadata or a process blueprint between business and IT teams. In the example above, you can see that the process has been developed in BPMN using Oracle BPA. Once the process is ready to be implemented, it was shared with the IT teams using a shared metadata or the process blueprint. This process blueprint is then retrieved by the process developer in the JDeveloper environment. You can see that the start event of the business process maps to a start event in JDeveloper, an automated activity is mapped to an automated activity bound by a scope, a human task is mapped to a human task, and an end event has been mapped to an end event.

The process blueprint view in JDeveloper allows the process developer to view the requirements as represented by the business teams on his desktop. Apart from the graphical view, the process developer and IT teams can also view the attribute information of the activities. The following example shows the details of the **Verify_Customer_Details** human task as we provided earlier.

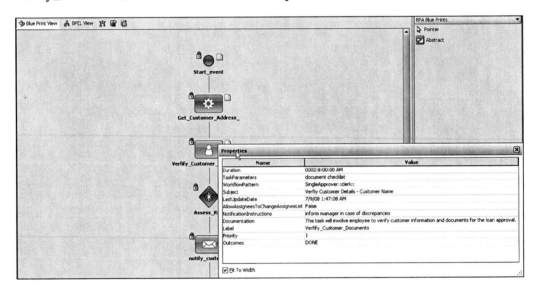

You can toggle between the blueprint view and the BPEL view in JDeveloper. Now, a developer can implement the technical details and execute the process using Oracle BPEL Process Manager.

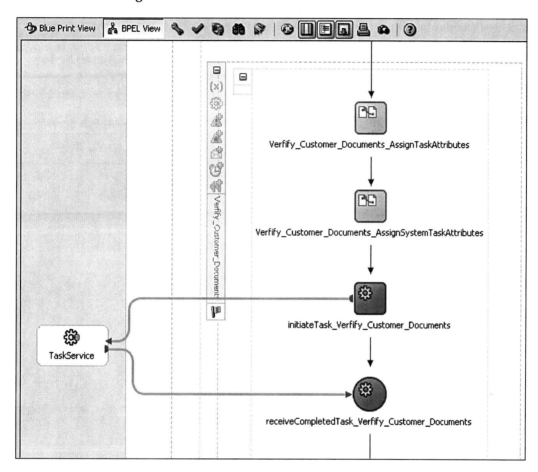

The metadata sharing between Oracle BPA and JDeveloper also provides an additional, valuable benefit. As business processes are dynamic assets of an organization, modifications and changes to them will be an ongoing task. Depending on the requirements of business or IT, the process models might need modifications from time to time. For example, businesses might realize that they need to provide a mechanism of assessing risk for customers asking for large credit. They should be able to make these changes while IT is still busy with an existing implementation. The IT developer, though, would primarily be involved in implementing details within a process scope, and might also suggest a process change that should be made available to the business for consideration.

The BPMN to BPEL Bridge provided by Oracle BPA allows us to maintain this concurrent synchronization of changes. The IT developer gets alerts upon creation of new versions of the Process Blueprint, and can view and modify these processes in parallel using the BPEL Process Designer component in JDeveloper. Business-level changes can automatically be merged with any changes made by the developers to ensure that their implementation details are kept safe, and the requirements being developed are always in line with business requirements. We can see in the following example that the JDeveloper blueprint view indicates that there is a new version available in Oracle BPA. IT teams can view the changes and merge these into their existing work.

In addition, IT developer can make changes to the business flow inside the Blueprint view, and these in turn get reflected in the Business Architect tool when the executable BPEL model is saved to the Business Repository. Business user can review these changes and incorporate them into the business process model to produce a newer version. As we can see in the following example, we have added a sample task called **Email_1** in our development environment, and that change is available to the business user as a change indicator. The user can decide whether to accept the change or reject the change by clicking the highlighted icons.

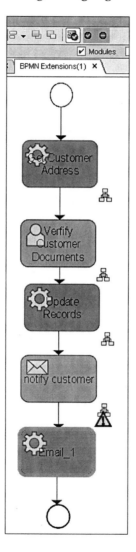

We will study the concept of BPMN to BPEL transformation in detail as part of a case study in subsequent sections.

Transformation Case Study

Let us understand the process of transforming of BPMN to BPEL using the example of a **Portfolio Account Opening** process at a bank. This example is a simplified version to help us understand and focus on core concepts. We will also be using this example to demonstrate the closed-loop BPM life cycle discussed in the next chapter.

Business Process Overview—What is 'Portfolio Account Opening?'

There is no business objective more important to banks and other financial services institutions than the acquisition of new customers for their products. This is enabled by having an efficient account opening process allowing customers to approach the institution and get the account opened in the least amount of time. Although customer acquisition is highly critical to the health of banks and financial services companies, the new account opening process for these banks and other institutions is typically costly and inefficient, and is plagued by mostly manual, paper intensive, error-prone, and inflexible processes, leading to silos of operations.

Business process driven process automation using BPM and SOA can help add significant value to these organizations by:

- Helping to maintain standardized processes across multiple channels of customer interaction

- Automating mundane tasks, and making most of the work straight through to enable faster account activation

- Reducing process cost by increasing process efficiency and process cycle time

- Creating a more responsive system for customers and providing enhanced service-level expectations

- Increasing process flexibility by allowing changes to be done rapidly, gaining a competitive advantage

In our example, 'Portfolio Account Opening' is a subset of 'New Account Opening' process, and is followed by the bank to service customers who want to open a portfolio account for conducting stock trading and investments. Typically, an account opening process has the following steps:

- **Customer contacts the bank**: The customer will approach a bank through any channel, such as the Web or the branch, and will complete an application form for the service or account they want to open. The customer might also be asked to share additional documentation for verification and regulatory compliance requirements.

- **Receipt of applications and verification by the bank**: The application forms and required supporting documents are received by a Bank employee who will carry out the necessary checks. If some required documents are missing, the bank will get in touch with employees, using email or phone, to sort out the gaps. Once the documentation is complete, the bank employee will check whether the customer is an existing bank customer or not. If the customer is an existing customer, a new portfolio account will be created. Otherwise, a new customer will be created in the system first. This is followed by an eligibility check, to see whether the new or existing customer passes the criteria for opening a portfolio account.

- **Opening of the account**: Based on the eligibility check decision, the account will either be created or the application rejected. The rejection information will be sent to the customer. Otherwise, once the customer's portfolio account is created, and in this case assuming he is a high net worth customer, a portfolio manager will be allocated to the customer for advising him on his investment portfolio.

- **Welcome Kit**: Once the allocation of an account manager is done, the customer is notified of the status, and a welcome kit is dispatched to his or her address. The documents for the customer are stored for safekeeping.

Let us look at what the BPD of 'Portfolio Account Opening' will look like, based on our high-level overview. This is just for your reference, and we will go through a step-by-step explanation of the BPD in subsequent sections of this chapter. The diagram is shown in two parts due to the size of the process.

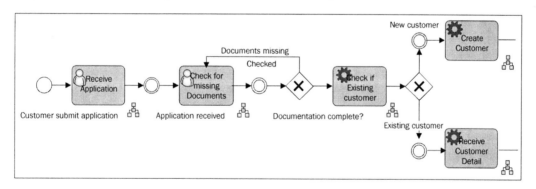

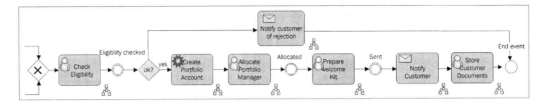

Now, we would like this process to be implemented in a way that will allow the customer to access the bank easily, and for the bank employees to cater to this request in the most efficient manner.

In Oracle, this can be achieved if we are able to map what has been proposed in the business process to the underlying IT process, reduce any gaps in information, and use work-flow to move from one step to another. This is the aim of mapping Business Process Management with SOA, allowing BPMN translation to BPEL, which in turn will bind various roles and application services as per the process.

Let us follow the transformation process we discussed earlier to model and transform the example process.

Business Process Transformation—Modeling and Analysis

The first step in this process is to model the Business Process for 'Portfolio Account Opening' using BPMN. We have to note that it is important that we understand the level at which a BPMN process should be created with implementation details. If the process is too high-level, then the IT teams will get very abstract processes that cannot be implemented without going into detail of every step. Hence, it's vital that the business process is at a level of abstraction that makes it ready for implementation. One of the ways of ascertaining this is to check if the current activity can have further sub-processes that haven't been elaborated. In our case, we are taking a process to a medium level of abstraction to make it easier to understand for users but this process can be further decomposed, if required.

Let's start by creating the BPD for the 'Portfolio Account Opening, process based on our understanding from the business scenario provided above. We will also use the extensions provided by Oracle BPA, to ensure that we can maximize the output to BPEL.

To ensure that the whole process is available for the users to view, the process has been split into two parts to help users visualize the end-to-end process.

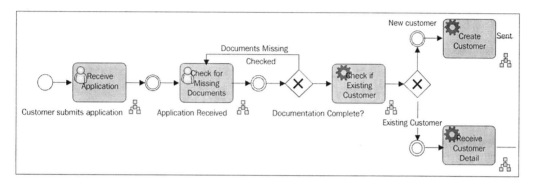

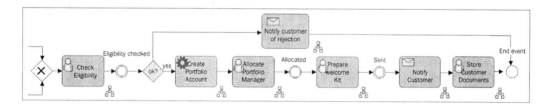

In this case, the process starts with a start event, **Customer submits application**. The application is received using a manual task, **Receive Application**. It is followed by another human task activity, **Check for Missing Documents**, which is a task performed to check if user has submitted the required documents or not.

The control is then passed through a gateway, resulting in two paths: one loops back to **Check for Missing Documents** if documents are found to be missing or incomplete, and another moves forward to the next manual task **Check if Existing Customer,** suggesting that all documentation is available and correct.

Check if Existing Customer can be a semi-automated task where the bank employee checks in a bank system to see if the applicant is already a bank customer or not. In this case, IT will use services provided by the bank systems to provide this information. If the customer is not an existing customer, then an intermediate event **New Customer** is sent to the systems using web services to help **Create Customer.** If the customer is an existing customer, an intermediate event, **Existing Customer**, is sent to help **Retrieve Customer Details.**

In both the cases, the next step is to check eligibility to open a portfolio account for the customer, which is carried out by an expert during the **Check Eligibility** human task. This leads to a decision to reject or approve customer's application for a new account. Once eligible, a new account is created using **Create Portfolio Account**. A portfolio manager is allocated to the customer using the **Allocate Portfolio Manager** manual task. A notification is sent as an email using the **Notify Customer** activity. **Send Welcome Kit**, which contains the necessary information and welcome note, is sent via the mail.

Finally, the customer application documents are stored in a warehouse for safekeeping by a bank employee. We can make the process of storing documents more efficient by automating the process by scanning and digitally storing these documents. In our case, the customer has a compliance requirement to maintain a physical copy of the application as well.

If the customer is not eligible for a portfolio account, a notification task is initialized to inform the customer of the reasons.

Business Process Detailing for Transformation

Once we have created the process diagram, we would want to add details to the activities and other objects to ensure that the process can be made ready for transformation to BPEL. These details can be added using another set of diagrams called **Function Allocation Diagrams**, which are created automatically for the activities based on the specific attributes we provide for Oracle extensions, that is, human task, automated, notification, and business rule activities.

Let us consider the following example. In the account opening process, we will need to provide details for the **Check if Existing Customer** automated task.

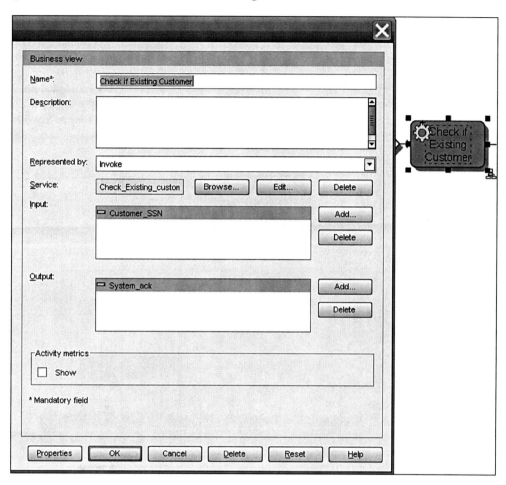

The highlighted fields are the ones that have been entered for this particular automated activity, an show that this activity will translate into an **Invoke** in BPEL. The name of the Service is **Check if Existing Customer**, which is a new service we are calling.

Once we have provided all of the details for the activity, clicking **OK** will automatically create a **Functional Allocation Diagram** or **FAD,** and will link it to this activity. The name of the service will translate into an **Application Service Type** FAD and during transformation to BPEL, will become a **PartnerLink** by that name. Similarly, the input and output fields will translate into **Technical Terms** in a FAD, and will later be used to understand which variables to use for input and output in BPEL after transformation.

Let's see what the resulting FAD looks like. You can access the FAD by double-clicking the icon next to the automated activity. This will result in the respective FAD being opened.

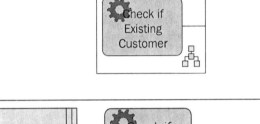

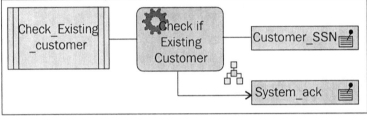

As we can see, the FAD now contains the automated activity **Check if Existing Customer** and the associated business service **Check_Existing_customer,** with input **Customer_SSN,** and output **System_ack.**

We provide similar information for the other activities including Human Task, and the tool will do the task of creating respective FAD. For normal processes and activities in BPMN, we will need to create a FAD manually. An example of FAD created for the Human task, **Check Eligibility,** with its properties and resultant FAD, is shown below

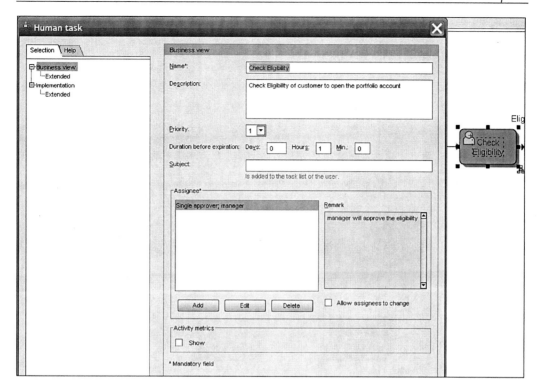

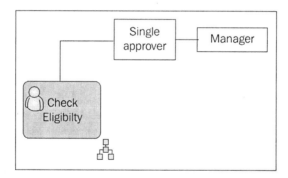

Similarly, we will add details to other activities and tasks.

Model Validation before Transformation

Once the process has been designed and the FADs created, we can use Oracle BPA to do a semantic check of the model to ensure that we are following the specification as per the tool's requirements. This can be achieved by selecting menu option **SOA | Validate Business Process**.

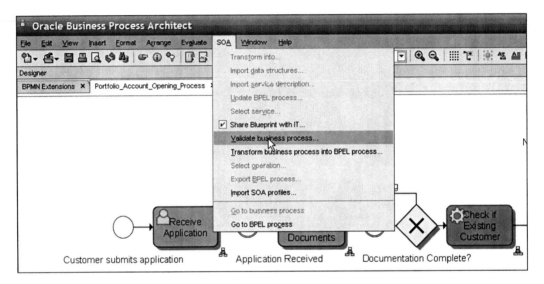

This feature allows us to identify any objects that are not modeled properly, or the areas where we haven't followed some key pointers. So, it's very helpful to run this feature before carrying out the transformation. This feature provides two outputs: one is a web report containing all objects, and the other is a report suggesting whether the semantic check has passed or failed.

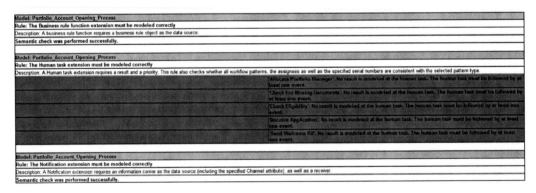

This report suggests that we should create an intermediate event after every human task activity. This is also shown visually in the tool as the second output.

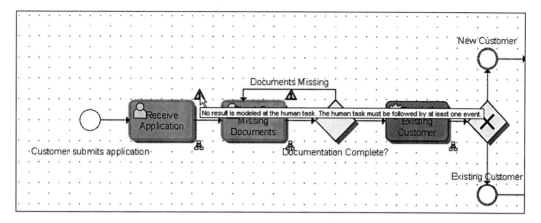

In the preceding figure, you will notice that the objects with issues are bordered in red, and there is a warning sign that provides details of the error. Details of most of the validation rules for Oracle can be found in the **Quick Start Guide** provided with the installation.

We can fix these errors by adding an intermediate event after each human task, and can also correct any other error flagged by the tool. Once the changes are done, we can revalidate the business process to check our changes.

Automatic Mapping of BPA Elements for BPEL

Some key mapping rules to keep in mind are:

- Gateways (XOR, AND, and OR gateways) are converted to switch and case statements upon BPEL transformation.

- Human tasks are translated to human task process activities upon BPEL transformation. Thus, Task Service and BPEL functions for invoking the Task service are also generated. The Notification attribute, and some of the other text attributes in the human task properties list, get translated to business annotations.

- Notification Services are transformed into a channel-specific process activity upon BPEL transformation. For example, if we have set the channel as 'Email', it will be transformed to an 'Email' type process activity in BPEL. The corresponding Notification service, as well as the BPEL artefacts for invoking the Notification service, is created within this business scope.

- Automated activities are converted to a Business Scope upon BPEL transformation. A Business Service, which is represented as 'Application Type' within the FAD, is converted to a Partner Link upon BPEL transformation. If 'Represented by' is set to 'Invoke', an invoke activity is created inside the business scope, and is linked to the Partner Link. If 'Represented by' is set to 'Receive', a receive activity is created inside the Business Scope, and is linked to the Partner Link. The activity metrics definition is converted into sensor variables within the scope. All Business Data or Technical Terms used in the FADs within the BPD are converted to variables upon BPEL transformation. The default variable type is string.

- Business Rules are converted into a decision service. However, this conversion is not supported in the current version. The free text in the Rules field is converted into business annotation.

Generate Business Process Blueprint

Now that we have checked our BPD for all aspects of transformation, we will perform the final step of Oracle BPA involvement in this cycle. Before the IT teams can start working on this diagram, it has to be made available to them in a format that is usable in their environment, namely JDeveloper.

We will create a business process blueprint that will provide a common format or metadata for linking JDeveloper with Oracle BPA. So, now that the business process is ready, we can use the **SOA** menu again to **Share Blueprint with IT**.

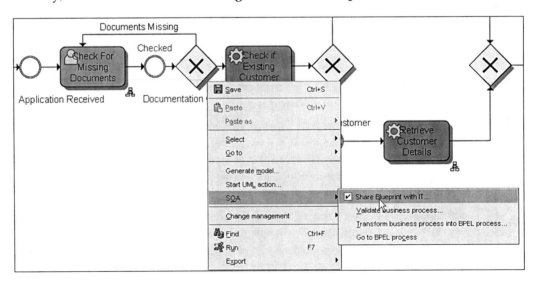

Select the option, and it will ask for re-validation of the process semantics. You can perform the check to ensure that there are no errors. If you are sure about it, then ignore the step.

The **Transformation Settings** window will allow us to set some common attributes to define the BPEL output in terms of the process type being **Synchronous** or **Asynchronous** and so on. We will enter a description and click **OK** retaining the default values.

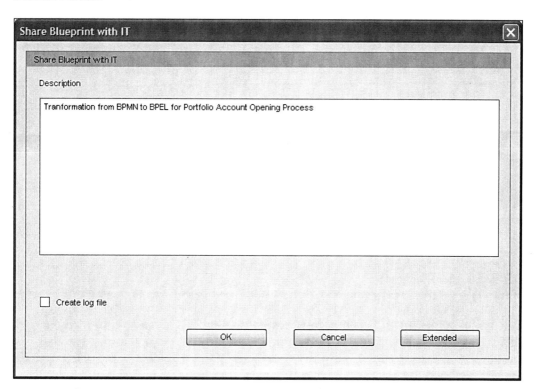

Further attributes to define the BPEL output in terms of process type being **Synchronous** or **Asynchronous** and so on can be provided using the extended options.

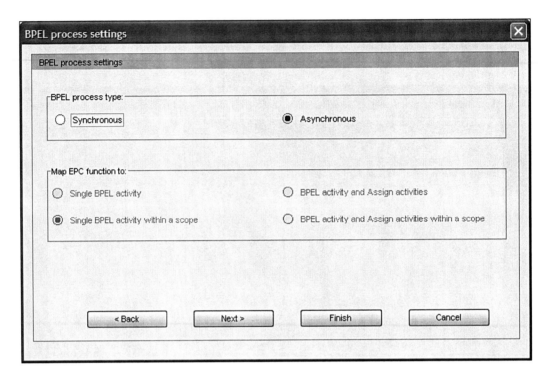

This will result in the BPD being transformed into a BPEL process within Oracle BPA. The finished BPL process is available under the IT Process folder. After the transformation is successful, a report is generated, in case there are any warnings. As we have defined the business services at a very abstract level in FADs, the following warnings are displayed, as the **PartnerLink** generated does not have defined **PartnerlinkTypes**.

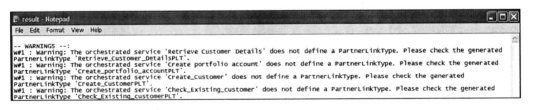

We can choose to ignore the warnings, and we will look to the IT teams to provide the necessary details to take care of these issues.

You will notice that in the BPA explorer, a new folder is created where the Business Process is being designed:

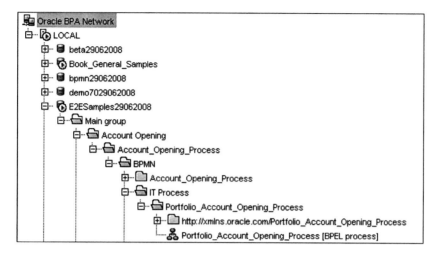

In this case, we have the **Portfolio Account Opening Process** within the **Account Opening Process** folder, under the **BPMN** subfolder. There is a new folder, **IT Process**, created by default, and this contains the generated BPEL that will be the Process Blueprint to be shared with the IT teams.

Retrieve the Business Process Blueprint

In this section, we will be creating a 'Portfolio_Account_Opening' BPEL project from a Business Process Blueprint in Oracle BPA from the JDeveloper interface.

This will involve the folowing three steps:

1. Create a BPA connection for importing the blueprint
2. Create a BPEL project
3. Blueprint view and BPEL view

The detailed discussion of these points is as follows:

Create a BPA Connection for Importing the Blueprint

In JDeveloper, the IDE performs the following steps to create a BPA Server connection. The installation documentation will provide you with details of to install a component called `pcbundle.zip` that is provided in the setup files. This component will setup a BPA Server connection. This connection will enable us to share the Business Process Blueprint with the IT teams for further implementation.

To create a link with a particular process blueprint, right-click the **BPA Server** node in the **Connections Navigator,** and then select **New BPA Server Connection**.

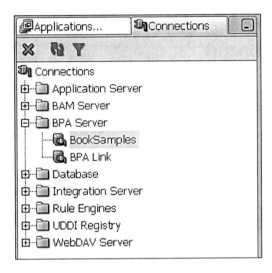

The following **BPA Server Connection** dialog is displayed:

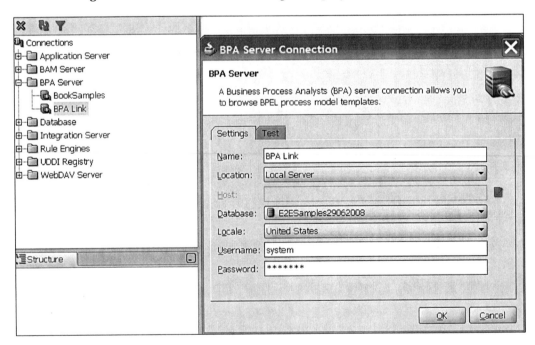

Now, carry out the following steps:

1. Enter an appropriate name for the BPA server in the **Name** field.
2. Choose the **Location** of the server, which can either be **Local**, or **Remote**. If using a local server, the location of the local BPA Repository will be retrieved automatically.
3. If using a remote server, enter the hostname or IP address in the **Host** field.
4. Enter the **Username** and **Password** for establishing the connection.
5. Test the connection by using the **Test** tab to check if the server connection details are correct.

Create a BPEL Project

In this step, we will create a new BPEL project, which will be based on the BPA process blueprint. In JDeveloper, you must create an application and a project to begin with. Follow these steps:

1. Select **File | New** from the main JDeveloper menu.
2. Double-click **Application** in the **Items** window.
3. Enter your application name in the **Application Name** field, **Portfolio** in this case, accept the default path or specify your preferred location in the **Directory Name** field, and then click **OK**.

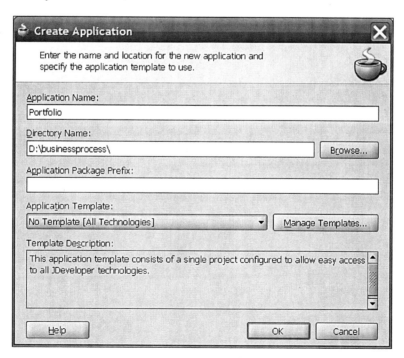

4. In the next step, click **Cancel** in the **Create Project** window.

5. Right-click on your new application node in the **Application Navigator** and choose **New Project,** to define a new BPEL process project.

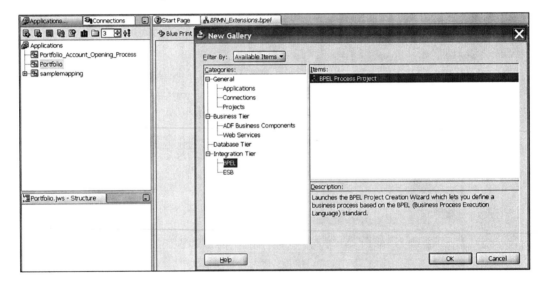

6. Double-click on **BPEL Process Project** in the **Items** window, to display the **BPEL Project Creation Wizard** window.

7. Select **Existing Blue Print** in the **Type** field.

8. The **Name** field is automatically populated with the blueprint name. All other fields are set to the correct values for creating an asynchronous BPEL process by default.

9. Click **Browse** to choose the Blueprint you want to use, from a BPD. What we select is the BPMN diagram, in this case, **Portfolio_Account_Opening_Process(BPMN)**. Based on the diagram, the tool selects the appropriate BPEL blueprint. Click **OK**.

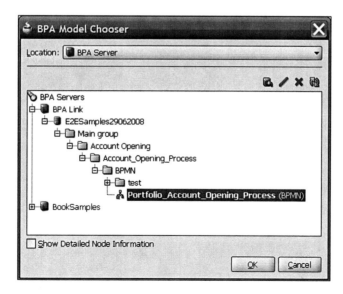

10. You will notice that the name of the process is automatically selected, based on blueprint. Click **Finish**.

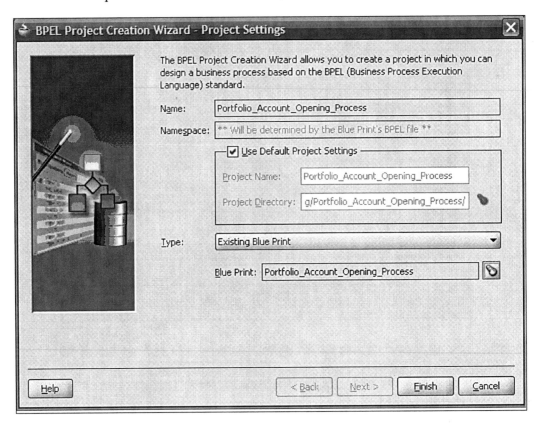

Blueprint View and BPEL View

The imported Blueprint in JDeveloper results in two views that are available to users of JDeveloper. The blueprint view provides a skeleton of the process.

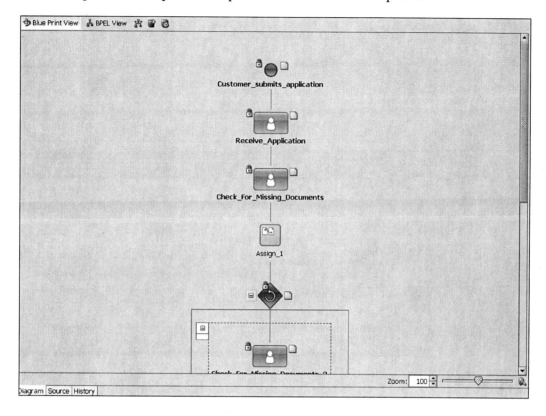

The details, which are provided by business users in various description fields, are available for the IT users as annotations, for verification purposes.

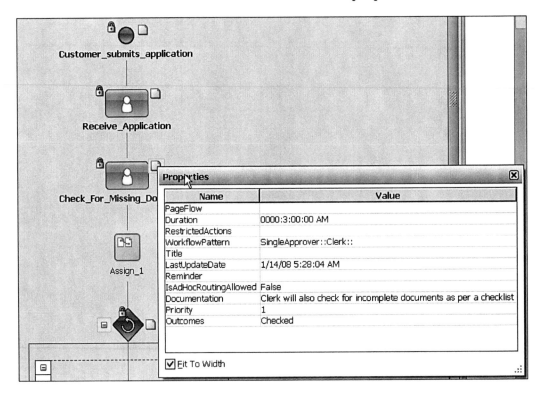

If a change is required to the blueprint, this can be made in BPA before being sent to JDeveloper, where it can be merged. A user can refresh changes from BPA on a regular basis, by synchronizing, as follows:

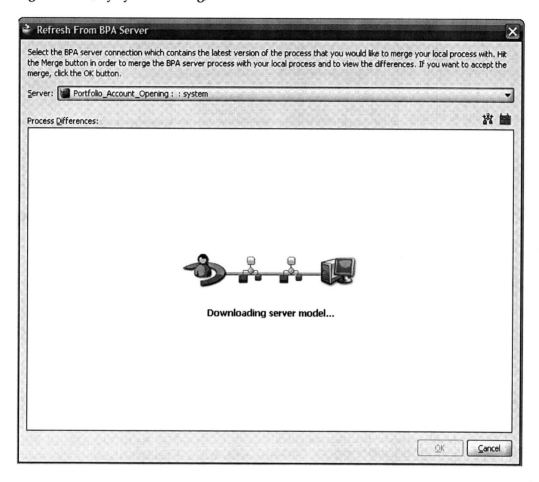

In our example, the result of refreshing shows a couple of server updates that have taken place, the same These need to be merged with the local blueprint.

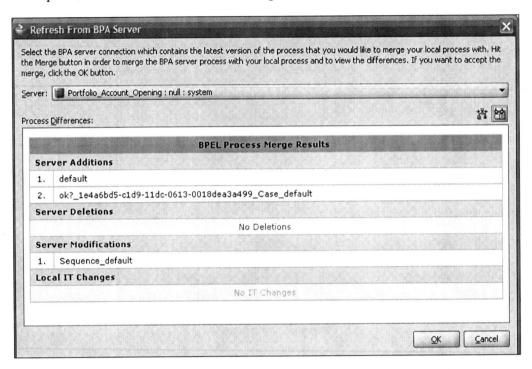

You can also view the changes made in BPA visually by choosing the **Visual** icon.

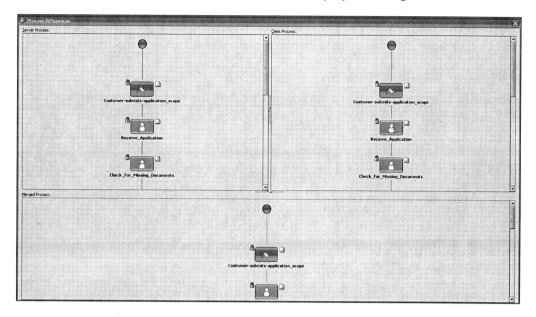

Add Implementation Details

In the BPEL view, the IT teams are able to see the details of the generated BPEL and the various errors it has due to its abstract nature.

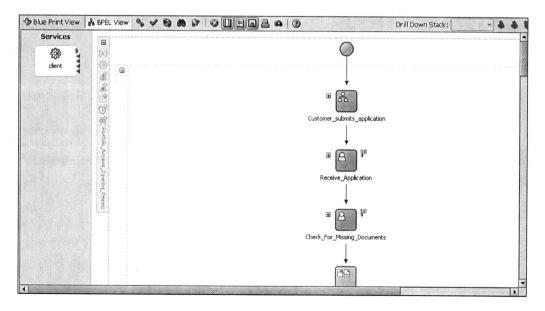

The developer can now modify the BPEL file, based on annotations and other information from the blueprint, and will update the BPEL file to ensure that the errors are removed, and the BPL is functionally ready to be deployed and tested.

Deploy and Test

Once the BPEL is functionally correct and error free, the developers can deploy the BPEL for testing or production, and subsequent use by the business users.

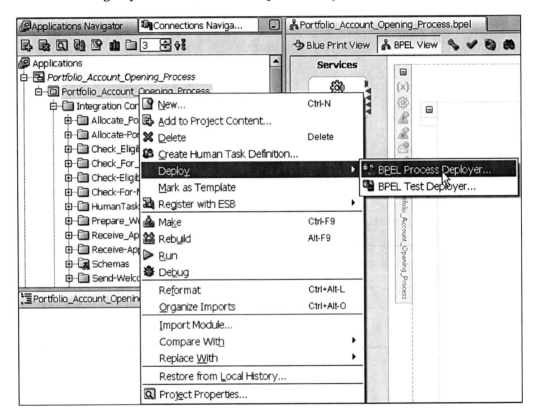

We will discuss the process of deployment and execution in greater detail in the next chapter.

Updating the BPA Server

Once the changes at the IT level are complete, these changes can be sent back to the BPA server as an update. They will be available to the business users as implementation details in the BPD.

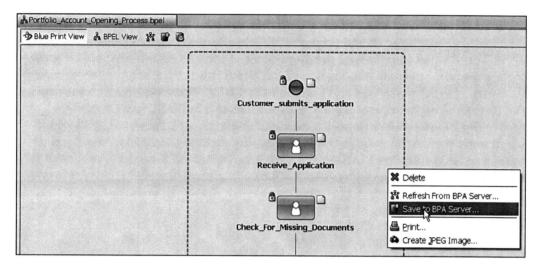

Any additions to the business process in terms of scope will be updated as improvements to the proposal in BPA. The business users can then consider the proposed changes to the business process and decide either to accept or reject the proposal.

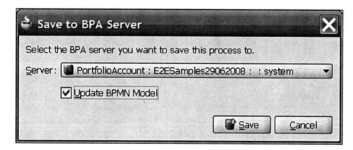

Summary

In this chapter, we covered two important aspects in the BPM process: process analysis using simulation and process transformation for implementation. The concepts learnt in this chapter will help the business analysts and process stakeholders to carry out simulation studies on processes and identify potential improvements before they confirm the process as being ready for implementation. We have also seen how we can prepare a BPD to allow efficient transformation to BPEL. This chapter emphasized the importance of tools to extend support for some of the gaps in the current standards, and the importance of transformation to reduce the issues of synchronization and process round-trips. The tool support from Oracle and its extensions have significantly reduced the gaps in BPEL, and Oracle are supporting these custom extensions over and above BPMN. However, while there is still some work to be done in terms of ensuring process standards maturity and respective tools adoption to achieve highest level of control for enterprise level BPM, the trend is moving in the right direction for agile, closed-loop BPM, and for further bridging the ominous Business-IT divide.

6
Business Process Orchestration for SOA

When discussing SOA, we need to understand its true value to the **organization**. Whether the service is basic or composite, its relevance is in its **capability** to support the business processes of the organization, and in turn help the organization to achieve its objectives. If we take a top-down view, our business processes are the main motivation behind creating a robust SOA infrastructure. SOA's main motivation is to provide a backbone for an organization's business processes.

This chapter discusses the concept of orchestrating business processes from SOA's perspective. We will introduce some core BPM concepts and collaborative technologies that add value in any BPM lead SOA initiatives.

To demonstrate the concept, we will use the Oracle BPEL Process Manager to execute and monitor the processes for a sample application, concentrating on the orchestration of an end-to-end process. We will also look at how Business Rules Management and BAM technologies play an important collaborative role in enriching BPM and SOA initiatives for an organization.

BPM Architecture and Role of Business Process Orchestration

Process Orchestration can simply be defined as the coordination of events and activities in a process at technical levels, to help achieve objectives laid down by the business. From an SOA perspective, orchestration involves direction and management of multiple component services to create a composite application or an end-to-end process. While orchestration tends to imply a single central engine performing the coordination act, another overlapping concept of choreography applies to sharing this coordination activity across multiple autonomous systems.

So, we can say that Business Process Orchestration is the act of implementing the business process requirements laid down by the business teams through BPMN models. In this case, it is achieved by using a process engine which can interpret the BPEL code and orchestrate the involved human activities and automated activities.

While we are covering orchestration and its detailed technology implementation of business processes for BPM and SOA, it is worthwhile to also discuss reference architecture for BPM, to understand how all components of technology fit together for modeling, executing, monitoring, and optimizing a business process. Following an architecture-lead approach, as always, is a good way to initially guide BPM projects. It is not necessary to implement all aspects of this architecture from day one, but as we mature with our BPM implementation, its coverage can be increased to gain maximum value.

From the perspective of this chapter, this reference architecture provides an understanding of how process execution and orchestration is a core activity in bridging the abstract business models and underlying SOA infrastructure.

If you look at the following architecture for BPM, you will realize that it is divided into layers and groups. The vertical right side covers the aspects of modeling the processes, business rules, and services.

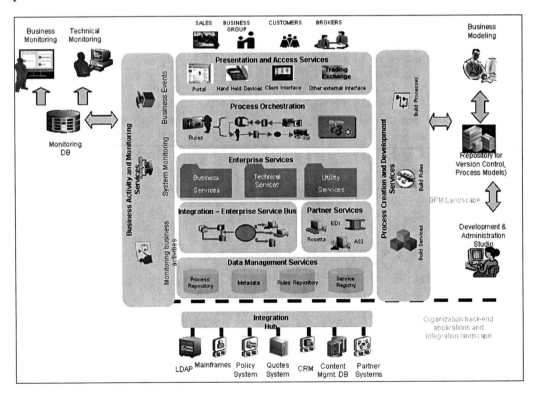

The horizontal stack starts with the presentation layer, which allows multiple channels through which a company's customers, employees, and partners can interact. It could be a web portal, a hand-held device, and so on.

These channels are supported by the process orchestration layer, which asists in orchestrating different aspects of a business process to provide information to respective users in a channel.

In this layer, we will have a process engine that will take inputs from the presentation layer and interface with underlying technologies and services to complete an end-to-end process. This layer will be responsible for ensuring that information is gathered from all sources at the right time, to enable a smooth process flow. The requirements for process orchestration will be fed by the activities performed by the business modeling team and the development teams, working on the process models using standards such as BPMN and BPEL.

The orchestration layer will then interface with what we call 'Enterprise Services', which could be business services, technical services, or utility services, available either as basic services, or a composition of multiple services required to support the process orchestration.

To enable access to these enterprise-level services, we will have an integration layer or an Enterprise Service Bus, which will provide a standards-based interface to multiple systems within or outside the organization, and also human service providers. We also have a layer of data management services that will be different high-level data sources that the BPM landscape will use. An example is a service registry to manage multiple services or metadata, which will manage information about all of the available data sources in the landscape to which this process has access.

On the vertical left side, we have the monitoring services, which will capture all the events generated by the process to help in analyzing the process performance against key performance indicators laid down by the business.

As we move ahead in this chapter, we will use this reference architecture to understand how various technology components fit together.

Let us now go ahead with an example to see how we can orchestrate a process using Oracle BPEL Process Manager.

Executing BPEL Processes in BPEL Process Manager

One of the fundamental benefits of using a BPM system for modeling a business process – in this case the Oracle suite of products – is to allow models created using BPMN at the business level to be executed, and to automate manual processes. It also allows a business to evaluate gaps in current processes and identify the remedial actions that can be implemented quickly using the execution engine.

When working on the example for the 'Portfolio Account Opening' process, we created the business process model using BPMN, analyzed the process, converted the BPMN model into a process blueprint to be shared by the development teams, filled the technical gaps, and enriched and finally deployed the process to the BPEL Process Manager.

Let us take the next step in understanding how our deployed process will work, and the functionality it offers to the users working on this process. Our aim is to make you aware of how process-driven SOA works for an end-to-end process. This explanation assumes that you have some working knowledge of BPEL constructs such as activities, partnerlinks and so on. XSD and WSDL are used with in the JDeveloper environment to create and deploy BPEL processes. For a detailed understanding of BPEL and its complex constructs, you may want to refer to these resources. For our case, we will use a simplistic representation of information, tasks and moving from one task to another.

Let us go through a series of steps to trigger an instance of the account opening process:

Initiation of the Process Instance

First, let us initiate the services related to SOA Suite. You can open them by selecting **Start SOA suite** from the Program menu.

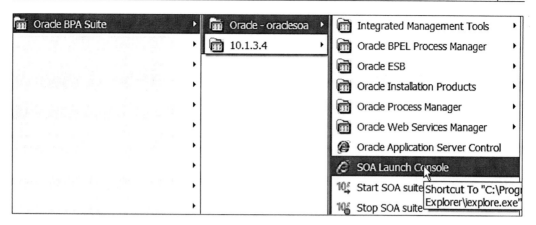

After the SOA suite services have started, we will open the SOA Launch Console, which provides a dashboard for all tools under the SOA suite that can be accessed from this location. To open the console, you can either enter the URL, which is typically `http://localhost:8888;` unless you have specified something specific during your installation. You can also access the console from the **Program** menu and select **SOA Launch Console**.

The following screenshot shows what the SOA Suite console looks like. And As you can see, it provides, in addition to from all the product literature and technical guides, links to the main components of the SOA suite including **BPEL Control**, which is highlighted in the image.

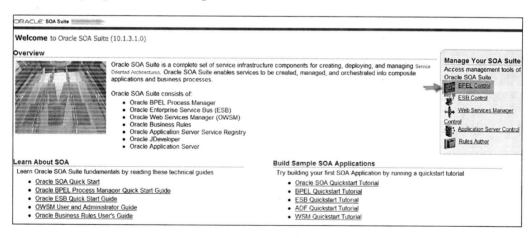

Open the Oracle BPEL Process Manager administration interface by clicking the **BPEL Control** link to access the details of the account opening process we deployed earlier.

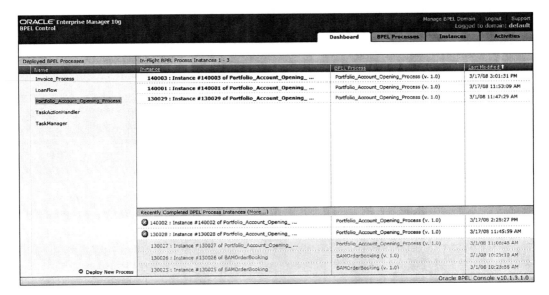

The first screen we see is the **Process Dashboard,** which provides us with the information on the currently-deployed processes in the database. As we can see, we have our 'Portfolio Account Opening Process'. There are currently some instances of the processes already running, and some instances have completed recently.

To test the flow of the process and its behavior, trigger a new process instance for the deployed process through this console. To do this, click on the 'Portfolio_ Account_Opening_Process' link on the dashboard to access details of our deployed process, and initiate a new instance. In a production environment, this step could be automated through a customized graphical interface. We will use the BPEL Process Manager to initiate this test process.

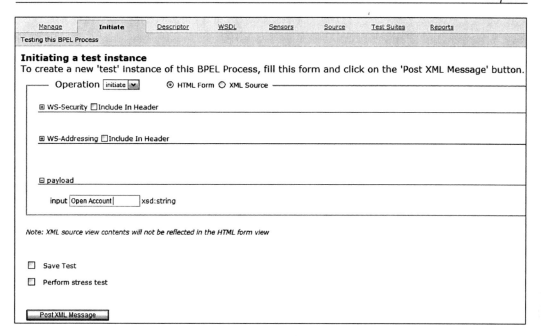

As you can see, the BPEL process **Portfolio_Account_Opening_Process** has been deployed from the development environment inside the BPEL Process Manager. To initiate the process instance, we have used a simple string as the input. In this case, we will just start the process by providing **Open Account** as the payload string, and posting the XML message to initiate the process instance.

To check whether the process instance has started, we can view the visual flow for the instance by clicking the **visual flow** link.

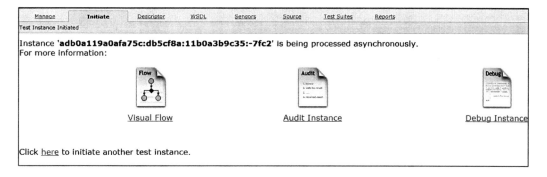

The following visual flow shows that we have triggered the instance of the process, and it has reached a stage where the bank has received the application.

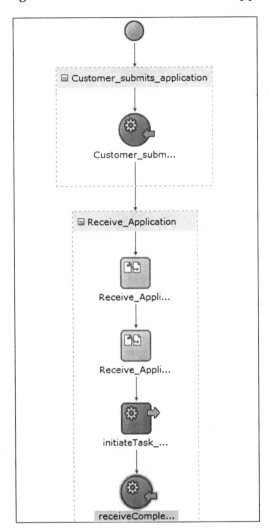

Accessing a Human Task through the Worklist Application

From our BPEL process, let us analyze the **Receive Application** activity, which is a human task involving the user to check whether or not the bank has received an application form from the customer. In this case, during development, the process developers will create a human task form to define how this task will work, and what data elements will be involved in the process.

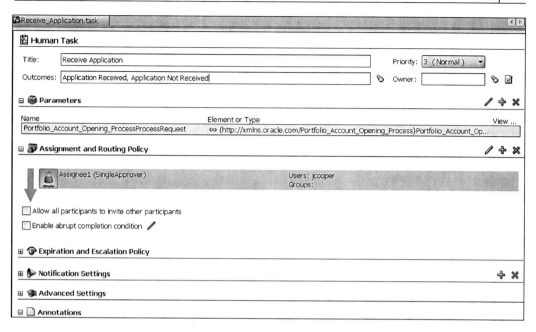

In the task form, we will add all details relevant for this task. For example, we want this task to be assigned to a bank employee who will analyze whether the application has been received or not from the customer. It does not need multiple steps of approval. Hence, we have selected **SingleApprover** workflow pattern from the many task allocation patterns available. You can access the details by double-clicking the assignment section.

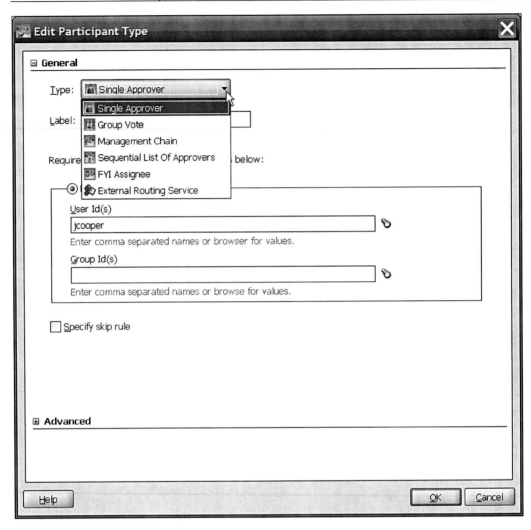

We have also chosen a particular user, who will perform this task, from the available user list in our application server. In this case, the task will be assigned to user **jcooper**.

Let us get back to our process instance, which has been initiated from Oracle BPEL Process Manager. At this moment, the process is waiting for the bank employee, **jcooper**, to verify whether the bank has received the application for the new portfolio account from the customer. For your reference, we have set up this user in our Oracle Application Server administration environment, which available from the SOA console, and you can have your own set of users defined.

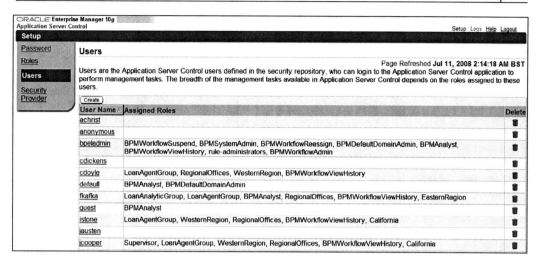

Our user, **jcooper**, can access this task form by using 'Oracle Worklist Application' which is a web interface that enables users to act on their assigned human workflow tasks. Using this application, a manager can approve employee leave requests, or a bank clerk can review a new account opening application that has been initiated as part of the BPEL process. The application can also be used by supervisors to analyze the allocation of tasks to his team or group, and to route and assign them appropriately. Worklist Application users can also update the payload for a task, attach documents or comments, route the task to other users, and conclude tasks through approvals and rejections.

This Worklist Application works on top of the workflow service provided.

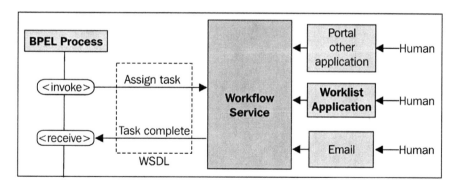

More details about the workflow service and **Worklist Application** are available in *BPEL for Webservices*, 2nd edition.

To access the **Worklist Application**, we can open the web browser and access the URL `http://hostname:portnumber/integration/worklistapp/Login`, or use the start menu as follows:

This will open up the login screen for the Worklist Application, which we will access using **Username**, **jcooper**, and **Password**, **welcome1**. This can be different for your setup.

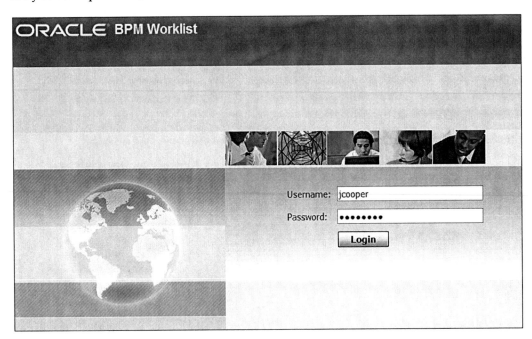

After we have logged in, the Worklist Application will appear as follows:

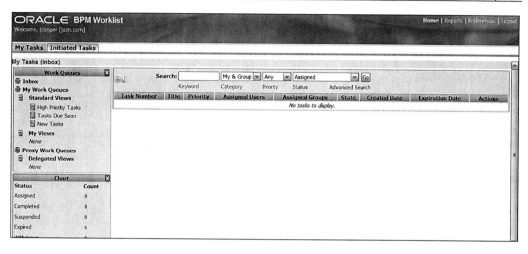

As we can see, the **Worklist** provides the user with a comprehensive view of the tasks and information meant for him, based on his role in the organization. The various tabs and menu items are meant to aid the user in managing his or her set of tasks and take relevant action. Also, the left-hand menu provides a view of a user (in this case **jcooper**) with an option to select tasks based on priority or deadline, and so on. There is also a chart option, which provides a snapshot of the user's activity in terms of their completed tasks. This is an important tool for managers as well, to ascertain the status of various tasks in the process that are active and are being worked on by his reportees. To further elaborate the concept, we will focus on the tasks that are being initiated by the account opening process.

Task Invocation from BPEL Process Manager and its Integration with Worklist Application

As soon as we trigger the process instance from the BPEL console, a task will be created for **jcooper** as seen in the following screenshot.

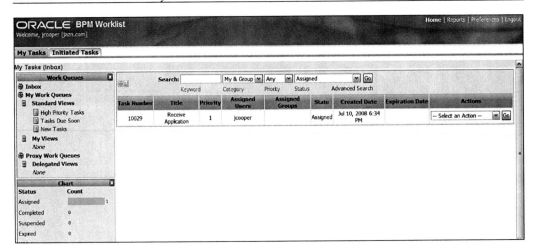

We will notice that a new task has appeared in the task list or **Inbox** with the title **Receive Application**. This is because this is the next activity in the BPEL process, and the human task is now behaving as we wanted it to, and is displaying the task information for the user, **jcooper**. You will also notice that the chart below shows that one task is currently assigned to this user.

As we can see, the process is currently in a wait state, because it has initiated the task to check whether the user has received application or not, and is awaiting a response from the user.

In the Worklist Application, user **jcooper** is now able to see the **Receive Application** task in their task list. The user can see the details of the task by clicking on the task, or he or she can choose from the various options that are available to them. In this case, the user has a choice to decide whether he or she has received the application or not. We will continue the process by selecting the **Application Received** option and clicking the **Go** button.

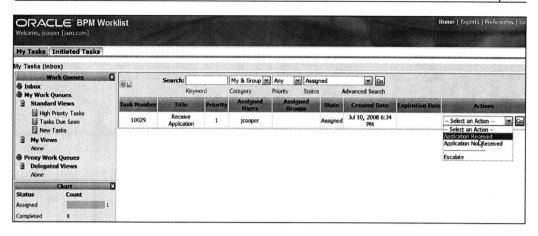

Once the task has been submitted, it will be moved out of the user's task box or work queue, suggesting that the user has completed this task. We can also validate this by checking that the number of completed tasks increases by one, and the currently assigned tasks count goes back to zero in the chart section.

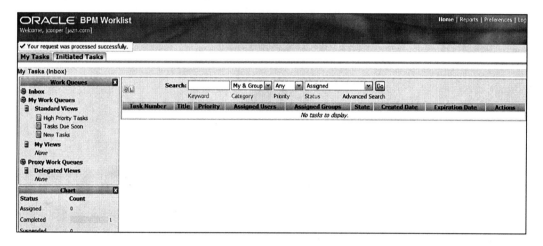

In BPEL Process Manager, we will see that the status of the process has progressed, and now the process has initiated another task to check whether there are any documents missing in the customer's application.

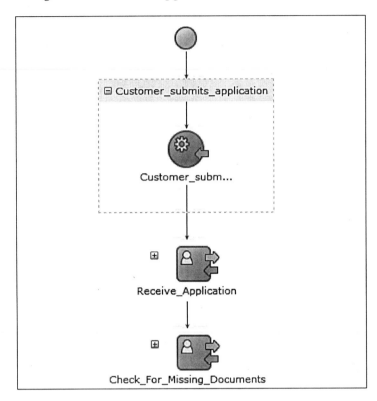

This will result another task item for the user in the **Worklist Application**, as seen in the following screenshot:

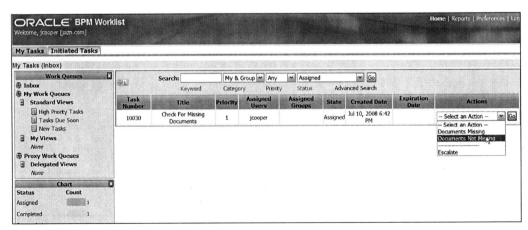

In this case, the user checks for the documents and decides that all are in order, and there are no issues. If the documentation was not complete, the user could have suggested an available alternative, which would have resulted in a loop to check at regular time intervals for document availability before progressing. In a real-life scenario, the logic could be more complex, where we can provide a checklist of documents received and follow-up on each of these with the customer.

The control now passes back to the Process Manager, where we have made a dummy activity that checks the bank's systems to determine whether the customer is an existing customer or not. In this case, we are taking the default value that the customer is an existing user of the bank's services. In real life SOA architecture, we would have made a service call to the banking system to perform this check, typically over the ESB.

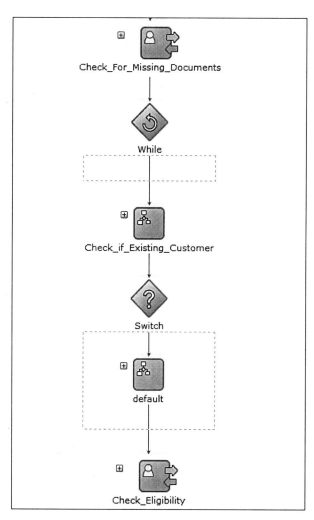

In our case, the process will quickly move to the next human task, to check eligibility, as we can see from the BPEL flow. Again in a real life scenario, the job of checking eligibility can be automated using a service call to a rules engine that is based on business policies of the bank, or it could be the job of specialized personnel in the bank to decide on eligibility. In this case however, we are sending the task to the default user jcooper for them to make a decision on the applicant's eligibility.

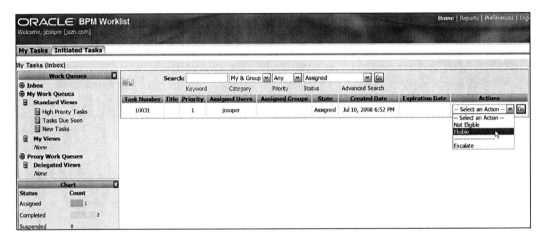

The control again goes back to the Process Manager, now that the customer has been found to be eligible to open a portfolio account. Based on this decision, the control passes on to the system to create a portfolio account, which we have created as a straight-through activity, considering that the backend systems will create the portfolio account, and will attach it to the details of the customer's existing details. When the account is created (we are assuming that the customer is a high-priority customer), we will allocate a portfolio manager to the customer.

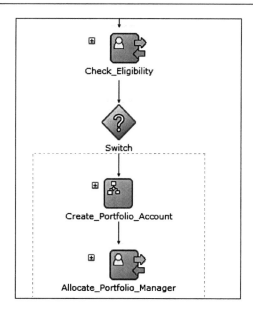

This, in real life, can be done by selecting from a list of portfolio managers automatically, based on criteria such as how busy the person is, or it could be sent as a task, for a manager to allocate a portfolio manager. In this example, we are taking a happy path of just asking the user to allocate a portfolio manager, although this could be developed as a straight-through process in most cases. This also demonstrates the fact that the implementation of a BPM project, and the way a process activity is automated, is driven by the business requirements' appetite for automation, and the capability of a system to implement such automaion in the most appropriate manner. Another benefit of a BPM-based system is that the activities can be deployed iteratively and more frequently than the typical application life cycle, allowing the business to improve their processes as they find bottlenecks and areas of potential improvement. So, we can have this example as a base, which could be iterated in real life to handle much more complicated, real world scenarios, with the fundamental concepts remaining similar.

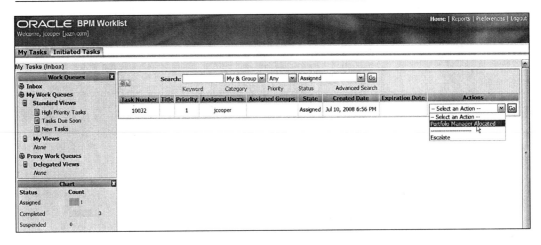

To take the execution example further, the control for the process now moves back to the process manager, where the next step is to prepare a welcome kit for the customer, to be sent to him or her by mail. Again, one way to do this is through a human task, where someone initiates the process of sending a welcome kit. However, nowadays these tasks are automated and the welcome kit is sent automatically or with minimal human intervention, based on the customer's data and choice of product request.

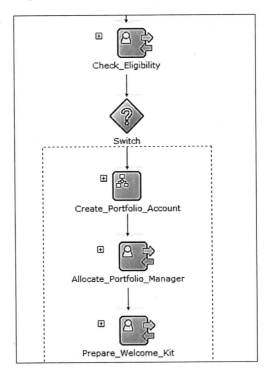

This initiates a task for the user to prepare a welcome kit.

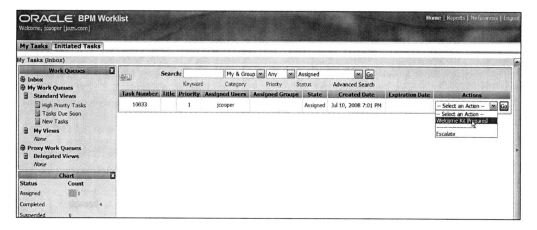

The control passes back to the process manager where the customer is notified via mail or any other channel that his or her request has been approved, and they should await the arrival of the welcome kit or any other communication message from the bank through an automated notification activity. Moreover, the bank, as part of their compliance and record keeping exercise, would like to store the physical documents in a warehouse for further reference. This will be the final activity in the process.

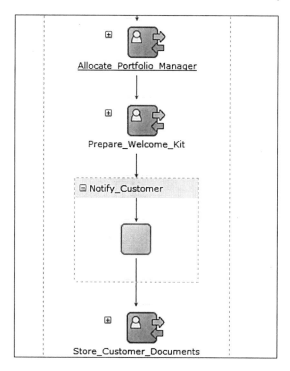

The assigned user will store the documents, or have someone store the documents, update the status, and send back the control to the Process Manager for the process to end.

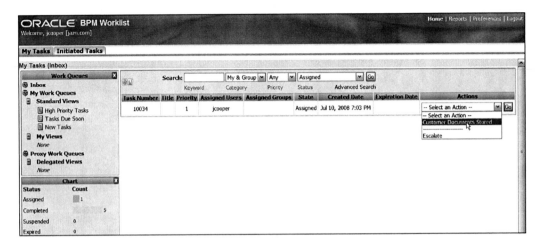

The following figure shows what the visual flow looks like at the end of the process execution of the 'Portfolio account opening process':

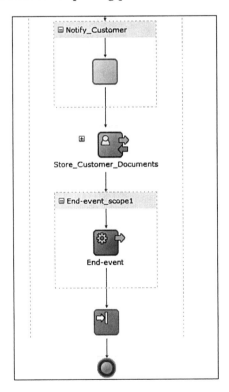

In this example, we can see how a process defined using BPMN by the business teams is communicated using a process blueprint from Oracle BPA to JDeveloper. This process blueprint then acts as the requirement specifications on which the process developers will work, and add technical details linking the process model to actual human tasks and technical services before executing the process in the process engine.

After covering the core flow of information from process models to process engine, we will shift our focus to other valuable complementary technologies that are part of BPM architecture, such as Business Rules Management and BAM, in the subsequent sections.

Introduction to Business Rules Management

This section will discuss the details of Business Rules Management from the perspective of its relationship with BPM and SOA, and how it adds value to a business. Let us start by understanding some key concepts around business rules.

What are Business Rules?

Business rules can be defined as the key decisions and policies of the business. Rules are virtually everywhere in an organization; an example is the rule in a bank to deny a loan for a customer if his or her annual income is less than $15,000. We can generally categorize business rules under the following categories:

- **Business Policies**: These are rules associated with general business policies of a company, for example, loan approval policies, escalation policies, and so on.

- **Constraints**: These are the rules which business has to keep in mind, and work within the scope of while going about their operations. Rules associated with regulatory requirements will fall under this category.

- **Computation**: These are the rules associated with decisions involving any calculations, for example, discounting rules, premium adjustments, and so on.

- **Reasoning capabilities**: These are the rules that apply logic and inference course of actions based on multiple criteria. For example, rules associated with the up-sell or cross-sell of products and services to customers based on their profile.

- **Allocation Rules**: There are some rules that are applicable in terms of determining the course of action for the process, based on information from the previous tasks. They also include rules that manage the receiving, assignment, routing, and tracking of work.

Business Rules Anatomy

To understand the anatomy of a business rule, we can divide a business rule primarily into the following four blocks:

1. **Definitions of Terms**: This helps in providing a vocabulary for expressing the rules. Defining a term acts as the category for the rules. For example, customer, car, claims, and so on define the entities for the business.

2. **Facts**: These are used to relate terms in definitions with each other. For example, a customer may apply for a claim.

3. **Constraints**: These are the constraints, limitations, or controls on how an organization wants to use and update the data. For example, for opening an account, a customer's passport details or social security details are required.

4. **Inference**: This basically applies to logical assertions such as 'if X, then Y' to a fact, and infers new facts. For example, if we have a single account validation rule (if an applicant is a defaulter, then the applicant is high-risk), and we know that Harry (the applicant) has defaulted earlier on his payments for other bank services, we can infer that Harry is a high-risk customer.

Automating Business Rules

As we discuss the externalization and automation of business rules, it's important to understand the distinction between implicit and explicit rules. An implicit rule can be viewed as a rule that is a part of a larger context within the system. It's like multiple rules that are implemented in traditional applications to implement decision logic, for example, assessing the risk level for a loan. Its implementation is usually part of the application it is being developed for, and is never considered beyond the scope of the application, perhaps to be re-used.

So Typically, in the IT world, these implicit rules are embedded within the complex application code and spread across multiple systems, making it extremely difficult to introduce changes quickly, and without creating a domino effect across systems. Some of these issues can be resolved by implementing a **Business Rules Management System (BRMS)** in collaboration with the BPM system in place. This allows the decision logic, which is being used by the process during its execution, to be driven by a central repository where all the rules are stored and managed. This repository provides a way to abstract the decision logic from the applications, and helps in managing this logic centrally, allowing for better management and flexibility for change and re-use. Hence, these rules are explicit in nature.

For the loan approval example, business rules such as these would traditionally be embedded in application code, and might appear in an application as follows:

```
public boolean checkAnnualIncome(Customer customer)
{
   boolean declineLoan = false;
   int income = customer.getincome();
   if( income < 10000 )
   {
      declineLoan = true;
   }
   return declineLoan;
}
```

The above example shows that this rule is obviously difficult for the business users to understand. In today's world, with the need for an organization to be agile, (considering our previous example) the business has to wait for weeks before a small change can be implemented by IT. What is required is the ability of the business users to define and control their own rules, and to be able to get the changes out in the market faster. Business Rules Management and related technology tries to solve this problem.

Automating Business Rules for Business Issues

Automation of business rules via BRMS is ideal for use, where the following issues are being faced by an organization:

- **Dynamism and Volatility**: Companies need to repeatedly change business policies, procedures, and products to meet the market needs. In this case, the rules change very dynamically, and having a BRMS can help in implementing these changes faster, and reducing the time to market and cost. of implementation

- **Time to Market**: In this case, the organization might want a particular set of changes to be released quickly due to market pressure, or to gain a competitive advantage. So, Even though the rules are not changed very often, a delay in their implementation could lead to a serious business loss. In this case, the organization needs to have the agility to get these changes in quickly, without roadblocks, which can be addressed by a BRMS.

- **Regulatory Compliance**: Failure to comply with regulatory requirements such as **Anti-Money Laundering (AML)** laws can result in millions of dollars in fines, and legal issues for the organizations. To solve these issues, institutions can combine business rules with SOA to create an effective strategy for enforcing compliance. Business rules technology helps in implementing these rules quickly, and helps them to be kept up-to-date across an enterprise.

- **Business Participation**: There could be rules which might be better off being controlled and owned by the business users. In this case, a BRMS can expose certain rules to be managed and edited by selected business users, providing an easy to use interface. Rules related to product configuration, customer eligibility, discounts and so on, are some examples where business users can manage the rules, and change them as required by changing scenarios.

- **Complexity**: Some scenarios, such as complex product and service pricing, require extremely complex dependencies between several rules to implement the scenario logic. These kinds of rules are best suited for implementation inside a BRMS rather than a procedural language, as is being done traditionally. Telecom Fraud Management, for example, is an area where rules management is being used along with BAM to identify potential frauds. There are similar applications in credit card and banking industries.

- **Consistency**: Rules managed centrally provides a more consistent way of managing certain policies requiring re-use and consistency across the enterprise. This is especially true in cases where inconsistency was an issue due to multiple applications, databases, and different lines of businesses.

Business Rules Management, BPM, and SOA

Business Rules Management, BPM, and SOA share a synergistic relationship, especially, when used together to provide agility to an organization. The term 'Agility' can be defined as "the ability of an enterprise to sense and predict change in their environment and respond quickly, efficiently, and effectively to that change." Agility, requires the organization to be flexible enough in introducing change and in modifying their current operations, to achieve higher levels

of performance or output. A process-driven approach to SOA allows business users to introduce changes to the process for faster execution, and with less cost. This value is amplified by using a Business Rules platform alongside process orchestration.
If we look at the BPM reference architecture again, rules functionality features in various layers of the architecture, in the initial rules discovery phase, during process mapping, and in its orchestration in the SOA environment.

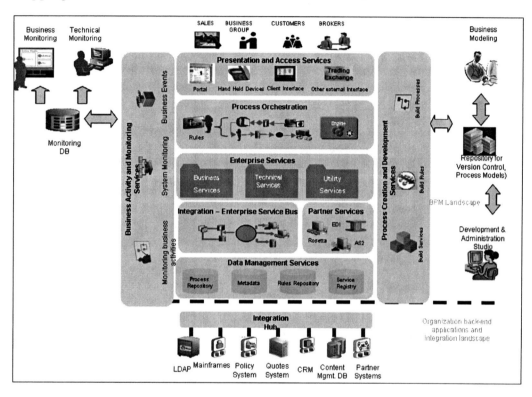

Business Rules-related technologies have been in the market for a number of years now. However, with the acceptance of BPM and SOA as enablers for increasing an organization's agility, today's enterprise are increasingly looking at using rules management to externalize their rules. Business rules management helps automate decisions and apply policies within processes. Automation of these decisions requires determining the meaning of a given situation, and applying a business policy in response to this. Business rules platforms provide tools to define this 'reasoning' logic for use by either developers or business analysts, and business stakeholders.

Organizations are looking at Business Rules Management to deploy rules related to policy decisions, work allocation, compliance and control, business exception management, and even data validation. For example, a major financial services company uses business rules to apply privacy and anti-fraud policies to all of its transactions. Even more, these Business Rules are being considered as an asset for an organization that should be managed centrally and re-used across departments and systems, instead of being hard-coded into an application.

So, it is important to ensure that business rules have a place in your SOA. Carefully defining and exposing your rules as services will enable all of the applications and services within your architecture to have simple access to a common rules repository. From an SOA perspective, before beginning a business rules implementation, you should:

- **Incorporate a business rules platform into your SOA**: This would be a service-enabled repository of your business rules, where instead of data you would maintain and execute rulesets using a business rules engine.

- **Create standards and best practices for developing business rules**: To maximize benefits from your rules implementation, you should focus on developing common standards and best practices for discovery, design, development, and interfacing of your rules. Some of the best practices for writing and designing business rules are:

    ○ **Declarative**: Business rules should be declared, and not stated as procedures as in coding. How a rule will be enforced should not be part of a rule definition. For example, "If the customer is a premium customer, offer him further 5% discount."

    ○ **Precise**: It's easier for business rules definitions to be misinterpreted due to the use of natural language syntax by business. One business rule should be open to only one interpretation, and would need rephrasing if it was found to be ambiguous.

    ○ **Consistency and non-redundancy**: Business rules should be consistent and not conflict other rules. Similarly, you should look out for business rules that are redundant.

    ○ **Business Focused and Owned**: Business rules should be declared using the business vocabulary so that they can understood by relevant business stakeholders. Avoid using technical jargons in business rules. Also business rules are best left under the ownership of the business, community, as that is the source for the rules.

Key Considerations for Selecting a BRMS

The following are some key considerations when selecting a BRMS to work with BPM and SOA:

- **Standards-based Integration capability**: The ability to integrate with the SOA landscape using a service layer.

- **Business User Interface**: The ability to provide the capability for business users to access and modify business rules through a user-friendly interface.

- **Rule Language**: The ability to provide support for natural languages for easily expressing a complex set of rules.

- **Performance**: The ability to provide support for high-volume transactions for mission-critical applications, which is normally measured in terms of the number of rules processed per second.

- **Rules Monitoring and Reporting**: The ability to feature support for rules debugging, rules reporting, and real time monitoring of rules.

- **Rules Repository**: The ability to provide a centralized repository for storing all rule-specific artifacts. The repository should also support change management by storing different versions of rules, and providing audit capabilities.

Key components of a BRMS—A Brief Look into Oracle Business Rules

Typically, a BRMS will comprise four main components:

1. **Business UI**: This is a user interface component for writing and editing business rules. Typically, it will be a web-based interface for business users to log in and access existing business rules, create new ones, and so on.

2. **Rules Development Environment:** Developers will be working in this environment to convert business rules defined by business users into code that can be implemented in the business rules engine. This will be also an environment where the service layer for the rules will be defined and implemented for integration with other applications and SOA components.

3. **Rules Repository:** This will be a centralized repository where all rules-related information will be stored.

4. **Rules Execution Engine**: This is the heart of the rules management system and will be responsible for executing the business rules in the run time environment. In SOA terms, this component will receive request for rules processing from the business process orchestration environment, based on which, it will run appropriate rules and provide decision information that will be sent back to the orchestration layer.

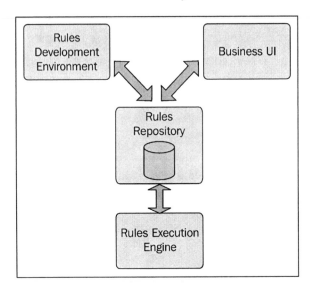

Oracle also provides a suite of components under its Oracle Business Rules product to support rules management and execution, which are as follows:

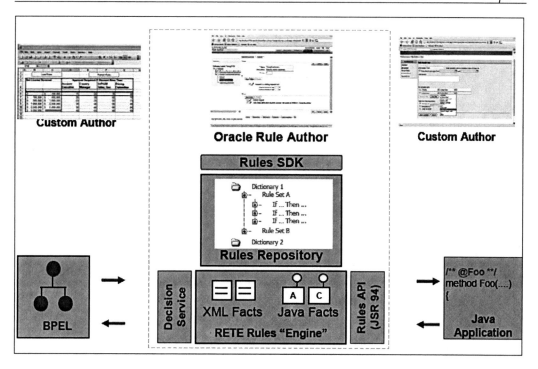

1. **Oracle Rule Author**: Rule Author provides a web-based graphical authoring environment that enables the easy creation of business rules via a web browser. The application developer uses Rule Author to define a data model and an initial set of rules. The business analyst uses Rule Author either to work with the initial set of rules, or to modify and customize the initial set of rules according to business needs. Using Rule Author, a business analyst can create and customize rules with little or no assistance from a programmer.

2. **Rules Engine**: This is the heart of the rules system and executes and manages rules in a proper and efficient manner. This allows inference-based rule execution, based on the very popular Rete algorithm. The Rete algorithm is an efficient pattern-matching algorithm used for rules and facts, and stores partially-matched results in a single network of nodes in current working memory, allowing the rules engine to avoid unnecessary rechecking when facts are deleted, added, or modified. Oracle's rules engine provides a data-driven forward-changing system. This means that the facts will determine which rules can be triggered. When a particular rule is triggered, based on pattern matching within a set of facts, the rule may further add new facts. The new facts are again run against the rules as an iterative process untill it reaches an end state. This allows rules to be interlinked and triggered in a cycle, also referred to as an inference cycle.

The rules engine also provides a web service interface with its SOA environment using 'Decision Services', which is available in a JDeveloper environment during the coding of business processes in BPEL. This can also be used to make a web service call to rules running in the rules engine. It also exposes a Rules API, which is based on JSR 94, a runtime specification for rules engines to integrate business rules application with other applications in an organization.

3. **Rule Repository:** A rule repository is the database that stores business rules. The Oracle rules repository allows rules to be grouped as rulesets, and make it part of the rules dictionary in a central repository. These dictionaries can be versioned for better governance. Oracle's rules repository supports a **WebDAV (Web Distributed Authoring and Versioning)** repository and a file repository.

4. **Rules SDK:** This allows users to develop and integrate the Rules Repository in to a custom authoring environment. This component also allows the development of a customized UI for business users to access and update the Rules repository, if required.

Implementing Business Rules—The Business Rules Development Process

We can take the approach of modeling the rules as part of the BPMN process flow, using decision points or gateways. We can also manage these rules (especially their business logic) either through a tool or by using simple tools such as spreadsheets, before importing them into a rules repository.

The process we are defining here allows business users to map a process flow using BPMN, and use either gateways or specialized activities (as provided in Oracle BPA) to specify a rules decision point. This is nothing more than a BPMN activity extended by the tool during export to BPEL. We would like to see more support for business rules being modeled in the BPMN specification, although at the moment, it is not supported. There are other standards initiatives, such as SBVR (Semantics of Business Vocabulary and Business Rules) by the Object Management Group, that might be worth considering if you are looking at evaluating standards around definition and development of business rules.

As an approach for BPM, it is essential that we view the rules as an integral part of business process, and enable a top-down flow of information from business to IT. This allows the business users to specify the details of workflows and the associated policies, procedures, and constraints at the process levels, and these can then be interpreted as rules during implementation. This is represented by the following diagram, where we can see the various layers of business rules implementation:

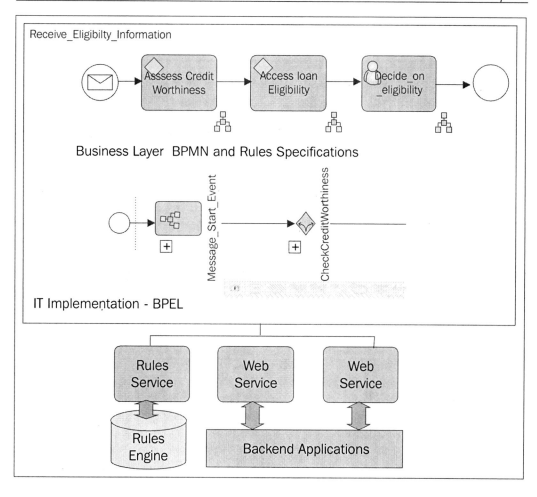

Business Layer BPMN and Rules Specifications

IT Implementation - BPEL

In the business layer, the business process is being developed using BPMN, and rules can be identified as decision gateways or activities. The business analyst will typically maintain a list of business rules discovered during the business process definition stage. The combination of BPD and rules specifications will be an input for the technical teams.

During implementation, the IT teams will maintain and manage the business rules with a development life cycle as for any other application. Typically, this will include analyzing the business requirements as part of the process, designing the data models for rules implementation, exposing the service layer from the business rules engine to integrate with the orchestration layer developed for the business process, and testing the deployed rules.

To understand rules development in the Oracle BPM suite, we can follow the steps shown below:

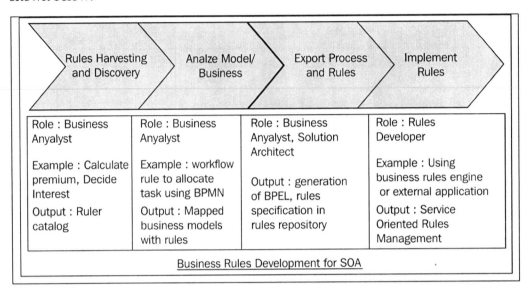

Rules Harvesting and Discovery	Analze Model/ Business	Export Process and Rules	Implement Rules
Role : Business Anyalyst	Role : Business Anyalyst	Role : Business Anyalyst, Solution Architect	Role : Rules Developer
Example : Calculate premium, Decide Interest	Example : workflow rule to allocate task using BPMN	Output : generation of BPEL, rules specification in rules repository	Example : Using business rules engine or external application
Output : Ruler catalog	Output : Mapped business models with rules		Output : Service Oriented Rules Management

Business Rules Development for SOA

1. **Rules Harvesting and Discovery**: At this stage, the business analyst and business communities will go through a process of understanding the various rules the organization currently possesses in relation to the given business process. This can mean understanding the various policies and procedures the company follows, as well as identifying rules embedded in existing systems. Many organizations go through a series of interviews and requirements workshops to identify the rules affecting the business process that is to be modeled. This process will also allow a variety of input information, such as policy documents, existing system's functional specification, and so on to identify the potential rules, to be structured in to logical groups.

2. **Analyze/Model Business Rules**: This is not about what is implemented as business rules, but what is not. As rules are virtually everywhere, there is a tendency to deploy all rules as business rules. An important part of business rules analysis is ensuring that the correct set of rules are managed and controlled by the business.

Although BPMN does not provide any specific construct for specifying rules, they are usually represented either through the gateway logic, for workflow-related rules, or via the use of a specific extension available in the process modeling tools. For example, with Oracle BPA, we can use the business rules function to enter details about the associated business rule in the process. Let us take a simple example to explain this concept. In this case, we are modeling a business process to decide eligibility of a home loan for an applicant. The process is represented by two business activities in Oracle BPA (Assess Credit Worthiness to check the credit background of the applicant and Assess Loan Eligibility), where a decision is made to decide which bank, and what intrests rates will be applicable to the applicant.

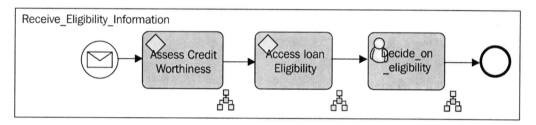

The attributes for the rules function can be specified here, to be used later as reference by other stakeholders in business and IT.

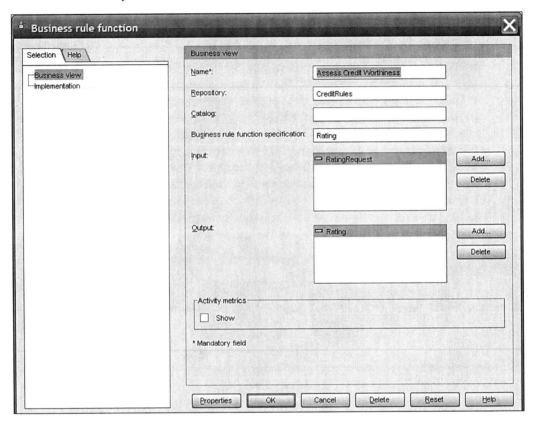

The business rules function also allows the business users to add details regarding the business rule, if required. This will allow the IT teams to use this information when configuring the data model for the business rules services in Oracle Rules Author, and modifying the BPEL to call these decision services.

3. **Export Process and Rules**: At this stage, after modeling and analysis of the process and rules, the BPEL for the BPMN model can be generated to incorporate the changes in to the process maps. This can be achieved by sharing the model in Oracle BPA with the JDeveloper environment using a process blueprint. The blueprint will provide details about the business process and the rules-based information, which can be used for configuring the business rules in BPEL.

At the moment, the exported blueprint for the business rule activity does not get translated to decision services in BPEL. It only creates a business scope in BPEL that can be modified further by IT to add detailed implementation information.

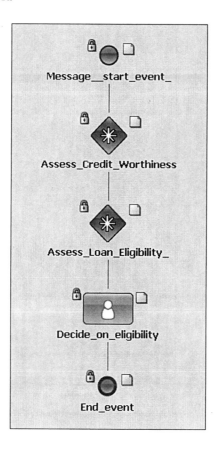

4. **Implement Rules**: The skeleton for the business rule specified in the process models is now available. We can represent this as a decision service in BPEL. An IT developer can now modify the decision services to create links with the rules engine, and implement the changes for the process along with the associated rule. As we can see, we are adding two 'Decide' activities to create interfaces with the external decision services.

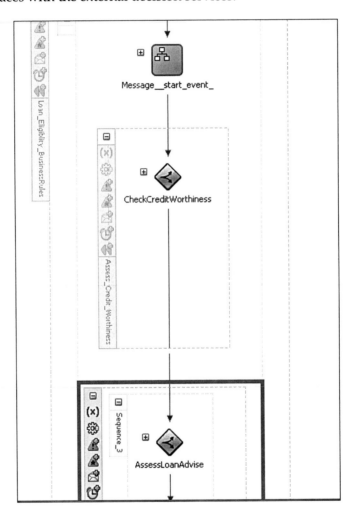

In this case, once we deploy the process **CheckCreditWorthiness** and **AssessLoanAdvise** during process execution, a service call will be made to the rules engine for the respective decision services. In this case, we are using a direct connection between the decision service and the Oracle Business Rules component using an available adapter. We will establish a connection to the repository and select the **Ruleset** or function to call using this wizard.

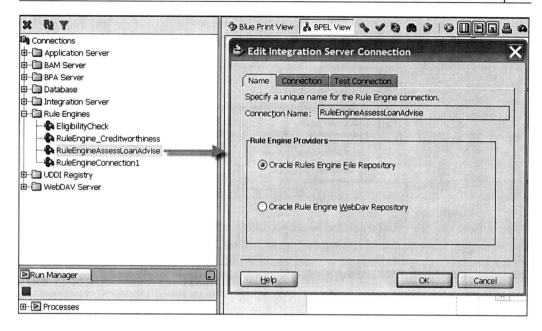

After the decision services have been called, we have created a human task in our BPEL to allow a user approve the loan based on the response from the rules engine.

From the Oracle Business Rules side, Oracle Rules Author will be used to define these business rules and will be configured to provide information based on service calls made from the decision services in BPEL. To access the **Rules Author**, we can use the link available in the Oracle SOA console.

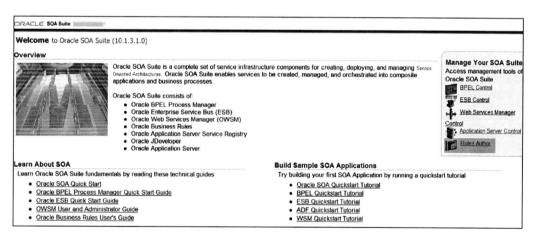

The Rules Author screen provides various tabs to start defining our **Rules Definitions**.

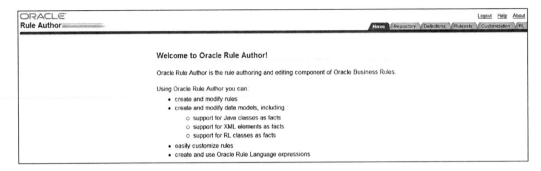

We can first start by creating a **Rules Repository**, which we want to be used for our example. We can either choose to connect to a file-based rules repository for managing rules in static files, or we can use a WebDAV-based repository. Let us use a file-based repository in this case. You can choose to either create a new **Repository** file or load an existing one.

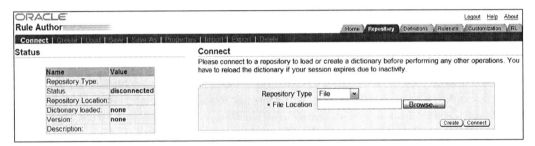

The rules can now be configured by choosing the appropriate **Dictionary** and **Rulesets**. In this case, we will take an example of the rules we have created as a sample for loan approval. We start by opening the file-based repository where our rules are stored, and load an existing dictionary. In this case, the existing dictionary we have is called **HomeLoanOffer**.

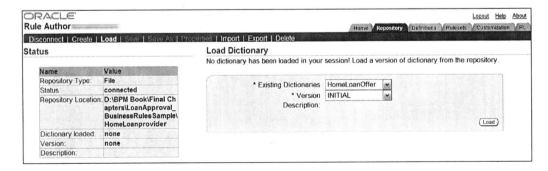

We usually start by creating **Facts** that will be used by the **Rulesets**. In this case, we have created a set of **XMLFact** by importing the XML schema for **HomeLoanOffer**.

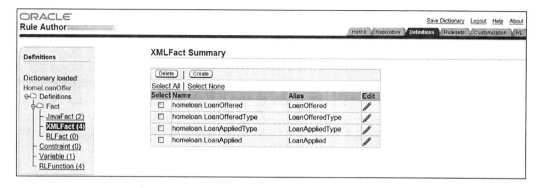

We are now in a position to create a **Ruleset,** as in this case, we are carrying out a simple check to see if applicant's credit rating is more than 200 points. In this case, the rule sends a response to the bank employee to approve the loan.

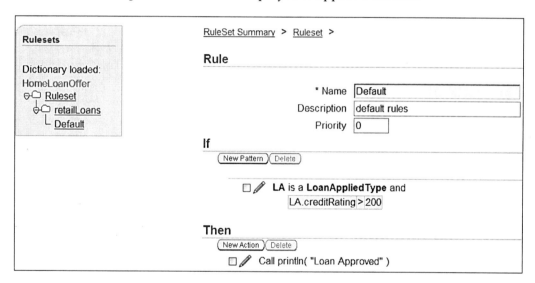

These rules, as we mentioned, will be available to the BPEL process as decision services during orchestration.

In a practical business situation, we would have a series of complex rules to be executed as required during the process orchestration.

Introducing Business Activity Monitoring

Typically, an organization's processes span multiple systems, channels, applications, departments, and external partners. In this case, how do we monitor such processes? What is the current state of the organizational processes? What is the benchmark for poorly-performing processes and exceptional processes? Most of the time, organizations are unable to answer such questions, or only have a vague idea for various reasons. Either they are monitoring the process with a very limited scope, or the mechanisms for monitoring the process are not in place to allow such details to be available. We rarely find organizations with process owners having an end-to-end view of a process. The big picture of a process is not available to the decision makers on a real-time basis.

Also, we have seen that a BPM cycle involves more than just automating a business process. Although modeling and analysis of the process plays an important part before a process is executed, the benefit is further highlighted by using Business Rules technology for added agility of the enterprise. One important factor that closes the loop for BPM is the aspect of monitoring the process on a continuous basis to pinpoint bottlenecks, as the process is executing within a business, and acts as a feedback for potential process improvement exercise. The need to monitor an organization's business processes, especially as part of a larger BPM initiatives, is gaining considerable acceptability and demand. Such monitoring is the primary job of BAM.

What is BAM?

BAM allows a business to monitor its business processes, and related business events being generated in real-time, and provides an assessment of business process health based on pre-defined KPIs. This allows greater operational visibility of the business to relevant process owners for assessment and decision-making via real-time information dashboards. BAM also allows users to take actions based on information available on the dashboards.

Typically, systems providing BAM capabilities use business events to capture information from varied sources such as ERP, workflow, BPM, legacy systems, external partners, and suppliers. These data sources provide the necessary business measures, which are evaluated by the BAM against set KPIs, and provide the information in a user-friendly dashboard for the users.

BPM, SOA, and BAM

BPM, SOA, and BAM can be used as independent, isolated technologies. However, their benefits are compounded for a business if used together in a complementary fashion. As we can see in the following reference architecture, BAM works along with the services and process components to capture event-related information from a business and IT perspective, for analysis and reporting purposes.

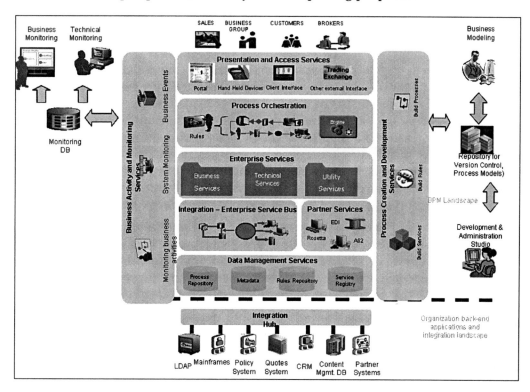

In this case, SOA enables an organization to have a robust and flexible IT infrastructure that can help it easily achieve its BAM goals by allowing events and data from different services to be available to BAM for decision-making and real-time analysis. In an SOA-based solution, the business events will be inputs for BAM that are provided from the services layer. The linkage is via the BPM route, or through an event-based integration layer provided by an ESB.

We can refer to this relationship between BAM and SOA as being **Service Oriented Activity Monitoring (SOAM)**, as today's organizational setup will provide this event information to various BAM services interfaces exposed by the business applications in an enterprise.

In case of BPM, the business process describes the key activities required to fulfill the specified business action and its associated KPIs. These actions are executed as transactions using an orchestration engine and the underlying service layer. These transaction occurrences result in multiple process events to be created for each step within a transaction. BAM's primary focus is on capturing, analyzing, and reporting on the transactions and events created by the process running over the SOA platform.

BAM usually looks at collecting information about a process based on the following attributes:

- **Quantity or Volume of Transactions or Events**: One of the primary areas covered by BAM is the volume of events generated by a process. This is not just an IT metric, but more of a business-related metric to help business stakeholders analyze information points such as the number of orders shipped in a day, the number of trades made during trading hours, the number of helpdesk tickets closed by a call centre, and so on. Usually, we will define these KPIs in a process definition, and use BAM to raise alerts to the portfolio manager if the process is exceeding those values, for example, "Send an alert as soon as the stock portfolio value decreases more than 3% ."

- **Time Bound Events**: In this case, the BAM concentrates on time-related metrics such as helpdesk ticket process cycle time for high priority issues, general process cycle times, supply-related waiting time, and so on. Again, based on certain thresholds, alerts can be sent out, or the reports can be viewed by the management in real-time using customized dashboards.

- **Faults**: These are situations where the process is not running well. This could be due to a hardware fault, or a process related issue such as deadlocks, or some other issue. BAM helps in these scenarios by helping to identify areas of problems, and providing important metrics with respect to frequencies of such errors and their potential damage on process performance, and other dimensions such as cost, schedules, and so on.

- **User Defined Events and Conditions**: Apart from the general dimensions of volume, time, and errors in a process, a business user might want to define KPIs around specific business issues that need analysis. For example, for compliance requirements, a bank might be required to keep track of all high-value transactions to prevent money laundering. During implementation, the business analysts can define this KPI in the process model, which will then be implemented mostly by a rules engine, and the events generated will be used by BAM to provide statistical reports and dashboards based on the frequency of these transactions, specific regions and user types involved in such transactions, and so on.

The real value of BAM, however, does not come only from analysis of individual events, and exceptions generated during process execution. BAM provides a mechanism to correlate aggregated process events to help with a cause and effect analysis, pattern matching, and so on, which provides immense value to today's businesses.

Although not in the scope of this book, another area which is gaining a lot of attention in this area is **Complex Event Processing** or **CEP**. This can be a perfect vehicle for implementing BAM in an enterprise in order to solve complex business issues. CEP is based on a concept of analyzing a set of specific events from a range of possible events, and identifying patterns that could be meaningful for an organization. Among the many applications of CEP, one example we can use is that of 'Algorithmic Trading', where CEP can be used to analyze a huge amount of market data, assess favorable patterns for trading, and initiate trading in a market based on this. A lot of banks are using this technology for performing low-value trades, and assessing risk positions simultaneously. CEP then records this information as a 'fingerprint', and maintains a history to use when deciding whether to execute similar trades in the future. As it gathers more experience and intelligence, the BAM tool supporting CEP can start to refine its predictive capabilities, and conduct more efficient calculations.

Oracle BAM

Oracle BAM is an integral part of the BPM suite (`http://www.oracle.com/appserver/business-activity-monitoring.html`). It is a message-based, event-driven platform that allows business users to link KPIs associated with the process being monitored on a real-time basis, and provides relevant information to the business using customizable dashboards.

The main architectural features for Oracle BAM are:

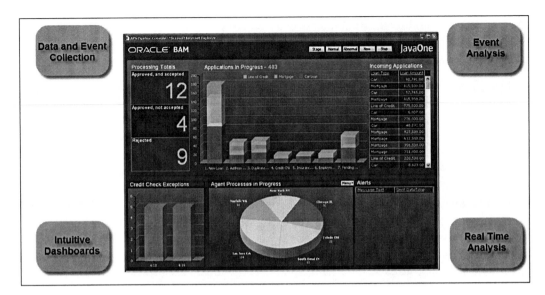

1. **Data and Event Collection**: The Oracle BAM provides mechanisms to collect event and data information from various sources, and it is integrated with Oracle BPEL Process Manager to link process-related events in real time.

2. **Event Analysis**: This allows the filtering and analysis of event-based information in line with the KPI information set by the users.

3. **Intuitive Dashboards**: This allows detailed reports regarding the process to be available to the users as per their requirements. It allows data from various sources to be made available using intuitive dashboards, which a user can use to take decisions or set customized alerts.

4. **Real Time Alerts**: The Oracle BAM provides the capability for setting alerts in case a business process is performing outside the range of acceptable standards.

From an end-to-end BPM perspective, Oracle BAM allows us to integrate with the Oracle BPEL process engine to provide process analysis in real time. In this case, the events will be generated via the process engine while the process is executing. These process-related events will be captured by Oracle BAM in real time for processing, analysis, and reporting via the **Business Activity Dashboard**.

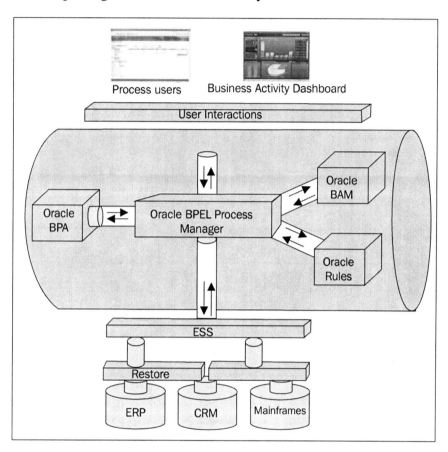

Oracle BAM and BPM

BPMN does not provide specific attributes for setting KPI information that could be used later by a BAM application. However, most of the tools have the extensions and capabilities necessary to store activity-specific KPIs for a process activity that could be translated during implementation by the IT. If we look at the the following figure, in the Business Process Layer, the BPMN model can be modified to include specific KPI information to be used by the technical layer.

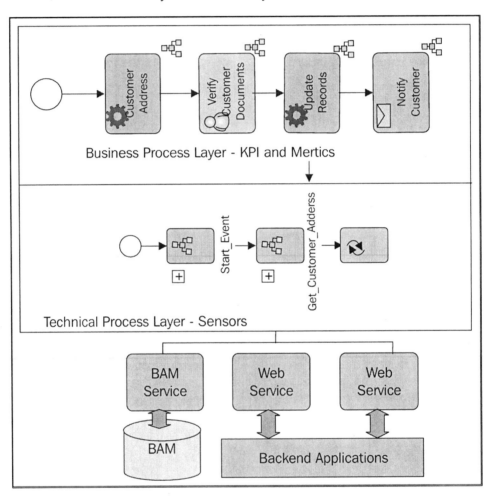

If we can see that a particular activity's attributes can be modified to include information in attributes for **Activity Metrics**, which is shown by a check-box which suggest that the process has a sensor attached to the process activity, and should be considered during implementation in BPEL.

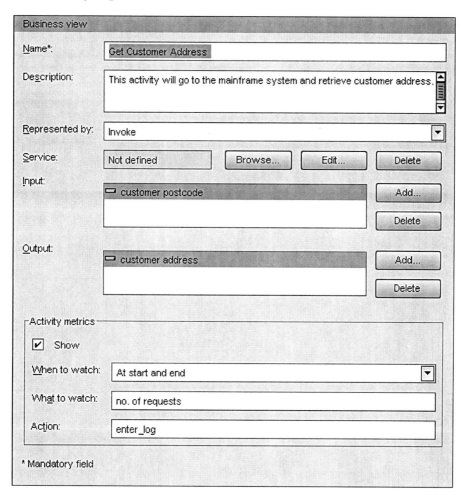

The user can then set other attributes such as "**When to Watch**", which will decide when a particular process activity should be monitored. In this case, you can set it for when the activity starts, or when it ends, or during an exception.

The next step is to transform this information to BPEL, which can then be implemented and deployed for the BAM application to monitor the particular process steps, and provide real-time reports. In the current release, the KPI information from a BPMN model gets converted directly to BPEL, and is available as the **Sensors** attribute within the activity **Scope**. As we can see in the following screenshot, the icon on the **Scope** activity indicates that there is a **Sensor** defined for this activity.

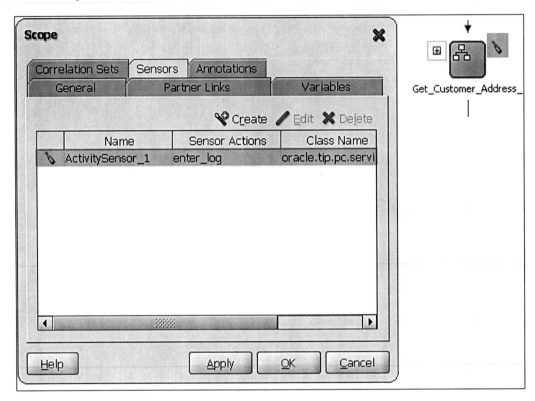

In BPEL, we can use the information provided by the process layer, and configure the BPEL process activities with the relevant sensors. In this case, we have sensor information available from the process diagram, and we can modify this by adding implementation details. This process activity can then be linked to Oracle BAM for performing real-time data collection and reporting. JDeveloper provides a BAM Server Connection adaptor to allow our BPEL activity to provide information to Oracle BAM during process execution.

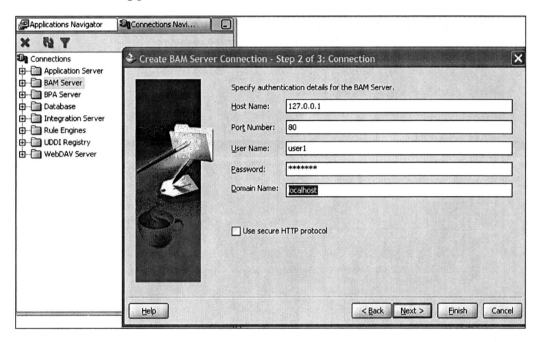

The information from the BPEL environment can be integrated with Oracle BAM to create customized reports and dashboards, which can be then published. Consider the following sample image:

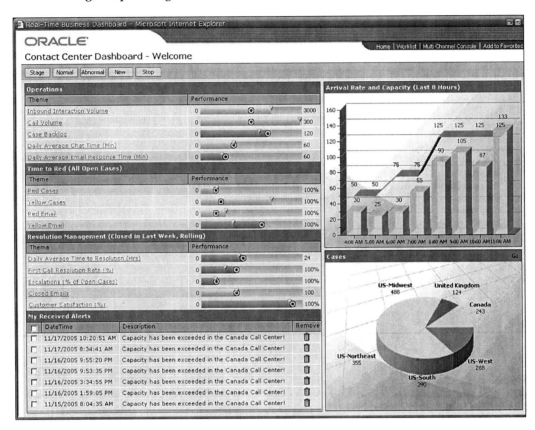

We can also configure alerts to be sent out via email or telephone to key stakeholders as required, based on KPI criteria.

The information gathered from the real-time dashboards provides a great mechanism for Business Analysts to determine the scope of process improvements and implement the changes back into the Business Process Model to be further implemented in an iterative fashion in BPEL and then re-deployed, allowing us to fulfill a closed-loop BPM to the maximum extent possible.

Summary

During the course of the book, we aimed at understanding the fundamental concepts of a standards-based closed-loop implementation for BPM and SOA.

We started by covering business process modeling using BPMN and process analysis using simulation techniques to allow business analysts to create iterative process versions, before reaching a selection point for process execution.

We covered the process transition from BPMN to BPEL, followed by process orchestration and execution using process engines such as Oracle's BPEL Process Manager, and saw how this fits into an organization's SOA.

While discussing standards and tools for implementation, we also discussed the coverage of standards in current technology, and potential areas of improvements in allowing end-to-end process automation in terms of interoperability between process models at business levels and IT.

The link between BPM and SOA with Business Rules and BAM also demonstrates the complementary nature of these technologies, and the synergies they provide to business and IT teams to realize real business benefits, and help create an informative and agile enterprise. We also evaluated some of the best practices for implementing various technology components to make this end-to-end process of BPM and SOA seamless. This will encourage the deeper involvement of organizations in the implementation of complex business processes and mission-critical applications in a closed-loop environment, further bridging the Business-IT divide.

Index

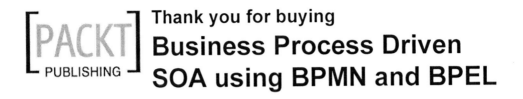

Thank you for buying
Business Process Driven SOA using BPMN and BPEL

About Packt Publishing

Packt, pronounced 'packed', published its first book "*Mastering phpMyAdmin for Effective MySQL Management*" in April 2004 and subsequently continued to specialize in publishing highly focused books on specific technologies and solutions.

Our books and publications share the experiences of your fellow IT professionals in adapting and customizing today's systems, applications, and frameworks. Our solution based books give you the knowledge and power to customize the software and technologies you're using to get the job done. Packt books are more specific and less general than the IT books you have seen in the past. Our unique business model allows us to bring you more focused information, giving you more of what you need to know, and less of what you don't.

Packt is a modern, yet unique publishing company, which focuses on producing quality, cutting-edge books for communities of developers, administrators, and newbies alike. For more information, please visit our website: www.packtpub.com.

Writing for Packt

We welcome all inquiries from people who are interested in authoring. Book proposals should be sent to authors@packtpub.com. If your book idea is still at an early stage and you would like to discuss it first before writing a formal book proposal, contact us; one of our commissioning editors will get in touch with you.

We're not just looking for published authors; if you have strong technical skills but no writing experience, our experienced editors can help you develop a writing career, or simply get some additional reward for your expertise.

Business Process Execution Language for Web Services 2nd Edition

ISBN: 190-4-811-81-7   Paperback: 350 pages

An Architects and Developers Guide to BPEL and BPEL4WS

1. Architecture, syntax, development and composition of Business Processes and Services using BPEL

2. Advanced BPEL features such as compensation, concurrency, links, scopes, events, dynamic partner links, and correlations

SOA Approach to Integration

ISBN: 978-1-904811-17-6   Paperback: 300 pages

XML, Web services, ESB, and BPEL in real-world SOA projects

1. Service-Oriented Architectures and SOA approach to integration

2. SOA architectural design and domain-specific models

3. Common Integration Patterns and how they can be best solved using Web services, BPEL and Enterprise Service Bus (ESB)

Please check **www.PacktPub.com** for information on our titles

Printed in the United States
142944LV00003B/19/P